Cognitive Pragmatics

Cognitive Pragmatics

The Mental Processes of Communication

Bruno G. Bara

Translated by John Douthwaite

A Bradford Book
The MIT Press
Cambridge, Massachusetts
London, England

Based upon *Pragmatica cognitiva: I processi mentali della comunicazione*, © Bollati Boringhieri, Milan, 1999

MIT Press books may be purchased at special quantity discounts for business or sales promotional use. For information, please email special_sales@mitpress.mit.edu or write to Special Sales Department, The MIT Press, 55 Hayward Street, Cambridge, MA 02142.

This book was set in Stone Sans and Stone Serif by Toppan Best-set Premedia Limited. Printed and bound in the United States of America.

Library of Congress Cataloging-in-Publication Data

Bara, Bruno G., 1949–.
Cognitive pragmatics : the mental processes of communication / Bruno G. Bara; translated by John Douthwaite.
    p. cm.
"A Bradford Book."
Includes bibliographical references and index.
ISBN 978-0-262-01411-3 (hardcover : alk. paper)
1. Pragmatics. 2. Cognitive psychology. 3. Communication. I. Title.
P99.4.P72B3713 2010
306.44—dc22
                                                                    2009039302

10 9 8 7 6 5 4 3 2 1

to Simona and Elena
sweetest strawberries
timeless promises

Contents

Preface

The basic idea behind this work is that communication is essentially a cooperative activity between two or more people in which the meanings of each transaction are constructed by all those actors together engaged in the shared task of reciprocally attending to the other communicants' words. The aims of the actors engaged in an interaction may differ, but to be able to say that communication has taken place successfully, all the participants must share a set of mental states. The responsibility for communication falls on the shoulders of each and every participant, for they act together in order to realize communication. Focusing on stereotypical roles such as speaker and hearer, or emitter and receiver, confounds the issue by fragmenting into isolated blocks an activity which acquires meaning precisely from being global and collective. Moreover, I shall claim that human beings, unique among animals, possess a basic communicative competence that sustains both the linguistic and the extralinguistic way of expressing it.

Furthermore, if we are to speak of communication and not simply of information transmission, then agents must devote themselves *intentionally* to such common activity. The intention to communicate must be a conscious one: no unconscious intentions exist in communication, even though, as we shall see, one can easily broadcast information unconsciously, about the world and about oneself.

The cognitive emphasis which can be seen in the title of the book itself is justified by the fact that communication will not be examined here from the viewpoint of an external observer, as happens in linguistics and the philosophy of language, where attention is focused on the finished product, whether this be an utterance or a discourse. Instead, I will take a standpoint within the mind of the individual participants, trying to explain how each communicative act is generated mentally—before being realized physically—and then comprehended mentally by the other interlocutors.

My intention is to describe the mental states of the participants in a communicative interaction. In addition to an analytical description, I will also furnish a formal definition of the various mental states, such as belief and intention, offering a number of innovations compared to traditional treatments, thereby offering solutions to problems which have hitherto not found satisfactory explanations. The mental states introduced will then come to constitute a logical model that accounts for both the production and the comprehension of communication acts in the ongoing process of their construction.

From a methodological standpoint, I take my stance within a cognitive science that has been revised from a constructionist standpoint. This corresponds to furnishing first and foremost a formal validation of the theory presented, something I have realized here essentially by deploying logic. From an analytical viewpoint, my standard procedure is to describe the stable state of communication as it is found in normal adults communicating among themselves.

The second important step is connected both to the evolution of the species and to individual development. It consists in defining how both the cerebral substratum, which renders communication possible, and the cognitive architecture, which realizes pragmatics properly speaking, come to be constituted. With regard to evolution, I have traced a possible developmental line, starting from primates and premodern humans.

With regard to individual development, the central point is to define the stages in the acquisition of pragmatic competence, from the first few seconds of birth to adulthood. Hence sets of experimental data taken from the literature and from my own work will be presented to support cognitive pragmatics. Finally, a valid theory should be able to correlate with the neurosciences, predicting how communicative capacities may decline with age, or suffer damage as a consequence of given pathologies that may be general—as in Alzheimer's disease—or focal—as is the case with brain injury. I will offer data supporting cognitive pragmatics in this area too.

In sum, I have attempted to corroborate the theory advanced in these pages with various scientific methodologies: with formal logic, with anthropology, with developmental psychology, and with the neurosciences. I take linguistics and psychology for granted. The book contains a number of formulas, which have helped me to clarify concepts that would have been difficult to express only through the medium of words. However, the number of formulas is relatively small and they are not too difficult to understand.

All the intellectual work presented in this book was carried out at the Center for Cognitive Science at the University and Polytechnic of Turin, a center I founded in 1994 together with Gabriella Airenti, Monica Bucci-arelli, and Maurizio Tirassa. Over the years, we have been joined by a number of colleagues, the closest of whom are: Mauro Adenzato, Cristina Becchio, Francesca Bosco, Livia Colle, Ilaria Cutica, and Giuliano Gemin-iani. This limited group of collaborators has been supported by other researchers, the most assiduous of whom have been Romina Angeleri, Rita Ardito, Angela Ciaramidaro, Marco Del Giudice, Ivan Enzici, Katiuscia Sacco, Valeria Manera, and our general manager, Cesare Bertone.

The objective of expressing thanks is to recognize debts, not to pay them off in full. In addition to the friends I have just mentioned, I owe a special debt to Philip Johnson-Laird, a model who cannot be equaled and who is an extremely severe judge when it comes to carrying out research; to John Searle, an affectionate and critical master of intellectual analysis; and to Steven Small, an ever-encouraging friend. I name the first last: John Douth-waite, who, in translating the book competently and generously, helped to creatively strengthen any weaker points in my analysis.

Marc Lowenthal and Judith Feldmann of the MIT Press gently and competently drove me through the unexpected, smoothing any asperity.

The first draft of the book was actually written during two consecutive stays as Visiting Scientist at the International Computer Science Institute (ICSI) in Berkeley, California. The research facilities at the ICSI and the people who work and study at University of California at Berkeley helped to make the writing of the book an easier and more enlivening task. The final version has been edited in front of a different sea: the Mediterranean, on the Ligurian riviera.

My daughters Simona and Elena provided me with a sense of proportion and detachment; all seasoned with their continual happiness, especially when they accompanied me on my trips to the United States, enriching weeks of paperwork with art, fashion, tennis and sailing.

All these good friends have shared with me their intelligence and their emotions, enabling me to pretend that what I was doing was called work when in actual fact, deep down, I was enjoying myself beyond belief.

1 Not Just Language: A Taxonomy of Communication

Communication is a social activity that requires more than one participant for it to take place.

The theme of this book is communication in general, not just communication that comes about through spoken language. Viewed in this way, speech is one of the modes of expression we use in order to communicate.

Other channels are writing, drawing, showing emotions, as well as any form of action, provided that the action was carried out in such a fashion as to make it clear to the receiver that ostensive communication was deliberately intended. Obvious examples include buying a ruby for one's beloved, or throwing an object of which she is extremely fond out of the window.

In order to take a unitary approach, we must start from a high level of generalization, at which the modes of expression are not the dominant spheres of discourse. In other words, we must start from a level at which the differences between linguistic and extralinguistic acts (both of which must be intentionally communicative) are of little or no importance. This will enable us to focus on those features that are common to all acts of communication, and leave the analysis of the specific modes in which a given interaction may be realized to later chapters.

Communication is a social activity of a combined effort of a least two participants, who consciously and intentionally cooperate to construct together the meaning of their interaction.

Cognitive pragmatics is the study of the mental states of people who are engaged in communication. Basing the analysis of communicative interactions on mental states means, first and foremost, examining *individual* motivations, beliefs, goals, desires, and intentions. The next step in the analysis is to examine how these states are expressed. The definition of communication as a process implies that communicating linguistically or extralinguistically will involve two different ways of processing data. The same input may be analyzed from both a linguistic and an extralinguistic standpoint, and except in special cases, it will be processed in two parallel ways. To examine how such mental states are expressed, I will investigate the specific features of the various channels of communication, analyzing both linguistic and extralinguistic communication.

In order to underscore the multiplicity of communicative channels, I will avoid the terms *speaker* and *hearer*, generally preferring, instead, the term *actor* to indicate the participant who takes the active role at the moment of communicating and the term *partner* to refer to the participant who has the passive role at that point in the interaction; in the flow of exchanging roles, both entities will be referred to as *agents*, or *interlocutors*. Conventionally, the actor (abbreviated to A) will be female; her partner (abbreviated to B) will be male; other participants will be abbreviated to C, D, and so on.

If, in the course of any potentially communicative activity—speaking, writing, carrying out an action—there is no partner to receive the message, then the communication remains private, a bridge that will never reach the other side of the river. Thus, if we speak to ourselves, if we write a letter that will never be posted, if we act out a scene in front of the mirror, we cannot classify these events as communication acts, no matter how expressive these activities might appear to us, for they are solipsistic acts, performed in a world in which we exist by ourselves.

The theory I am about to outline does not consider the presence of two people a sufficient condition for there to be communication. A further set of conditions must also be stipulated. The first assumption is that the global meaning of the interaction is *agreed on* by the participants, irrespective of whether they take the role of speaker or of hearer. In other words, a mental representation must be constructed of the event that is taking place which is shared by both interlocutors: I call this structure a *behavior game*. It will be introduced in chapter 3. The game represents what both agents believe they are engaged in, the meaning they are giving to the entire sequence of interactions. The sequence may be extremely short, as when asking the way to the station, or extremely long, as when two lovers are debating whether to leave each other or to get married. In both of these examples, all the participants must be fully aware of what is happening, what social and personal obligations are involved, what one may legitimately expect from the other partner, and what one may not expect.

The linguist François Recanati (2004) goes so far as to claim that the meaning of every single term employed in an interaction must be agreed on by the participants in that conversation. Lexical bargaining, term by term, might seem a rather extreme argument; however, the objective behind arguments of this type is to underscore the fact that interaction is something that is constructed by those involved, in which each participant takes on full responsibility for what happens. It will help clarify matters if I momentarily draw the reader's attention to the alternative paradigm that will be analyzed shortly. This view holds that the emitter reflects on the message she wishes to convey to the other interactant, plans it syntactically, and finally generates it physically, at which point it becomes the receiver's task to interpret what he has received, and so on turn by turn.

The second assumption is that in order to be able to speak of communication, all the agents must make explicit their own conscious intention to take part in the interaction. The second chapter will justify the need for a fully conscious communicative intention. In sum, my argument is that it is not possible for A to communicate something to B if she has no intention of doing so; if this were to happen, then it is B who has autonomously inferred some information from A's behavior without A's participation. Furthermore, if A intends to communicate something to B, she must be aware of the fact: although unconscious intentions do exist, unconscious communicative intentions do not.

Language is the means of communication par excellence; it is thus obvious that its appearance is connected with the social nature of human beings. The problem of the origin of language will be dealt with organically in chapter 6. However, it would be a totally pointless exercise to attempt to establish whether the language capacity developed because it was the most promising means for the realization of smooth and successful communication, which would thus appear to be its basic function, or whether development ran the opposite course, according to the hypothesis that language emerged as an aid to the formulation of priorly existing thought, and that it was subsequently exploited in a parasitical fashion to satisfy the needs of communication.

Both positions attempt to establish a simple, linear system of causality (of the type "X causes Y"; for instance, a hammer blow causes the vase to break) in a world that is incommensurably more complex. In a complex causal system, events exert reciprocal influence on each other, each one acting as a means of regulating the other. For example, the endocrine system modulates the release of each individual hormone based on a series of differentiated and interdependent factors, such as one's biorhythm, the concentration of a series of substances in the blood, the presence of release factors, general physical tone, the mental state of the individual, together with the situation the individual is in at that particular moment. In their turn, the hormones influence all the above-mentioned factors, sparking off a complex system of interactions. In cases such as these, speaking of linear cause and effect is overly simplistic, to say the least.

By the same token, the relationship between communication, thought, and language must be viewed as one in which the three domains press each other on to reciprocal future improvement, rather than as a competition over which domain will determine the ultimate destiny of the human race (thinking, inasmuch as we are intelligent beings, or communicating, insofar as we are social animals?).

Before we proceed, one key feature of communication must be pointed out: only a phenomenon that resists or helps resist the constantly increasing entropy of the world may be considered as constituting a genuine message. In other words, we humans realize that something is to be construed as a meaningful message only if that something produces a change in the world, in a direction that may be classified as *nonnatural*, one that combats the increasing disorder exhibited by the world. We only perceive pronounced variations, not the continuities. Thus, I realize my daughter has been in the kitchen because I see a tennis sock perched on the fridge; or Sherlock Holmes realizes the landlady has come into his flat because despite his precise orders that nothing be touched, everything is in its correct place, and disorder does not reign as it normally does. Violated expectations are densely packed with information; this explains why silence is communicative when one expects words.

Norbert Wiener, the inventor of cybernetics (Wiener 1948), identified one important feature that is common to any form of communication among living beings on our planet: a piece of information defies the entropy that is continuously on the increase in the world, thereby diminishing natural disorder. For any being built to live in a world of increasing entropy—whether he be gifted with natural life as are human beings and sloths, or whether it be equipped with artificial life as are cybernetic robots—to be able to perceive change as information, that entity must perceive that information as resisting entropy. Hypothetical negentropic beings, which have developed in a world with the opposite characteristics of ours, where entropy decreases naturally, would never be able to communicate with an earthly creature: we would interpret their messages as natural events, events that do not express meaning; similarly, such creatures would not even perceive an attempt made on our part to communicate with them.

For instance, if the book the reader is reading were to rise from the table, or if the chair on which the reader is sitting were to start dancing, then the reader might think that something significant was happening; but how could he realize that the *non*motion of a book or of a chair also constituted a message? Perhaps, by means of not tearing this page, an Arthurian knight of the negentropic Vega VII is trying to say something that, unfortunately for us, will never be understood.

Whatever may be classified as change can become a communicative message from one person to another. If a living being cannot classify that phenomenon as change, then that phenomenon cannot become a message.

1.1   Social Interaction

We may speak of social interaction every time that two or more people enter a situation of mutual exchange, that is, a situation that enables one person to influence another and vice versa. Commonality may be spatial and temporal, as is the case with a conversation; it may be spatial but not temporal, as happens when one reads a letter sent by another person; or it may be temporal but not spatial, as in the case of a telephone call.

I will deliberately define the concept of social interaction in a wide manner, so that it may accommodate any type of action that may influence others. It therefore goes well beyond communication proper, because it comprises a mode of interaction I will call *extraction of information*; it is important to recognize the distinctive features of both modes of reciprocal influence. Figure 1.1 introduces a first set of differences that will be progressively analyzed.

1.1.1   Information Extraction

A first and extremely important mode of interacting with others is represented by information extraction: I will begin with this mode since it is the most ancient, phylogenetically speaking, for we share it with all other living creatures. In order to explain it, I will avail myself of a distinction first introduced by the ethologist Marc Hauser in his work on animal communication (Hauser 1996); in this sphere, he distinguishes between a cue, a sign, and a signal.

A *cue* is an attribute exhibited by an individual that is always active, or *on*, thereby enabling other animals to make inferences; a cue costs nothing to that given animal, because it is part of its phenotype: it cannot be abandoned. Examples of cues include the golden plumage of a pheasant

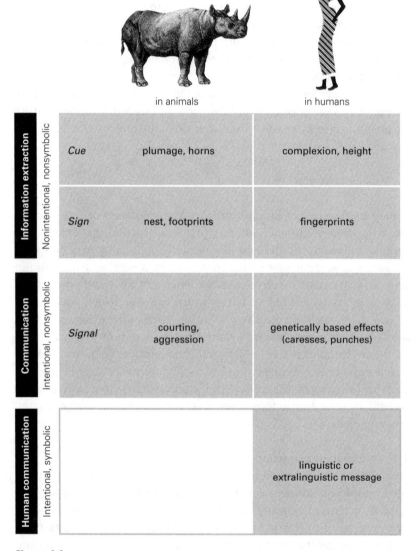

Figure 1.1
Social interactions of a communicative type.

or the horns of a deer. The pheasant's plumage and the ramifications of the deer's horns allow other animals to infer a good deal of information: a female searching for a mating partner may comprehend that the animal she has set eyes on is a male and may gauge the degree of suitability of adaptation of that specimen to the environment; she is thus in a position to evaluate his genetic quality; a male rival may estimate how dangerous his adversary would be in combat; a predator would be able to assess its potential as food, and so forth.

In human beings cues refer to physical constitution, even though we are capable of modifying at least a few of these, as, for instance, dying our hair so as to look younger, or using plastic surgery to become more attractive.

A *sign* is a parameter that is separate or distinct from the organism itself and may take on different values: it is produced by the individual itself, sometimes with a precise aim, but without any communicative goal. Examples of signs are the footprints left by an elephant or the nest built by a bird. In going to the river to drink, the elephant has no intention of communicating to anyone that this is the course it has taken, but another animal may obtain this information from its footprints and from the feces it leaves behind. A bird builds a nest to lay her eggs in it and to bring up her little ones, not to convey to other animals that that is the exact spot she has chosen to build her nest; yet, other animals are able to extract a fair amount of information simply by noting the presence of the nest.

In humans, the concept of sign is intrinsically ambiguous, for any trace whatsoever of activity may turn into communication. A crumpled newspaper, an unmade bed, dirty dishes may be signs that a person has looked at a newspaper, slept in a bed, eaten breakfast. But in certain circumstances, all of these signs could be taken as fully communicative, that is to say as symbols deliberately left to inform the observer that the newspaper has been read, that the bed has been slept in, that breakfast has been eaten. In the case of humans, therefore, signs may easily become signals, provided they have been left intentionally. For example, fingerprints left by an incautious burglar at the scene of the crime are signs that a good detective may make note of. It is no difficult matter, however, to imagine a situation in which the criminal was anxious to expiate his guilt and so deliberately left his fingerprints as signals to be discovered.

One of my patients, a fifty-year-old male, an insurance agent with psycho-somatic problems, had never cooked anything in his life: if his wife went away for a couple of days, she left a number of coffee pots ready in the fridge, equal to twice the number of days she would be away. After a year's

therapy, the man had decided he wanted to increase his autonomy, starting from morning coffee: each time he managed to prepare the pot of
coffee, this also became a message to his wife indicating that he was well
enough to look after himself.

Conversely, a twenty-five-year-old female student who, for a year, had
been cohabiting with a man who was slightly older than her and whose
work kept the couple, was offended every time she found an unwashed
coffee cup around the house. She thought it was a precise message which
was aimed at reminding her of her state of dependency, underlining the
fact that he could allow himself the luxury of not looking after household
affairs: his work was more important than her study course.

A *signal* is a communication act that the individual directs to other
animals. It may or may not be active (*on/off*), it always has a cost each time
it is emitted, and it may either be directly exhibited by the individual, or
be temporally and spatially separated from its organism. Examples include
the mating dance of two herons, or a rhinoceros staking out his territory
by urinating. The herons wish to convey their own sexual availability to
each other, while the rhinoceros intends to communicate his presence to
fellow rhinoceroses in the area.

The second case of information extraction belongs to the domain of the
hard sciences and not to ethology, and is represented by the mathematical
theory of communication, developed by Claude Shannon and Warren
Weaver (1949). This is the most influential theory in the field of engineer-
ing. Its applications range from telephony to robots. Despite its enormous
success in the artificial sciences, it cannot be applied to the sciences dealing
with human beings for reasons we will now examine.

Shannon had already propounded the theorems on which the theory
is based when he worked at the Bell Telephones Laboratory, that is, at the
largest U.S. telephone company, which is committed to discovering the
laws that govern the transmission of information from one system to
another. The first problem consisted in measuring the quantity of information transmitted; the first approximation was obtained thanks to the
concept of the maximum quantity of information conveyable along a
given channel. It became immediately obvious that the communication
channel was affected by a number of forms of interference, as well as by
unpredictable accidents that occurred during transmission. This rendered
that maximum quantity an imprecise measure.

The first thing that must immediately be stressed is that we are speaking about the quantity and not the quality of the information: the meaning of the message cannot be measured. Hence, it does not come within the domain of the mathematical theory of communication. The quantity of information contained in a message may be defined as a constant feature of the message no matter what means is employed to encode it; furthermore, it is independent both of the modality of transmission and of the systems of emission and reception. For there to be information, there must be a variation in the signal; the most elementary variation is represented by the difference between presence and absence, between yes and no, between on and off, between zero and one.

We now turn to the definition of the unit of information measurement: the *bit*, which is an abbreviation for *binary digit*. One bit is the quantity of information necessary to discriminate between two equally probable alternatives: for example, knowing whether the person now reading this book is male or female requires one bit of information. To discriminate between four alternatives calls for two bits: one to halve the alternatives from 4 to 2, and one to distinguish the remaining two alternatives. Analogously, choosing between eight alternatives requires three bits: each bit reduces the alternatives by half (8/4/2/1). If we call the information transmitted *I*, we obtain the following formula:

$$I = \log_2 \text{(the number of alternatives)} \tag{1}$$

Formula (1) means that the informational content of a message corresponds to the logarithm to base 2 of the number of possible alternatives. Given that the probability $p(m)$ of a message is inversely proportional to the number of alternatives possible, we obtain:

$$I = -\log_2 p(m) \tag{2}$$

Formula (2) is tantamount to saying that the information contained in a message is measured by the negative logarithm to base 2 of the probability of the message itself.

The informational value will vary not only from message to message, but even within a message itself, because it is linked to expectancy, that is, it depends on how much the receiver is able to predict the signal. For instance, the first letters in a word are highly informative; as the word proceeds, the letters become increasingly predictable, thereby progressively decreasing their informational value. In *California*, the initial *C* transmits a greater quantity of information than the final *A*, which could be lost in the course of transmission without impeding the comprehension of the message, for the word is highly recognizable by the time the final letter is reached.

Shannon turned to probability theory in order to calculate the differing informational value of the various parts of a message; in his basic theorem, the message is considered to be a sample extracted from a statistical set of messages that may be generated from a source, and its information content is connected to the probability that that message will be emitted by that source.

Shannon and Weaver (1949) consider a message to be a model distributed over time. The more improbable the message is (in the sense that the less the receiver is expecting it), the greater the information it will contain. Vice versa, the more the message contains predictable and expected information, the less information it contains. For instance, a Christmas card conveys little information even if the message is long: in the final analysis, the only thing that is really important is the sender's signature at the end. By contrast, a two-line telegram announcing the tragic death of an extremely rich uncle contains a wealth of information, in stark contrast to its brevity.

The question, then, is why can we not apply the mathematical theory of communication to human communication? The most important reason is that human communication is intrinsically *qualitative*, in the sense that it is based on the subjective significance a message bears for the receiver, and not on the quantity of information the latter has received without errors from the source.

For human beings, the degree of unpredictability is only one of the indicators of meaningfulness. A message that is highly unpredictable does not necessarily have a correspondingly high value in quantitative terms. Let us compare, for example, a list of twenty-five randomly selected numbers—which, for the mathematical theory of communication, represents the most informative message possible—with the following twenty-five keystrokes, whose entropy is smaller:

All's well that ends well   (3)

From a psychological point of view, measuring the degree of probability of incoming information is insufficient to grasp its importance. Instead, what is crucial is evaluating the significance of that information to the system. It is the subjective goals of the system that determine the importance of the message, and not how statistically probable that message is. It is significant that Shannon and Weaver (1949) understood this point; they therefore never tried to apply their theory to human communication.

However, their warning went unheeded, one reason perhaps being that there was nothing available that was better suited to the human sciences.

The second reason accounting for the weakness of the mathematical model of communication when it is applied outside the specific domain is evident in its sarcastic nickname, the *parcel post model*. The mathematical model treats communication as if it were a process in which messages are transported along a conduit, without taking into account the continual adaptations made by the interlocutors that are necessary for the successful enactment of even the simplest of conversations. At the roots of the information transfer model of communication lies the separation between knowledge and the transfer of that knowledge by means of a conduit. Dealing with knowledge as an entity that exists independently of the participants in a speech event, information becomes an object that may be physically moved from one place to another through a series of conduits.

If we apply a stance of this type to human communication, we obtain an analogous clear-cut division between information and people exchanging information. The task of the source and of the receiver consists in ensuring the channels remain clean in order to avoid polluting the purity of the information that must pass through those channels. As I suggested at the outset, and as I will be trying to demonstrate throughout this book, I will be arguing the opposite standpoint: human communication is generated in a common process by all those people taking part in the interaction, and no meaning can exist outside that constructed within the relationship existing between those people.

The best application possible of the mathematical theory of communication to human sciences was developed by anthropologist Gregory Bateson. Bateson's intuitions are important enough to minimize the technical errors he committed, a phenomenon that is quite understandable given the historical period in which his wide-reaching and fruitful work took place. Bateson (1972) took the viewpoint of total ecology, which holds that any model of communication must be applicable to all living and nonliving systems. His intention was to develop a general theory of communication that would be valid for every form of interaction between systems, and which would therefore be able to account not only for interactions between human beings, but also those involving animals and plants.

The concept of a message in cybernetics corresponds to quantitative information; stated differently, the quantity of information contained in a message is a constant feature of that message no matter what code the message is encrypted in, and independently of the mode of transmission and the systems of emission and reception. For example, anatomy speaks of the necessary relationships between each organ and the body as a whole; these relationships are determined by specific genetic instructions on how each individual organ must develop within the context of the growing organism in its entirety: the legs must be symmetrical, they must occupy a given position with respect to the pelvis, they must interrupt their growth when they reach a predetermined length. In order to formulate laws that would be equally valid for both living and nonliving systems, Bateson (1979) was obliged to remove from his analysis that part of communication which is specifically human, namely intention.

The crucial change comes about through use of the concept of *ostensive communication*, by which is normally meant that the meaning of a term may be clarified by extralinguistic means. For instance, the difference between anatomical forceps and surgical forceps may be clarified to a student by showing him an example of each. Bateson stretches this concept by amplifying it to the point that he renders it equivalent to nonintentional communication. The example he gives is that of meeting one's friend Bill in the street, from whom one receives ostensive information (his appearance, the way he walks, etc.), whether Bill desired to transmit this information or not. In this way, Bateson manages to include nonintentional communication as part of the general category of communication. Note that the case he describes differs radically from a standard intentional communicative event: it is one thing to decide to wear a King's College tie to dinner in order to convey to one's fellow diners that one is a member of King's; it is quite another to put on a stained tie without realizing it is soiled, unwittingly signaling the fact that one is perhaps absent-minded.

Grouping together intentional and unintentional communication allows one to speak of communication even when this term is not strictly speaking correct. Think of the situation in which one of the actors does not even know that there are others present: is the chaste Susan whom the prophet Daniel speaks of in the Old Testament communicating to the old men information concerning her beauty? To take an extreme case, one in which one of the two interlocutors is dead, in what sense during an autopsy can the corpse be said to be intentionally communicating to the anatomopathologist information regarding the cause of his death?

Given Bateson's interest in interaction between nonliving as well as living beings, this extension is readily comprehensible. However, it also leads us astray: in the case of interaction between nonliving systems, treat-

ing such interactions as communication means one is anthropomorphiz-
ing these interactions (for example, the relationship existing between a
plant and its environment). Analogously, when Bateson speaks of communication between living systems and nonliving systems, he is *attributing
intentionality* to the latter. For instance, in a situation of total immersion
in the environment one may have the sensation of talking to the sea, of
receiving messages from the waves, from the wind, from the sun.

Despite the fact that Bateson is a scholar who scrutinizes levels of communication with the utmost care, he falls into the trap of using a metaphor
in its literal sense. In the preceding example, in which the difference
between anatomical forceps and surgical forceps was cleared up by showing
an example of each type, those instruments convey information to the
student only in a metaphorical sense; the real agent of communication is,
quite clearly, the instructor who accompanies his words with the gesture
of exhibiting the forceps. Neither the words nor the forceps communicate
autonomously—it is the person employing those words and those forceps
in a specific context that does so.

If we were to remove the condition that states that the actor must have
a communicative intention, then the interlocutor would be free to interpret the other's act in any way he pleases. Any utterance, even distracted
silence, on A's part could be taken by B as conveying affection, insult,
or any other meaning he wishes to place on that act, without A being in
any way able to influence or control B's interpretative process. Even the
simplest conversation would become an insoluble exercise, carried out in
a climate of unrestrained paranoia: the license to interpret is something
different from the act of communication. If Bill has no intention of communicating anything to his friend Gregory, then nothing is communicated. In parallel fashion, spying through the keyhole on Romeo and Juliet
kissing is not the same as being openly informed by them that they are in
love. This demonstrates why it is no accident that extracting information
from people who are unaware of divulging or who do not desire to divulge
information is an act that is socially condemned: individual privacy is a
right that is recognized and defended by the law.

For example, if Charles reads an e-mail which Alice has written to
Bernard without the author knowing it, then the content is known both
to Bernard and to Charles. The difference lies in the fact that in addition
to Alice and Bernard both sharing the contents of the e-mail, the two
people also share that Alice has sent the e-mail to Bernard. Contrariwise,
Charles cannot openly refer to either the contents of the e-mail nor to
Alice's intentions to communicate it to him. The difference is even more

glaring if we assume that the e-mail message contains a lie: Bernard can accuse Alice of having lied to him, while Charles cannot.

We thus speak of *communication* when reciprocal intentionality is involved. We speak of *extracting information* when one of the actors does not possess the intention to communicate; in this second case, it is of no importance whatsoever whether the actor is alive, dead, or inanimate. The second type of situation may be accounted for by extending the concept of *natural meaning* introduced by the philosopher of language Paul Grice (1975). On Grice's view, natural meaning is that meaning which may be inferred from events that take place in the world. His examples include:

Those black clouds mean rain.   (4)

Those red spots mean measles.   (5)

In both cases, the only source of intentionality is that of the person extracting the information from the clouds or from the spots, for the clouds and the spots have no intention whatsoever of communicating anything to anyone. It is the meteorologist or the doctor who infers that a certain type of cloud or of exanthema will probably have certain consequences.

Cases of social interaction, which are the ones that interest us in this book, may be explained using the same approach, in a crescendo of intentionality on the part of the actor. My daughter might quite simply have the measles; she may, however, show me the spots as a means to be kissed and cuddled. The color of Muhammad Ali's is genetically determined, but he may sometimes emphasize the social significance of the color of his skin. Marilyn Monroe is naturally well endowed; nevertheless, by wearing certain outfits she explicitly emphasizes her natural condition. It is as well to note immediately that the only judge of the intentionality or otherwise of a behavioral act is the actor who performs that act: sometimes the observer has no way of deciding whether an act was intentional or not. When we are dealing with human beings, what would be considered cues in animals veer sharply toward signals in the true sense of the word.

We may therefore conclude that naturally possessing a set of features is different from exhibiting those features in such a way that red spots, the color of one's skin, or the opulence of one's body induce the interlocutor into drawing a set of inferences, and perhaps into behaving in a certain way. However, even exhibiting natural characteristics comes fully within the definition of communication.

This argument also applies to signs. In extracting information, an agent influences the mental states of the other agent through his behavior, without there being any intention on his part to do so. For instance, stupid people tend to behave like stupid people, and in acting in this way they allow others to infer their stupidity. This instantiation may be considered a clear case of information extraction, inasmuch as the actor has no desire to convey to others the fact that he is stupid; quite the opposite, despite the fact that others will inevitably understand the fact. In the way they act, for instance in the way they characteristically damage others without reaping any benefits for themselves, stupid people are nevertheless conscious and intentional—they have explicit objectives. The case is not very different from that of the elephant who leaves signs of its passage as it proceeds to its drinking place in the savannah. A stupid person has a conscious objective: he wants to act in a particular way, which others deem stupid (he consciously and deliberately wishes to carry out that senseless action he has decided on), but in so doing he does not openly intend to communicate to others his own stupidity; it is up to his partners to infer this fact, if they wish, by extracting the pertinent information from his behavior. To sum up, mental states may exude stupidity, leaving obvious signs of this condition, but without the condition ever being intentionally communicated.

Bad taste is a similar case in point. A person who buys a certain suit and a certain tie is fully aware of what he is doing; he is also fully aware of that he is matching the two items. In fact he is creating a hideous match, whose bad taste is evident to all who observe him. What the example shows is that intentionality guides part of the behavior (buying and matching) while another part is excluded from one's conscious intention to communicate (the bad taste of the match made): if an observer perceives or infers the unconscious part, it is to this latter part that he must refer when talking of information extraction.

In conclusion, all these cases may be referred to as information extraction—or attribution—but not as meaning, because the creation of shared meaning requires two parties, both of whom must be reciprocally interested in constructing that meaning.

1.1.2 The Communal Construction of Meaning
In my definition, communication is an activity consisting of a combined effort of actor and partner, who consciously and intentionally cooperate to construct together the meaning of their interaction. All these terms will be given a precise definition in the second chapter; in the present chapter we will have to make do with an intuitive treatment. In actual fact, to be able to speak of communication proper, the analyst must have among his

tools the concepts of symbol, consciousness, and intentionality, instruments I will introduce in formal terms later in the book.

The fundamental idea is that communication is an activity in which all those agents active in the process take an equal share together in the interaction, independently of the roles they play, such as whether they be speaker or hearer, roles that nevertheless may change in the course of the interaction. The meaning of what they are doing is constructed together, and it includes both the specific content of the communication and the relationship within which the individual relationships are played out.

The problem that the agents who wish to communicate among themselves must face is how to manage to progressively agree on what activity they are engaged in, attributing to this activity a meaning that is not purely individual, but that must in some way be shared. The efficacy of a communication is measured by the degree of satisfaction expressed by all the participants in relation to the shared component *after* the completion of the interaction, compared with what was considered to be the shared component *before* the interaction got under way. Viewed in this light, communication consists in constructing together an acceptable interpretation of the reciprocal communication acts, at all levels at which the participants consider it significant to do so.

I will use Grice's (1989) notion of communication as a composite of meanings and intentions as my starting point. Grice asserts that by means of a given behavior someone means that q if and only if, by means of that behavior, he intends to induce in the hearer the belief that q." The innovation Grice brings about with respect to preceding treatments is in comprehending that to be able to assert that A wishes to say something by means of a given behavior, A must have the intention of bringing about a given effect in her interlocutor, an effect that is realized at least in part thanks to the fact that the hearer recognizes that the speaker intends to convey something to him.

Translating Grice's words into my own notation so that terminology may be kept homogenous in this book, Grice specifies that:

A wishes to communicate something (that q) by means of utterance x, if A intends:

1. to provoke a certain type of reaction in listener B by uttering x (namely that listener B believes that A thinks that q);
2. B to recognize that A intends to provoke this reaction, and that this intended reaction is at least in part the result of A's uttering x;
3. that B's conforming to the intention mentioned in (2) is at least in part a result of B's having conformed to the intention mentioned in (1).

Later I will deal with each of Grice's points concerning communication in detail, but it is as well to point out from the very beginning that it is its recursive nature that distinguishes communication from other activities.

The attempt to understand the mechanisms of communication involves developing a theory that is capable of accounting for both the linguistic and the extralinguistic aspects of human interaction. Language—the main means of communication—is constantly attended by extralinguistic elements that facilitate reciprocal comprehension. We may even go so far as to assert that in some situations, language turns out to be an instrument that is singularly ill suited to transmitting what we desire to express; when grief is to be conveyed, for example, embracing or weeping are much more effective than verbal utterances, which are necessarily standardized.

The nature of the analytical tools which will be introduced in the second chapter is such that they may be applied to any form of communication, whether it be linguistic or extralinguistic. Based on the mental states of the participants in the interaction, each actor freely decides how to express her own intention; the only constraint is that the other participants should be in a position to comprehend that intention.

Thus, A may signal she likes another person in a direct fashion:

"You're a marvelous person!" (6)

or indirectly:

"It's my lucky day today." (7)

A may even convey the idea by means of a radiant smile directed at B. The important point is that B understand what A wanted to communicate to him through the signal employed. It is obvious that some signals are more effective than others; producing a suitable communication act is not always a simple matter. An infinite number of linguistic forms exist to express a given message, just as there are a high number of extralinguistic signals that may convey the same thought; in addition, words and gestures may be combined in an infinite number of ways.

In normal communication, linguistic, paralinguistic, and extralinguistic aspects are constantly mixed, modulating constantly and in a variety of ways in order to achieve the desired effect. For instance, a person may be obliged to carry out a given action by using forcefully significant expressions:

"If you prefer not to do this, you may hand in your resignation." (8)

Alternatively, the words may be neutral, while the tone clearly indicates an imposition:

"Please do as you have been told."   (9)

Or the words may convey a literal meaning that is obviously untrue, while the real message is signaled by a heavily sarcastic tone:

"Do just as you please. I'm sure you'll find it's the best solution."   (10)

And this is not to mention a meaningful glance, a pointed finger, or a threatening silence.

This explains why I will deal with extralinguistic aspects of communication together with linguistic aspects, considering them not as two rigidly distinct domains, but, concurrently, as two modes of expression that complete each other. In their turn, both domains are integrated by paralinguistic aspects that determine their mode of emission. It is therefore necessary to introduce a concept that enables all the various aspects of communication to be unified into a single theoretical construct. I therefore define any action, whether this be linguistic or extralinguistic, as a *communication act*, provided the actor intends that action be interpreted as communicative and provided that it is recognized as an act of communication by her partner.

Having established that I will take an integrated approach, I will nevertheless differentiate between different types of communication in sections 1.2 and 1.3. Before dealing with these domains, however, it is necessary to clarify what I mean by paralinguistic devices. I define *paralinguistic* aspects of communication as those aspects that modify meaning, typically adding an emotional dimension. Normally, such emotional features are produced unwittingly. Despite this fact, they are generally congruent with the goal of the interaction. They are subsidiary features of language and communicative gestures; they are parasitical in the sense that they are not autonomous; finally, they improve the effectiveness of the communication acts. The most important paralinguistic structure is *prosody*, which consists of tone, pitch, stress, volume, speed, and so forth in speech, and discourse organization through page layout (paragraphing, spacing, etc.) and modes of signaling emphasis such as underlining and character type (e.g., capitals, italics, bold type) in writing (Levelt 1989).

For example, tone of voice gives a special coloring to the meaning of the words uttered, helping the interlocutor to distinguish between a serious and an ironic statement; and when one receives a letter, the type of paper, the handwriting, and the layout transmit information about the sender that fills out what is conveyed by the written words. Such symbolic devices are language-specific; thus English (Pierrehumbert and Hirschberg 1990) and Japanese (Pierrehumbert and Beckman 1988) employ different devices to signal a given type of meaning.

Paralinguistic aspects can be tuned or not tuned to the semantic content expressed through language or extralinguistic gestures. When the semantic content and paralinguistic components diverge, a *paralinguistic contradiction* emerges (Sacco et al. 2008). In such cases, the agent's expressed content is contradicted by the paralinguistic indicators revealing a different mental state.

Angeleri et al. (2008) showed their experimental subjects some video-taped scenes in which paralinguistic aspects were in contrast with the linguistic content expressed by the actor, for example situations in which a person says "What a nice present!" with a disappointed tone of voice and a puzzled attitude, or "So nice to see you again!" with a forced smile. My colleagues and I found that normal adults give more credit to paralinguistic cues, correctly interpreting the actor's real mental states, whereas people affected by traumatic brain injury are more likely to believe in the linguistic content (Angeleri et al. 2008). Moreover, we show (Bosco et al. forthcoming) that the ability to correctly infer the actor's actual mental state, ascribing sufficient weight to the paralinguistic aspects, emerges gradually during middle childhood: initially—at about 5 years of age—children pay more attention to linguistic content and then, by degrees, they become able to better integrate the different kinds of information.

Just as language may be spoken or written, so prosody employs two different systems depending on whether the agents are writing or speaking. Conveying emphasis is realized differently depending on the medium employed. In speech, emphasis may be signaled by tone of voice; in writing, the same emphasis may be conveyed by underlining the phrase to be stressed.

I stated earlier that such devices modifying meaning may affect both linguistic and extralinguistic communication: a pointed finger may tremble with indignation, or a smile may appear artificial because it is overdone. Strictly speaking, cases such as these should be classified as paraextralinguistic devices, but this neologism sounds so prolix that we may have no qualms in limiting ourselves to the term *"paralinguistic,"* whether the devices be linguistic or behavioral.

Permanence and impermanence   In the taxonomy I am about to construct, a distinction must be added that is orthogonal to the other dimensions developed so far, depending on whether or not the communication act leaves any trace of itself in the external environment. I have attempted to capture this distinction by creating two categories—*permanent* and *impermanent* communication. I define the *permanence* of a communication act as the protraction of the act in time, a duration that goes beyond the time necessary to emit the act itself. Reciprocally, *impermanence* exists when the duration of an act is strictly limited to the time required for its emission. The permanent act remains; the impermanent act disappears immediately.

The distinction is not a rigid one, because it is impossible to establish a priori what is meant by permanence: drawing a heart in the air is different from drawing a heart in the sand, from drawing a heart on paper, and from engraving a heart on a gold ring; depending on context, all four cases bar the first could possess the attribute of permanence.

The dichotomy between permanence and impermanence is thus not a dichotomy at all but a cline along which various degrees of permanence may be distinguished: from a few minutes, to a few days, to a few centuries. Furthermore, permanence is always provisional, never eternal.

Figure 1.2 lists the various types of communication, exemplifying the basic cases of permanence and impermanence. In this figure, I have placed drawing in the extralinguistic category of communication. This decision gains support from scholars of developmental psychology who have collected firm evidence in favor of the existence of two distinct modules that control writing and drawing. Investigations from neuroscience lend further weight to this stance, for the findings are that the two abilities are realized by different neural networks. In line with this general result, both architecture and the figurative arts have been situated in the same area, namely extralinguistic communication.

Relevance   The most controversial wide-ranging theory in the domain of pragmatics is undoubtedly the theory of relevance advanced by Dan Sperber and Deirdre Wilson in 1986 and revised in 1995 (Sperber and Wilson 1986, 1995). The authors set themselves the ambitious aim of laying the foundations of the entire field of cognitive science, uniting communication and cognition. And they deserve our praise, if for no other reason than their courage in undertaking such a daunting task, as well as for having survived such an ambitious enterprise.

The theory of relevance is based on an underlying general principle, called the *cognitive principle*, since it refers to cognition in its entirety: "Human cognition tends to be geared to the maximisation of relevance" (Sperber and Wilson 1995, p. 261). What this principle means is that cognitive resources tend to be allocated to the processing of the most rel-

Type of communication		Impermanent	Permanent
Linguistic	Acoustic medium	*spoken language*	*audio recordings*
	Visual medium	*sign language*	*writing*
	Kinesthesic medium		*Braille*
Extralinguistic	Acoustic medium	*music, crying, laughing, shouting*	*audio recordings*
	Visual medium	*gestures, smiles, tears*	*video recordings*
	Kinesthesic medium	*caresses, slaps, kisses*	
	Olfactory medium	*perfume, scent, smell*	
	Figurative arts		*drawing, painting, sculpture*
	Manufactured products		*shop signs, street signs*
	Environmental modifications		*architecture, garden design*
Paralinguistic		*prosody (tone, pitch, volume, speed, pause)* *intensity of gestures and actions*	*space, emphasis, underlining*

Figure 1.2
Types of human communication. Paralinguistic devices may be applied to both linguistic and extralinguistic communication.

evant inputs available, whether they originate from internal or external sources.

This first principle gives rise to a second principle, termed the *communicative principle*, since it is specific to communication. It is usually referred to as the *principle of relevance*. "Every act of ostensive communication communicates the presumption of its own optimal relevance" (Sperber and Wilson 1986, p. 158). The essence of this second principle is that an actor is implicitly asserting that simply by communicating something, she has something pertinent to communicate. By *ostension*, the authors mean behavior that makes manifest an intention to make something manifest.

The second principle asserts that each communicative act must guarantee its relevance, in the sense that the speaker must make it clear that her own contribution is sufficiently important to merit the listeners' making a cognitive effort to understand what she is saying. Stated differently, the components of each communicative act are structured in such a way as to make the communicant's first objective that of gaining the listeners' attention, thereby rendering the effort required to interpret the message worthwhile; the second objective of structuring the message in the way chosen is to try to reduce the cognitive effort that must be made to understand a message, thereby facilitating the act of comprehension.

Sperber and Wilson (1986, 1995) argue that Grice's cooperative principle is excessively specific. They therefore attempt to substitute it with the single property of relevance. This property has a far wider area of applicability, since it covers all of cognition. In order to render the principle effective in communication, however, they must equip it with central unspecialized inference processes applied to the output of specialized linguistic processes. But the inferential engine the authors have recourse to, even if in a nonradical fashion, is connected to a notion of mental logic based on the assumption that human beings possess deductive rules that are represented and applied as such.

Sperber and Wilson's line of reasoning may be summarized as follows: since a set of deductive rules, as part of one's basic mental equipment, would be extremely useful in carrying out the inferences we need to make, then let one assume that humans possess such a system, given that they manage to communicate, and hence to make the deductions that relevance theory lays down as indispensable. Now, after two decades of heated debate, the theory of mental models (Johnson-Laird 1983, 2006) has decidedly gained the upper hand over the theory of mental logic (Rips 1994). Human beings reason not by applying innate logical rules, but by constructing and manipulating mental models that subjectively represent states of affairs in the world (Bara, Bucciarelli, and Lombardo 2001). This cuts the ground from under the Sperber–Wilson deductive framework, given that their principle of relevance is not powerful enough by itself to account for all the inferences humans must make to integrate communication. The ubiquity and importance of inferences in the communication process will be illustrated in section 1.5.3.

Leaving aside the technical problems related to how the inferential apparatus may be realized physically in the brain, there are serious doubts as to whether a single principle can be sufficient to explain all of the phenomena that make up communication. These reservations notwithstanding, Sperber and Wilson's work constitutes a point of no return in the study of pragmatics. Indeed, it is thanks to their work that the enormous importance of the inferential apparatus, which Grice had only begun to explore, has been realized. The impetus their work created led to the sweeping away of any pretension to a priori absolutism in pragmatics, demolishing both semiotics ("a history . . . of simultaneous institutional success and intellectual bankruptcy," Sperber and Wilson 1986, p. 7) and literal meaning: the content is selected to maximize its relevance; it does not represent primary data constituting the point of departure for establishing relevance.

Their work has been most influential in pragmatics; furthermore, the theory of cognitive pragmatics shares with relevance theory its constructivist starting point: meaning is constructed by participants together; it is not a message that the speaker encodes and the listener decodes.

1.2 Linguistic and Extralinguistic Communication

It is now time to specify explicitly the differences between the two basic forms of communication. In so doing, I will keep fairly closely to the approach adopted by Bara and Tirassa (1999). The issues raised with regard to the differences between verbal and nonverbal behavior have been historically imprecise rather than controversial, for the distinctions that have been made are, first, based on intuitions and, second, contradictory. The difference between the two forms is founded principally on the nature of the input: spoken language is defined as *verbal*, as is generally the case also with written language. *Nonverbal* language refers to all other forms: posture, facial expressions, gestures, space (between conversants), and time (between two following communication acts) (Hinde 1972).

This distinction creates many problems, all of which are substantial. The most serious is that the category nonverbal includes structured languages such as those for the deaf (for instance, ASL, American Sign Language). Other issues also produce devastating criticisms, highlighting the weakness of input as a distinguishing criterion: why should the visual medium be assigned to the verbal category in the case of writing and to the nonverbal category in the case of observed behavior or of gestures? Which category should Braille, the language of the blind, be assigned to? Since it is written, it should be classified as verbal; however, since it exploits tactile medium, it may be equally correctly categorized as nonverbal. In general terms, placing so much weight on the acoustic medium thus seems excessive; in particular, this excessiveness is underscored by the fact that the criterion is not applied in absolute terms: prosody, which incontestably employs the voice, is classified as nonverbal.

I will therefore advance an alternative to the distinction based on input that is based instead on the way data are processed: *linguistic* communication is based on the communicative use of a *system* of symbols, whereas *extralinguistic* communication consists of the use of a *set* of symbols. Intuitively, the essential difference lies in the principle of *compositionality*: language may be subdivided into smaller constituent components bearing autonomous meaning, that is to say words, whereas extralinguistic communication comes about through the use of components that cannot be decomposed into smaller, autonomous units: a smiling face is a smiling face, and not the sum of many small parts each of which is smiling.

As we shall see in chapter 6, extralinguistic communication is both phylogenetically the oldest mode of communication and ontogenetically the first mode of communication available to humans, since it is potentially active barely a few hours after birth. This particular mode of expression is especially rich. Such wealth is due to its phylogenetic origins, and is therefore connected less to the abstract and conceptual dimension of human life and more to the emotional and behavioral features of higher mammals.

After recalling the definition of communication as the declared and intentional attempt to influence the mental states of others by means of an open act of communication, we may take up the distinction outlined earlier between communicative and noncommunicative gestures. Our behavior toward others does not always take on the features of intentional communication: a person gesticulating, laughing, getting red in the face may modify certain mental states in the observers; however, such behavioral acts may only be considered communicative when they are consciously and openly employed with the intent to communicate. Otherwise, they must be considered cases of information extraction. Only the agent may discriminate—and sometimes not even she can do so, in certain borderline cases of consciousness—between intentional and unintentional acts of communication.

For example, a person may burst into tears because she has been moved, though it might not be her intention to convey this fact; quite the contrary, for sometimes tears are repressed so that bystanders may not notice them. Compare genuine emotion with the artificial tears of a theatrical actress who displays those tears to the audience in order to communicate to them the pain felt by the character she is interpreting on stage; or with the skill certain adolescent girls have in producing tears in order to embarrass the interlocutor—father, or fiancé, for instance—flooding the scene

Conventional gesture
symbolic, culturally determined

Actions open to interpretation	*bereavement*
Gestures with fixed meanings	*gestures signaling "Hi," "OK," "Victory"*

Nonconventional gesture
these gestures possess both a genetic component, which is mediated by automatic autonomous cerebral reflexes, and a symbolic component, which is culturally determined

Genetic component	*the sensation of being touched*
Symbolic component	*the meaning of a caress*

Figure 1.3
Types of extralinguistic communication.

with indubitably intentional tears whose objective it is to convey the tragedy of misunderstood youth.

Extralinguistic behavior hovers between two polar opposites; it is not always possible to distinguish clearly between the two poles. At one extreme we have the fully symbolic and conventional gesture (for example, raising one's middle finger to the driver who will not let one overtake him), and at the opposite extreme those nonconventional gestures that activate cerebral and behavioral reflexes. Both are schematized in figure 1.3.

I define a *conventional gesture* as a culturally stable mode of behaving that is recognizable by all those who belong to that culture, a carrier of an autonomous, context-independent meaning. The specific gesture is symbolic in the sense that it "stands for" something else, just as a handshake indicates acquaintance, friendship, and like meanings.

A conventional expression has a socially shared meaning and may thus be analyzed at the lexical level. The ethologist Desmond Morris (1977) has attempted to apply this axiom to gestures. Although the results obtained are not definitive, they are undoubtedly valuable. Gestures with a fixed meaning constitute a subset of conventional signals. Social convention has established that each of these gestures has only one meaning. This meaning is not, therefore, subject to alternative interpretations. Such gestures include, for instance, joining thumb and index finger to describe a circle in order to convey the message "okay," and showing the forefinger and middle finger stretched and pointing upward to indicate "victory."

Conventional expressions are culturally determined and modulate extralinguistic communication with exactly the same precision with which they regulate linguistic communication. Think, for instance, just how different the forms of behavior deemed appropriate to mourning are in different countries. Actions range from burying the body, to burning it, to symbolically eating a part of it. Crying goes from silence in Native Americans to screaming in Southern Italy. David McNeill (1998) has extensively analyzed the subset of gestures generated by movements of the arms and hands in a spatial region reserved for symbolic expression, typically in front of the torso.

I define a *nonconventional gesture* as an action that is totally inscribed in the neural circuits as regards expressive modality and the ability of others to recognize it. Whereas a conventional signal has a margin of variation inasmuch as innate behavior may mix with acquired behavior, nonconventional signals are indissolubly linked to genetic design.

The fact that nonconventional signals are fundamentally genetic in nature, namely directly inscribed in the neural circuits, has an important consequence: the first reaction to the signal is triggered automatically, almost as if it were a reflex action made up of a neural and a behavioral component. A second reaction to the signal may be produced once the signal itself has been comprehended. Nevertheless, nonconventional signals belong to the sphere of communication, and must thereby be clearly distinguished from signs that others may detect and interpret, but which are never intentional in a communicative sense (see fig. 1.1).

For instance, a caress activates the automatic reaction of increasing the endorphins in the person being caressed. This reaction is due entirely to the purely physical contact between hand of the caressor and body of the caressee. The reaction is not symbolic. It is guided directly by the neural circuits in a reflex manner. When, however, the communicative intent behind the gesture is interpreted by the partner, and when, therefore, the partner understands that the gesture was carried out deliberately and with the intent that this deliberateness should be recognized as such, only then does the physical signal become a caress, with all the potential symbolic content this type of gesture may convey (love, affection, eroticism; or the opposite: fastidiousness, anger, disgust).

Nonconventional extralinguistic modalities are often connected to basic emotions and are consequently recognizable interculturally. The anger of a Samurai would be patently obvious in Arizona just as the happiness of a Bedouin would be evident in China (Oatley 1992). Nonconventional gestures may nevertheless be influenced by culture, even though they may not be ritualized in the way conventional signals can (an embrace is always an embrace, though the way one embraces one's fellow beings will not be the same in both Russia and England).

The moment brushing someone is interpreted as a caress, it may convey irony or deceit, for the very fact that it is symbolic makes it interpretable in a variety of nonliteral ways. Thus A may brush away B to make him understand she can no longer bear his presence, or she may feign a tenderness she does not feel. On the contrary, the act itself of touching another body can be neither pretense nor irony. It is simply a physical action.

I may convey my aversion toward another person with a gesture that explicitly transmits intolerance: I refuse to shake his hand, looking him straight in the eyes. In this case, the failure to carry out the socially expected gesture immediately activates a symbolic interpretation. If, instead, I slap that person, my gesture first triggers off a brain circuit causing him to feel pain; this is then followed by my gesture being interpreted as a deliberate offense, and therefore as a gesture with symbolic value.

This dual possibility applies only to extralinguistic communication, for language immediately activates the symbolic system. Naturally, language may give rise to physiological reactions—endorphins, c fibers, and so on— but only *after* the words employed have been assigned a symbolic function. For instance, we would expect some physiological reaction to also take place when the following utterance is expressed in the appropriate context, respectively by King Arthur to the unhorsed Black Knight:

"Your head, severed from your body by my invincible Excalibur, will remain as a warning to all traitors and evil-doers!"   (11)

and by the seductive witch Morgan le Fay to Merlin, who is madly in love with her despite the fact that he knows she will bind him in chains for the rest of his life:

"Kiss me, Merlin, uncover my desire."   (12)

The knight's fear and Merlin's sexual arousal follow on their comprehending the utterances directed to them. They do not occur independently of those utterances, as is the case with extralinguistic communication.

Permanent extralinguistic communication, whose effects on the world exhibit a certain amount of stability, does not enable conventional signals to be distinguished from nonconventional signals. The two aspects inevitably dissolve into thin air, since they are closely connected to the context that gave rise to the state of impermanence. Drawing is the prototypical exemplification of this fact. Indeed, Tolchinsky-Landsmann and Karmiloff-Smith (1992) postulate a specific cerebral module for this ability (fig. 1.4). The figurative arts in general, from Apelle to Picasso, may be considered a variant of the same ability.

Various types of manufactured products constitute other significant modifications made to the environment with the intention of communicating, prime among them being modes of artistic expression, represented by sculpture (fig. 1.5). Finally comes the design of closed spaces, namely architecture, and that of open spaces, namely urban design. Figure 1.6 reproduces a garden whose design is artificial. Here, the enlightenment of the painter-gardener Soami offers a sense of extreme spontaneity: in this sense, Zen gardens may be considered as nonconventional natural signs, realized thanks to a total command over the effect of conventional signals.

In the rest of the book, we will focus on conventional signals, since it is these that realize the communicative intention of an agent. However,

Figure 1.4
Paleolithic graffiti: wall paintings in Lascaux, depicting enormously powerful bulls.

Figure 1.5
Venus of Willendorf, opulent and callipygian, a symbol of generative sexuality, sculpted approximately 30,000 years ago.

bearing in mind that we are dealing with a continuum and not a binary division, we will also refer at times to nonconventional signals, both in humans and in animals. In actual fact, as soon as an actor is conscious of emitting a signal, any natural signal may become communicative in the full sense of the term. I might suddenly find that I am spontaneously smiling at a charming lady with intelligent eyes; the moment I become conscious of what I am doing, I may use my smile to communicate to her openly that I like her and that I want her to become aware of my feelings toward her. A signal that is neither conventional nor conscious is transformed into an intentional communicative expression directed at another person.

This discussion clarifies the nature of nonconventional gestures that accompany linguistic communication. Such gestures are typically unconscious. For this reason they do not set out to realize communicative goals, even if interlocutors may extract information from them. For example, those gestures that generally accompany spoken discourse are typically nonintentional, even though they are usually goal-related. The goals may be related to the content of the speech event, or to the relationship

Figure 1.6
The rock garden of the Zen temple at Ryonanji, designed in 1525 by the enlightened gardener Soami to enter into emptiness.

between the participants (for example, a person may gesticulate in a different manner depending on the identity of the other participant).

Thus, nonconventional signals may become conscious, and hence become part of the domain of communication, at any moment. The same strictures apply to the third type of communication, paralinguistic communication. Normally, paralinguistic communication is unconscious and nonintentional. For instance, prosodic intonation is not modulated intentionally; it adapts automatically to the flow of interaction, voices being raised and lowered in harmony with what is being said. It may happen, however, that a speaker may consciously begin talking in a loud voice, to convey a sense of authority (to a child) or irritation (to an adult); or volume may be kept at a high level in order to explicitly convey intensity of emotion, and so forth.

1.3   The Difference between Linguistic and Extralinguistic Is a Process, Not a Product

The alternative to distinguishing between types of communication according to how the linguistic symbols are codified is to consider the different ways in which the two types of communication process data, independently of the way in which the signals are codified: communication is a process and communicating linguistically or extralinguistically will involve employing two different ways of processing data. The same input may thus be analyzed from a linguistic and from an extralinguistic standpoint, and, presumably, except in special cases, it will be analyzed in two different ways. These ways will be parallel and will integrate each other—one will not exclude the other. Whereas from the perspective of verbal and non-verbal communication, the incoming data may be processed in only one fashion—the process being established by the intrinsic structure of the data itself—from the perspective I am proposing, each set of data is simultaneously analyzed by two different procedures, one of which is linguistic, the other being extralinguistic.

Linguistic communication: Compositionality Linguistic communication may be defined as the communicative use of a *system of symbols*. This means that language is an entity based on *compositionality*: language is built up recursively from separate components that may be joined together. Some linguistic expressions have an atomic structure, that is, they may not be subdivided into smaller, constituent units. Other expressions have a molecular structure, that is, they are composed of smaller constituents which may in their turn be either atomic or molecular. The semantic content of an expression—be it atomic or molecular—depends both on its global structure and on the semantic content of its constituents.

For instance, the meaning of an expression such as:

The leopard was observing the gazelle   (13)

is determined by the meaning of its molecular constituents (*the leopard*; *was observing*; *the gazelle*), by that of the atomic subconstituents (*the*; *leopard*; *was*; *observing*; *the*; *gazelle*), and, finally, by the global structure of the expression, for the structure as a whole yields further information that the individual constituents and subconstituents do not provide. Finally, the global structure of (13) bears a different meaning from that conveyed by

The gazelle was observing the leopard   (14)

When the number and nature of the constituents is identical, it is the global structure of the expression that gives that expression the meaning it bears. In the case of (14) subject and object have been inverted. Similarly, it is the global construction that robs the following variant of any meaning whatsoever:

Observing the the gazelle leopard was   (15)

The principle of compositionality means that language has the following characteristics, which in turn determines the way communicative expressions will be processed by the linguistic procedure:

Systematicity One fundamental aspect of language is syntactic structure (Chomsky 1957). Linguistic expressions cannot be composed or decomposed in an arbitrary fashion: the ability to generate and comprehend given expressions is intrinsically—and therefore not arbitrarily—connected to the ability to generate and comprehend other expressions of a certain type, namely expressions that are syntactically related to the original expression, because a set of basic conditions related to lexis and general knowledge has been respected. Thus a speaker who can produce and understand (13) will also be able to produce and understand examples such as the following:

Humphrey was observing Laureen.

Robespierre was observing the guillotine.

Buddha was observing emptiness.   (16)

Productivity Linguistic competence enables a speaker to generate and comprehend an infinite number of lexical meanings; in turn, these enable the speaker to generate and comprehend an infinite number of well-formed and meaningful expressions. A speaker capable of using abstract compositional principles may generate and comprehend an infinite number of specific instances.

Displacement Spatial and temporal reference made in the discourse may be spatially or temporally different from the spatial and temporal location of the speech event. For instance, an interlocutor may immediately grasp what is meant by a phrase such as:

"Let's meet tomorrow evening at Lonely Pine Beach."   (17)

The utterance may be generated and comprehended even if the interlocutors are distant in time and space from the moment and site of the planned event. This possibility is guaranteed by special-purpose referential markers called *deixis* (for instance, words such as "yesterday," or verbal suffixes indicating the past tense or the gerund). The important concept, one that was first advanced by Hockett (1960), is that language systematically allows the speaker to create spatial and temporal displacements with respect to the time and place in which the speech event occurs. In this way, it is possible to generate expressions such as "at time T" and "in place P," where T and P may be substituted by entire domains of referents.

Sign languages such as American Sign Language (ASL) belong to linguistic communication, inasmuch as they fully respect the three essential criteria I advanced above for this type of communication. In fact, ASL possesses a lexicon that is largely arbitrary, and the iconic part may be assimilated to what are onomatopoeic words in any language. Its syntax is arbitrary, compositional, and productive; acquisition processes in children are identical to those by which children learn to speak (Petitto 1987). Finally, neuropsychological evidence shows that brain areas responsible for the management of ASL are identical to those dedicated to language in speakers. In particular, in cases of speech deterioration following brain trauma, the cerebral lesions produced are identical to those observable in the deterioration of spoken and written language (Poizner, Klima, and Bellugi 1987).

Extralinguistic communication: Associative Passing on now to extralinguistic communication, this form of communication may be considered as the communicative use of a *set of symbols*. This mode is essentially *noncompositional*: that is, it consists of *parts* and not of *constituents*. Extralinguistic signals are molecular blocks that cannot be decomposed any further, inasmuch as they are equipped with intrinsic, global significance. The parts do not possess atomic meanings into which they may be further subdivided. The pirouette performed by a ballerina is a pirouette performed by the entire body, and not a pirouette that is performed by the left leg plus a pirouette that is performed by the right leg plus the torsion of the trunk and so forth. This creates a number of essential differences between extralinguistic and linguistic communication:

Associativity The property that distinguishes a noncompositional structure is that of associativity. Since there exists no systematic fashion for putting together elementary meanings to generate a global meaning that is richer than the simple sequence, each extralinguistic meaning remains an independent atom: no superordinate, or molecular, structure, is possible. This does not mean that each extralinguistic expression must stand alone, an isolated phenomenon, an entity to itself; it is obviously possible to create a sequence of symbols whose meanings are connected. The real point, however, is that the meaning of the sequence of extralinguistic acts will always derive from simple association between the various elementary symbols; it will never be the result of compositionality as happens in language.

For instance, when Aeneas flees from burning Troy obeying the orders given him by Pallas Athene, he signals to his family and servants not to speak, pointing to the groups of Achaeans warriors who are sacking the town. He would have obtained the same result if he had employed a linguistic utterance such as:

"Be silent, so as to avoid being recognized as Trojans and so being
killed by the Achaeans."   (18)

But whereas (18) exhibits a complex syntactic structure, with a main clause and two subordinate clauses, in Aeneas' imposing silence with a gesture followed by the act of indicating the enemy with a finger, we obtain a direct association between two elementary gestures. Each of these represents an entire clause; each symbolizes a concept, as the following meaningful strip demonstrates:

Silence! Enemies!   (19)

However, note that the sequence of the actions performed is meaningful. In fact, associativity (and hence extralinguistic communication) possesses a *zero-order syntax*, that is, a syntax based solely on the consecutivity of meanings.

In a similar fashion, Mirdred of Cornwall indicates to the knight she is in love with that the King is sleeping, pointing to the empty chalice that had previously contained drugged wine. She then offers him a dagger, while kissing him. The corresponding linguistic utterance would sound something like:

"My husband is sleeping a drugged sleep, because of the wine I made him drink: kill him now with this dagger, if you want to inherit his throne and nuptial bed."   (20)

Instead of a linguistic structure consisting of two coordinated main clauses, each with its own subordinate clause, the extralinguistic communicative act associates the following deictic meanings:

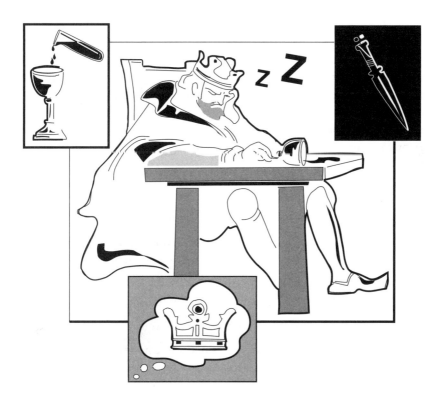

Sleeping husband! Drugged wine! Kill him! Become king!   (21)

The sequence of gestures, emitted in a given context, makes the communicative intent of the actor quite clear. The reconstruction of that intent is not determined by any syntactic rule related to communication acts, but only by consecutivity and by the interlocutor's knowledge of the world.

Theoretical Limits and Practical Impossibility of Productivity and Displacement
Productivity does not necessarily depend on systematicity: in principle, the hypothetical situation of an agent continually generating new gestures conveying shared conventional meanings is quite possible. A community consisting exclusively of agents behaving in this fashion would develop a vast and ever-increasing repertoire of gestures: the main constraints would be represented by memory capacity and by learning mechanisms. In actual practice, however, extralinguistic communication systems exhibit a highly restricted number of gestures that may be shared; clearly, the constraints imposed by memory and learning severely limit shareable signals to at most a few hundred.

This is not due to the fact that each gesture only conveys one predefined and unalterable meaning. I have already stated that meaning is constructed in the "here and now" by the participants, and this is true of any form of communication. The real point is that extralinguistic communication is in no way systematic. This means that there is not much sense in inventing a new symbol to convey a complex meaning if that new symbol will never be used again. For instance, it is unlikely that a gesture bearing one of the following meanings will be commonly employed in a community:

The evening wind coming off the sea after a hot day.

A green jacket thrown haphazardly down onto the divan.

An apple pie with almonds cooked without butter.   (22)

Enriching the extralinguistic repertoire in this way is unthinkable because it is impractical. Consider, instead, the following situations. In (23), A touches his left ear lobe to signal the following message:

"Take the car and wait for me outside the Morocco café."   (23)

If, instead, A pinches his nose, the message transmitted is:

"The Inspector suspects something is afoot. I'll leave the packet with the pearls inside in the secret drawer in the desk."   (24)

In these two cases the agents have come to a prior agreement as to the complex and secret meaning of a gesture or an action. The action thus stands for a complete speech event and therefore falls squarely—even if unusually—within the realm of symbolism.

Displacement, we will recall, is the ability to refer to time and place that go beyond the here and now. An analysis similar to that of productivity also applies to displacement. Here too, provided the constraints of learning and memory are respected, it is not theoretically impossible to construe the social construction of a gesture that denotes meanings such as:

At 2.30 PM of June 13, 1989.

In four months and fourteen days' time.

The Monterey beach cliffs.   (25)

It is, however, quite obvious that such gestures would have no possibility of becoming firmly established in the communicative repertoire of a community, because the inability to reuse them would render their acquisition pointless: the cognitive cost would be the total waste of collective memory and culture.

Figure 1.7 summarizes the features of the two types of communication.

We may now complete our discussion of the difference between linguistic and extralinguistic modes of communication. Any type of communication may be produced and processed by employing one of the two modalities described above. Nor must it be forgotten that a third form must be added to these two modalities: paralinguistic communication. There are

	Nature	Productivity	Displacement
Linguistic	compositonal: system of symbols	infinite	possible
Extralinguistic	associative: set of symbols	theoretically limited, unrealizable in practice	theoretically limited, useless in practice

Figure 1.7
Essential differences between linguistic and extralinguistic communication.
Source: Bara and Tirassa 1999.

types of input that may be processed using both types of modalities concurrently. This is the case with normal, face-to-face communication, where the two interlocutors employ the linguistic components provided by the dialogue while simultaneously employing extralinguistic elements stemming from the observation of each other's gestures and actions. In this case, the two forms cooperate to construct a coherent meaning to attribute to the conversation. Whenever possible, both modalities increase the quantity and quality of knowledge to be shared. Collaboration, in contrast to competition, means that the final result is a composite of all the participants' contributions.

Some types of input privilege linguistic communication, such as an audio recording or a letter. In the latter example, the paralinguistic mode is realized by the type of paper, the handwriting, and so forth, provided that they have been consciously and deliberately employed by the writer in order to convey something to the reader. It should be noted that a linguistic structure may also be processed by employing the extralinguistic modality. For instance, if a tourist does not have a great command over the language of the country he is visiting, he may try to understand the main points of the news published in the newspaper by trying to comprehend the few words he is acquainted with, thereby ignoring syntax, which he is weak on, and privileging elementary associationism.

Vice versa, other types of input favor the extralinguistic modality, as do an emotionally important bodily interaction such as a heartfelt embrace conveying gratitude or a silent film. However, in these cases too it is not the nature of the input data that determine the processing mode, because the linguistic mode may be activated in an attempt to extrapolate a linguistic interpretation.

If we accept the fact that both communicative modalities are activated independently, and then work together to build what will be the shared meaning attributed to the interaction, this poses a series of questions. The first concerns the type of relationship between communicative modalities and the development of the human system: the evolution of communication will be dealt with in chapter 6.

The second question is whether independent communication-specific modules exist. The philosopher Jerry Fodor furnishes the definition of a *cognitive module* as "domain specific, innately specified, hardwired, autonomous, and not assembled" (Fodor 1983, p. 37). The concept of a module is still the subject of heated debate, especially because of the misuse that has been made of the concept by a certain brand of psychology and by a certain brand of neuropsychology that, by claiming that any process is capable of being modularized, authorized the independent study of micro-phenomena without having to worry about the connections between the phenomenon being investigated and the global activity of the mind or of the brain. A similar concept proposed by the neuropsychologist Tim Shal-lice (1988) has been widely adopted in the neurosciences. Shallice's concept is, however, structurally less rigid. He adopts Tulving's definition of an *isolable functional subsystem*: "a system that can operate independently of the other although not necessarily as efficiently. The operations of one system could be enhanced without a similar effect on the operations of the other; similarly the operations of one system could be suppressed without a comparable effect on the activity of the other. The functional difference also implies that in important, or at least in non-negligible ways, the systems operate differently, that is, that their function is governed at least partially by different principles" (Tulving 1983, p. 66).

I will treat the two communicative modalities as two *isolable functional systems*, not as two separate modules. The relationships between them and the principal processing procedures are represented in figure 1.8. The two systems are virtually independent of one another. This mirrors their different phylogenetic origins, a point confirmed by the fact that they may be dissociated when neurological lesions occur.

The central procedures process the information coming from the two communicative systems in different ways, in the sense that the incoming information is not of the same kind from the two systems, and the information itself is specifically pertinent to one of the channels employed. For example, the linguistic system may furnish displaced referential data while the extralinguistic channel activates emotional systems directly realized in the brain.

At a certain level, however, the information acquired through both the functional systems must become equivalent from a processing standpoint; to be exact, at the point at which the actor's communicative intent has to be reconstructed, central inferencing processes use any type of information whatsoever to produce an acceptable meaning.

Whatever form perception may take (sight, sound, touch, smell, etc.), sensory activation precedes the attribution of meaning. Once meaning has been comprehended, however, it may influence the neurophysiological functioning of the system. We may thus conclude that the information coming from the two communication channels differs in the way it activates central processes depending on which channel the information comes from. However, once the two different types of information have been adequately symbolized, they are dealt with in the same manner,

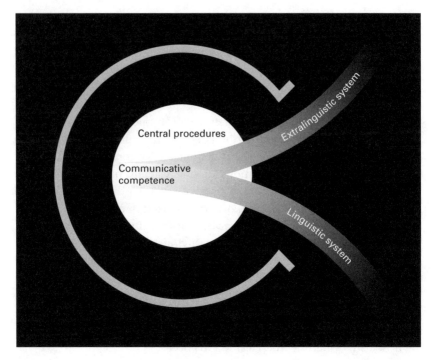

Figure 1.8
Relationships between the linguistic functional system, the extralinguistic functional system, and the central processing procedures.

barring the specific systems that may have been automatically activated in the first stage. At bottom, an actor's communication acts must in some way be attributed meaning (the part that is common to both channels in central processing), whatever channel the acts have been received through and analyzed by (the separate part of central processing, which takes into account the specific communicative channel).

The fact that the two modules are functionally independent may sometimes lead to a discrepancy between the results obtained from one channel and those obtained from the other channel. In this case, central processing will solve the dilemma, giving credence to the more reliable of the two channels in that specific context, or, for instance, by systematically preferring one of the two channels. For example, if an assertion conveying apologies to one's superior is not accompanied by appropriate deferential behavior, the inconsistency between the two types of information would be solved depending on whether the interlocutor were to give more importance to the emotional relationship (preferentially conveyed by the extralinguistic channel) or to the official part of the interaction (typically conveyed by the linguistic channel).

Extralinguistic communication is more effective in transmitting basic meanings precisely because it is more elementary. For exactly the same reason, extralinguistic communication requires greater knowledge and a greater effort on the part of memory and inferencing processes in order to be understood as soon as it attempts to convey more complex messages. By contrast, the compositional structure of language simplifies communication enormously: it is easier to communicate using constituents rather than parts, once the constituents are accessible and the actor has mastered the principles of compositionality. From an evolutionary standpoint, linguistic structure is an important conquest, one that makes it possible to communicate with ease what, instead, constitutes an insurmountable difficulty for extralinguistic communication.

1.4 Communication Acts

The origins of the pragmatic approach to language are to be found in the philosophy of language, a movement that developed in Oxford and Cambridge in the 1930s thanks respectively to John Austin and Ludwig Wittgenstein. With his *Tractatus Logico-philosophicus* (Wittgenstein 1922), which ended with the optimistic seventh aphorism "What we cannot speak about we must pass over in silence," Wittgenstein contributed to founding and spreading the theory of verificationism that had stemmed from within the logical positivist movement. Verificationism stated that any utterance that cannot be verified, that could not be attributed a truth-value, was meaningless.

Utterances which are philosophically meaningful, namely those whose truth-value may be established, include:

Napoleon Bonaparte was born on August 15, 1769.

Tahiti is an island in Hawaii.

Tahiti is an island in Polynesia.   (26)

The following utterances are philosophically nonsensical from a rigorously verificationist standpoint, for they cannot be tested for their truth-value:

I wish you loved me as much as I love you.

Verdi does not reach the supreme heights of Mozart.

All living beings are entitled to respect.   (27)

Verificationism poses logical problems that cannot be solved. The most important of these concerns the difference between the meaning of an utterance and the procedures by which its truth conditions may be verified. The truthfulness of many assertions may be discovered quite simply by consulting a book. This is the case with the assertions in (26). However, it may be practically impossible to discover whether the assertion:

The headmaster has fallen in love with the new secretary.   (28)

is true or false. Notwithstanding this, a listener is quite capable of comprehending the meaning of (28), independently of what he would have to do if he decided he wanted to find out what the headmaster's true sentiments were. Matters become even more complicated when we move to the free world of literature:

Ulysses killed the suitors.   (29)

What does checking an action carried out by an imaginary character mean? Even more difficult is validating the case of a metaphorical action carried out by a historical figure. Think of Count Ugolino, who is to be found in the ninth circle of Hell, that of traitors to their guests, eternally eating the skull of Archbishop Ruggieri (Dante: *Hell*, Canto XXXIII):

Lifting his mouth from his horrendous meal,
this sinner first wiped off his messy lips
in the hair remaining on the chewed-up skull.

Difficulties of this nature weaken the verificationist position in favor of a less rigid, less abstract, and less "objective" position, one that takes into account daily, "subjective" criteria, connected to what people really do when they speak. In the most important work of his mature period, Wittgenstein (1953) modifies his position by introducing the concept of the language game, which allows him to identify the meaning of language as the actual use to which language is put. Austin (1962), who at Oxford was studying daily language use independently of Wittgenstein at Cambridge, reached virtually the same conclusions.

1.4.1 Saying Is Doing

The spirit of the philosophers of language was that of abandoning the abstract research carried out by linguists in order to concentrate on the use people make of words in their day-to-day lives—not the study of the linguistic norms, but the investigation of everyday conversations, of the linguistic games people actually play with each other. "Saying is doing" thus becomes the motto of pragmatics, and attention is focused on how people construct verbal cooperation among themselves. The key concept at the roots of pragmatics is the *speech act*. Austin notes that in precisely given circumstances and situations, certain utterances expressed in the declarative form (*performatives*) modify the world in exactly the same way as do actions. Furthermore, talking about whether such utterances are true or false is senseless. What matters is not their truth-value, but whether they are successful or not, whether they are "felicitous" or "infelicitous." For instance, the utterance:

"The accused is sentenced to a fine of £900 pounds or to thirty days' imprisonment."   (30)

if uttered by the judge in the proper context imposes upon the condemned man a fine or a prison sentence, and certain people (court officials, prison officers) are consequently obliged to carry out actions that will ensure that the punishment actually is inflicted. Similarly, the utterance:

"I baptize thee Julius John."   (31)

if uttered by the vicar in the appropriate context determines the imposing of the name "Julius John" on the baby, and that that baby will be called by that name from that moment on. Performatives may be successful, modifying the world in the desired direction, provided that the speaker respects what Austin calls the *felicity conditions* governing the complete execution of a conventional procedure.

If the conditions do not correspond to those laid down for the successful completion of a given act, then the performative will fail. For example, a judge can condemn no one to prison if he is not sitting in a courtroom, or if the law on procedure in criminal trials has not been followed to the letter. In those cases, one would say that "the sentence is not valid" or that "the trial is not fair." It is incongruous, however, to comment on the sentence in terms of truth and falsity.

One of the fundamental consequences of considering language in terms of speech acts is that language is then considered within the framework of the general laws regulating actions: in particular, focus is brought to bear on intentionality.

Considering speech acts as actions, Austin (1962) posits that a speech act has three separate constituents: a locutionary act, an illocutionary act, and a perlocutionary act:

The *locutionary* act corresponds to the emission of an utterance having determinate sense and reference.

The *illocutionary* act corresponds to the speaker's communicative intentions in uttering the message.

The *perlocutionary* act corresponds to the effect the speaker wishes to achieve in the mind of the of the interlocutor by means of uttering the expression.

The locutionary act represents what is said, the illocutionary act represents what is done in saying something, and the perlocutionary act what one wishes to obtain through saying something. A few examples will shed light over this tripartite distinction:

Locution: "Don't move or I'll shoot you!"
Illocution: threatens the addressee;
Perlocution: induces the addressee to stand still.   (32)

Locution: "I didn't break the vase!"
Illocution: protests her innocence;
Perlocution: convinces the addressee of her innocence.   (33)

Locution: "Do it for friendship's sake."
Illocution: begs a favor of the addressee;
Perlocution: obtains the favor from the addressee.   (34)

Locution: "Have pity on me!"
Illocution: implores;
Perlocution: moves addressee to pity.   (35)

The three parts of a speech act are governed by different sets of felicity conditions determining the success or failure of each phase. In addition, success at one stage does not automatically imply success at the following stage.

If we take example (32), the locutionary phase may fail if for instance B is deaf or if he does not understand English, or if a sudden noise drowns out A's words. But even if the locutionary phase meets with success, this is no guarantee that the illocutionary phase cannot fail—B might think A is joking, or that A is incapable of pulling the trigger, or he may be convinced that the gun is not loaded. Finally, illocutionary success is not necessarily followed by perlocutionary success. B might decide to move in spite of the threat, in the hope that A will miss him, or because he does not care whether he lives or dies, or perhaps to show how courageous he is.

We may immediately note a first difference between locutionary and illocutionary aspects, on the one hand, and the perlocutionary aspect of a speech act, on the other. The first two are essentially conventional and are enacted in an area of linguistic knowledge shared by both speaker and listener. By contrast, the perlocutionary act is strictly private, pertaining exclusively to the world of the listener—it takes place in the listener's mind, and there is no direct way the speaker can discover if the perlocutionary effect is felicitous or not. The addressee may have comprehended assertion (33), but might not believe it; may have understood the request for a favor (34), but not concede it; may have heard the cry for pity (35), but not be moved.

1.4.2 Conversational Implicature and Conversational Maxims

The most important bridge between language and communication is constituted by the concept of *conversational implicature*. To comprehend the origin of this special type of inference, reference must be made not to language, but rather to the norms regulating social and conversational interaction. Paul Grice (1975) illustrated how everyday language use has contents that are transmitted through the use of words, but that in no way derive from the meaning of the words themselves. In other terms, some things are not said directly, but are rather "implicated" by what is said. These implicatures are intentionally communicated by the speaker to the listener. Consider the following conversational exchange:

A: What's Claire's boyfriend like?
B: I can't understand why she is content with a man like that!   (36)

B has not furnished a literal reply to A's question. Nevertheless, he has indisputably given her reason to believe that the characteristics that attracted Claire are unknown to him. In order to explain the norms governing this particular type of inference, Grice's first point was that every conversation is the result of cooperation between two people who share a common goal. The conversation also presents a mutually shared development, rendering certain moves acceptable at certain stages in communication and not at others. Grice therefore formulates the following *cooperative principle*: "Make your contribution such as is required, at the stage at which it occurs, by the accepted purpose or direction of the talk exchange in which you are engaged" (Grice 1975, p. 45).

This general principle is specified in four maxims, recalling Kant's four categories:

1. *The maxim of quantity*
1a. Make your contribution as informative as is required in relation to the goal of the conversation.
1b. Do not make your contribution more informative than is required.

2. *The maxim of quality*
Try to make your contribution one that is true.
The quality maxim may be specified further into:
2a. Do not say what you believe to be false.
2b. Do not say that for which you lack adequate evidence.

3. *The maxim of relation*
Be pertinent.

4. *The maxim of manner*
Be perspicuous.
Unlike the other maxims, the maxim of manner does not refer to the content of what is said, but to how it is said. It may be further specified into:
4a. Avoid obscurity of expression.
4b. Avoid ambiguity.
4c. Be brief.
4d. Be orderly.

It should be noted that the four principles do not apply exclusively to language, but to action in general:

1. *Quantity*: I expect a contribution that is quantitatively adequate. For instance, if I am making the mayonnaise and I ask you to add two egg yolks, I expect you to add two, not one or four.
2. *Quality*: I expect an authentic contribution. For example, if you offer me a glass of what we take to be cognac, I expect the glass to contain cognac, and not colored water, or even brandy (if we are in a civilized country).
3. *Relation*: I expect a contribution appropriate to the stage the exchange has reached. For instance, if we are at dinner, I do not expect to start off with apple pie, which will be acceptable later on, when we get to the dessert.
4. *Manner*: I expect my partner to clarify what he is doing, and to do so rapidly and in an orderly manner. For example, if we are working together on assembling the video recorder, then I must know what you will be doing, and I expect you to carry it out in a reasonable time and without any incongruities.

Grice's aim is not to furnish a book of etiquette on conversation, even though children are indubitably taught to respect something of the sort in a more or less explicit fashion. Rather, the goal of the maxims is to clarify the kinds of criteria we use to create the inferential chain that,

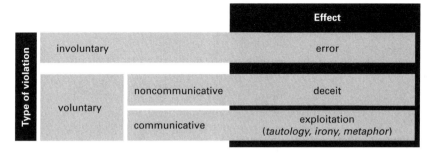

Figure 1.9
Types of violation of Gricean maxims and their effects.

departing from the speaker's utterance, extends to the comprehension achieved by the listener. Returning to example (36), if A can assume B is cooperating, then she is in a position to understand what B is seeking to communicate to her, namely that Claire's fiancé does not appear to possess any attractive features; otherwise the reply would seem to have no connection whatsoever with the question asked.

The maxims are respected in a well-conducted conversation. Naturally, they may also be violated, thus giving rise to various interesting cases. The possible types of infringements are shown in figure 1.9.

Error Error consists of an involuntary violation of a maxim, unfortunately a frequent occurrence in everyday conversation. Examples of chronic, nondeliberate violations (the maxims being violated are signaled in square brackets) are those committed continually by prolix speakers [1b], by superficial speakers [2b], by distracted speakers [3], by disorganized speakers [4d].

Naturally, anyone, including even generally cooperative speakers, may flout a maxim without realizing it, or realizing it too late. Error does not intentionally transgress the cooperative principle, because the speaker lacks the intention to communicate something misleading. Errors may or may not be detected by the listener. At an examination, the teacher will presumably discern the mistakes of the examinees, but the client of a financial advisor or of a lawyer is not usually able to detect mistaken predictions or bad advice. If it is the speaker that possesses the greater quantity of information, the error will escape the listener. If it is the listener who finds himself in this privileged position, then the error will be recognized as such. From this derives the fact that if the addressee infers something from the lack of respect of a maxim, the addressee does so over and beyond the intentions of the addressor, since the latter is normally far from desirous of having an error she might have committed detected.

Deceit   Deceit is a deliberate but not communicative violation of one or more of the maxims, in which the addressor attempts to deceive the addressee by inducing the latter into drawing incorrect inferences. The deceiver has both the conscious intention of deceiving and also the equally conscious intention of preventing the addressee from discovering the deceit. Full-fledged lies violate the quality maxim [2]. For instance:

Doctor Bovary: Are you faithful to me?
Emma Bovary: But of course, darling.   (37)

There is a whole category of lies consisting in withholding a significant part of the truth, without ever reaching the point of openly asserting a falsehood. The doctor failing to inform the patient as to the real gravity of his illness, the adolescent hiding something from her mother to avoid causing her worry, the benevolent critic who does not speak out when she cannot utter praise: these are all instances of deceit through the violation of the maxim of quantity, provided nobody realizes that something has been omitted. In British law, witnesses in a trial are wisely made to swear they will not only tell the truth (commitment to respecting the maxim of quality), but will tell the whole truth (commitment to respecting the maxim of quantity), and nothing but the truth (commitment to respecting the maxims of relation and manner).

Violations of the maxim of relation may be achieved by changing the subject without the addressee realizing. The concept of dissimulation is tied to the simultaneous flouting of the maxims of relation and manner, avoiding the commitment of the more socially serious infringements of the maxims of quantity and quality.

The key point in deceit is that the deceived must not realize that the deceiver has deliberately violated a maxim. The deceiver attempts to do so in a noncommunicative manner, that is, trying to ensure the deceived does not become aware of the violation. Naturally, the deceived party may detect the deception, in which case two choices are open to him: unmasking the deception, or effecting a counter-deception, in other words attempting in his turn to induce his partner into drawing the wrong inferences. Countless examples are furnished by the double-crossing rampant in espionage and counter-espionage services: a person discovered to be a spy may be deliberately fed false secret information passed off as true, thus deceiving the deceiver by playing a double game.

Exploitation Exploitation constitutes a communicative violation of a maxim in which speaker A induces listener B into making a series of inferences based on the fact that he has realized that speaker A openly intends to flout the maxim by communicating to B that she was violating the maxim. The difference between deceit and exploitation lies in the fact that in the former the violation is hidden, whereas in the latter it is openly displayed for communicative purposes. We shall now examine a few examples of exploitation of the various maxims. Tautologies, utterances devoid of informative literal content, exploit the maxim of quantity (first specification):

A woman is only a woman, but a good cigar is a smoke.   (38)

Both the speaker—in this case male chauvinist Rudyard Kipling, in his poem "The Betrothed" (circa 1885)—and the hearers know full well that women remain women forever, and also that cigars turn to smoke. Yet, the juxtaposition implicates the repetitiveness in being a woman among women, as compared to the absoluteness of a Havana cigar.

The maxim of quality may be exploited in various ways, the most frequent case being irony. Another way of infringing on the quality maxim is by using metaphor. Here the utterance is obviously false from the literal point of view, but the implications of the comparison are significant. Powerfully evocative examples are provided by the Song of Songs:

Your eyes are like doves.
[. . .]
Like purple ribbon your lips,
your mouth an invitation:
segments of pomegranate are your cheeks.
[. . .]
Your breasts are like two roe-deer,
two twin gazelles,
browsing among the anemones.   (39)

The above two cases merge in ironic metaphor, where literality is flouted, and at the same time the quality named is inappropriate to the referent. For example, a person behaving in a particularly treacherous manner may be rewarded for his efforts by sarcasm:

"You're a real sweetie-pie."   (40)

Working within a sociological perspective, the philosopher Jürgen Habermas has advanced a set of *validity claims* that coincide in part with Grice's maxims and are intended as a prolegomenon to a universal pragmatics. In Habermas's (1976) view, speech acts are founded on four consensual presuppositions that define the *valid assertions* in an utterance. In other words, in uttering a speech act, a speaker *claims* that:

Her contribution is true: this first presupposition corresponds to Grice's quality maxim.
Her contribution is comprehensible: this second presupposition comprises Grice's maxims of quantity, relation and manner.
Her manifest expression of intention is truthful.
Her utterance is right and appropriate in relation to the recognized normative context.

Habermas (1979) focuses his analysis on the concept of *commitment*: the essential presupposition for an illocutionary act to be successful is that the speaker make a commitment so that the listener may trust her—she must commit herself to taking certain courses of action if certain conditions hold. Both Winograd and Flores (1986) and Cohen and Levesque (1990a,b) have considered commitment to be a central tenet. The former have made it the cornerstone of their considerations on the nature of interaction between human and machine. The latter have based their idea of communicative interaction on this concept. A reciprocal assumption of commitment is to be found as a basic component of a behavior game. The latest development of this approach may be found in philosopher Margaret Gilbert's work on joint commitment (Gilbert 2006).

1.5 Principles of Communication

Each and every use of a communicative tool is subject to the general constraints of communication itself. Hence, both linguistic and extralinguistic pragmatics must respect these rules. We may term such constraints *general principles of communication*. They are valid for every form of communicative behavior. These principles will be analyzed in chapter 6, when I deal with the theme of the evolution of language.

In addition to general principles, there also exists a set of constraints that are specific to linguistic communication as a special communicative mode. This second set of *rules specific to linguistic communication* is embodied in the lexicon, syntax, semantics, and pragmatics of language, and is determined by both genetics and culture.

Finally, there is a third set of constraints, which, although they are less open to formalization compared to linguistic rules, I will nevertheless call *rules specific to extralinguistic communication*. This third set of rules is also determined by both genetics and culture. Such principles may characterize a specific domain, such as those that underlie the transcultural recognition of basic emotions. Or else they may pertain to a particular mode of perception, such as the olfactive perception of sexual pheromones, or the visual or auditory perception of signals of aggressiveness and danger.

General principles of communication   Each of the following principles will be discussed and justified starting in the next chapter. Figure 1.10 provides the general taxonomy of communication, which summarizes all of the basic components I have introduced so far.

Cooperation.   Communication is a cooperative activity in which both the significance of each communication act is agreed on by the agents and the global significance of the interaction satisfies the motivations of all the participants. The latter concept underlies the notion of behavior game, that is to say of a structured and shared interaction among agents. The relationship between agents in a communicative interaction thus presupposes some form of stable cooperation.

Common attention.   For communication to take place, contact conditions, or their equivalent, must be met: the partner must have understood that the actions executed by the actor are expressive, that is to say, they constitute an attempt to establish a communication with him. The very fact that A tries to attract B's attention implies that A is doing something expressive.

Communicative intentionality.   The communication is openly intentional. That is, the actor wants her partner to recognize not only the informational content of the communication act but also that she is attempting to communicate something relevant. This implies that communicative activity is always conscious.

Communication is symbolic.   What is considered the meaning of the interaction is constructed by both participants together. Acting is not communicative in itself. It only becomes such when all the participants agree that it has the status of communication. In other words, the action becomes an act of communication when it is attributed a shared meaning, that is to say, the action is taken to refer to something else in order to be comprehended.

Information extraction		
nonintentional, nonsymbolic		

	Cue	*Sign*
In animals	plumage, horns	nest, footprints
In humans	complexion, height	refuse, fingerprints

Animal communication
intentional, nonsymbolic

Signal
courting, aggression

Human communication
intentional, symbolic

Linguistic
compositional, system of symbols

	Syntax	Semantics	Pragmatics
Permanent (alphabetical writing)			
Impermanent (dialogue)			

Extralinguistic
Compositional, set of symbols

	Conventional signal (symbolic, cultural)		Nonconventional signal (genetic + symbolic)	
	actions open to interpretation (bereavement, wedding)	gestures with fixed meanings (hello, victory)	part hard-wired in the brain (effect of being touched)	symbolic part (meaning of a caress)
Permanent (drawings, pictograms)				
Impermanent (music)				

Paralinguistic
devices modifying meaning

Linguistic devices prosody	Behavioral devices emotional dimension of gestures

Figure 1.10
Taxonomy of social interaction. The dimensions of permanence and impermanence of communication are orthogonal in respect to the other distinctions.

Sharedness. Communication takes place on the basis of increasingly shared knowledge. The greater the knowledge shared, the more effective the communication will be.

Conversation. Interactants must employ forms of conversation that are appropriate to the situation: they must follow precedence, comply with turn taking, ensure discourse coherence, and so on.

Cultural dependency. A society's cultural norms must be respected. Hence communication acts must conform to those norms. In particular, global communicative effectiveness derives from the successful integration of the linguistic mode of communication with the extralinguistic mode, and the congruence of the two. Successful integration also depends on the genetic structure being compatible with acquired social structures.

Linguistic and extralinguistic functional systems. Linguistic and extralinguistic communication are two modes of realizing communication that are not in competition with each other but which must integrate harmoniously with each other. They are to be viewed as functional subsystems that may be isolated, even if both have the same objectives.

2 Tools for Communicating

Before laying out the points on which cognitive pragmatics is based, I would like to outline certain fundamental methodological aspects. What instruments are available for validating theories? How may a theory be falsified, in order to confirm it if it manages to resist all attacks (Popper 1934)? The philosopher of science Thomas Kuhn (1962) insists that a successful theory should convince one's fellow scientists, and his colleague Imre Lakatos (1970) asks the question of how wide-ranging and fruitful is the research program proposed by the theory. Both these issues are important, but the answers to them will come not from the author of this book but from readers and colleagues. It is the latter who will decide whether a theory is successful and fruitful.

What, then, is the author's task? I believe it consists in furnishing all the possible evidence in favor of the theory he or she is advancing. The evidence must conform to the criteria of scientificness holding in the relevant domain. In the present case, the domain I will be investigating is that of developmental cognitive science. Since I have already gone deeply into the question of methodology in my handbook on cognitive science (Bara 1995), I will here recall only the key points of this methodology: formalization, construction (in its dual aspect: evolutionary and developmental), neural correlation.

Formalization A theory must be formalized. Formalization may be achieved using either logic or the computational method. A theory that has not been formalized, even if only partially so, cannot be considered as belonging fully to the domain of cognitive science. A computer implementation of a model of the theory is to be considered as constituting an equivalent alternative to formalization in terms of logic. In classic cognitive science, the role of artificial intelligence is to provide a common methodology: it must be possible, at least in theory, to simulate models of different functions expressed in different terms through the use of a computer program.

The aim of this criterion is to eliminate those theories exhibiting internal contradictions, or which are irredeemably metaphorical or irreparably vague. The price readers must pay is a set of logical steps that must be made explicit if they are to comprehend how the theory has been constructed. The entire book abounds in such illustrations. Readers may take consolation in the fact that such illustrations are functional to the economy of argumentation and explanation.

Construction   This criterion was inspired by the physicist and Nobel laureate Percy Bridgman who asserted that a state or a phenomenon may be defined by the operations required to reconstruct it. According to Bridgman (1927) an event cannot be fully understood if, once a given set of initial conditions have been satisfied, we are unable to reproduce it. The prototype of a scientific theory is a recipe: given the basic ingredients (flour, milk, eggs, etc.) and the necessary tools (pot, oven, etc.), anyone who is sufficiently experienced should be able to follow the instructions in the recipe to obtain the desired result at the end (e.g., an apple pie).

The objective of this criterion is to eliminate all those theories that do not guarantee duplication of a procedure inasmuch as they fail to make all the steps in the procedure explicit (as in magic), or which tie the phenomenon being investigated to some characteristic of the investigator (as in the case of the fairy who can change pumpkins into carriages, where ordinary mortals cannot). The reader should be wary of smiling at this example, for psychotherapy is teeming with fairy stories whose effects, no matter whether the stories are told in good or bad faith, always have dramatic consequences for the patients and our students.

In our domain, constructivism may take one of two possible forms: *evolutionary* or *developmental*.

The construction of a theory from the standpoint of the evolution of the species constitutes an attempt to establish how probable it is that a given mental function developed, both through the global tree that goes from mammals to apes, and through the specific evolutionary line that goes from australopithecine to modern man. For instance, the bond between mother and child is best understood if we possess knowledge about the relationships between mother and little one in other animal species, and if we are in a position to make well-founded hypotheses about these relationships in the various stages in the evolution of hominids. Many of our hypotheses on evolution are not directly observable, but derive from inductions based on indirect evidence obtained from archaeology and anthropology.

The construction of a theory from the standpoint of individual development is based on the claim that to be able to understand how a given function operates in the adult system, in other words at the stage of full and stable maturity, it is necessary to understand how that function developed from infancy through childhood and adolescence. For example, adult sexuality is indissolubly linked to a series of stages experienced in infancy and adolescence: if one possesses knowledge of these stages, then one can fully understand what each adult individual can and cannot do, as far as his or her sexuality is concerned.

Neural correlation   Mental states and psychic processes are all realized in the brain; they are not the abstract processes of a virtual machine. The importance of embodying psychological concepts emerged with great force thanks to the recent successes obtained in the neurosciences. In particular, cognitive neuropsychology has made it its business to establish the neural correlates of our mental functions. Researchers use a variety of techniques in pursuing this goal, of which the most important are anatomical and functional investigations and selective dissociation.

When techniques of anatomical and functional investigation are employed, subjects are asked to carry out a series of tasks while enveloped in equipment that monitors their neural activity. The areas that are selectively active when a subject is carrying out a task (such as understanding a sentence, imagining she can see a camel and rotating it in space, solving a problem using deduction) are specific and highly pertinent to the task at hand.

Techniques of selective dissociation aim at establishing correlations between functional inabilities and neural lesions. If one area of the brain has been damaged, and the patient is no longer capable of carrying out a particular task, then it is hypothesized that the damaged area was dedicated to that task, or at least necessary for the execution of that task. For example, a focal lesion in Broca's left parietal lobe brings about aphasia, a fact that enables us to connect Broca's area with language capacity.

The objective of this criterion is to establish the connections between mind and brain: a theory that can predict that given pathologies will lead to specific psychological problems is a theory that is more wide-ranging and fruitful than a theory that is unable to establish any connections whatsoever. Increasing the constraints on a theory increases its heuristic value, furnishing indications that sometimes have important washback effects, for example, for clinical and rehabilitation purposes.

Analyzing communication from a cognitive standpoint means, essentially, considering a mental act as the product of all those participating in its execution, and then breaking it down starting from the individual mental states of each participant. Philosophers of mind agree to a reasonable degree on the nature of some of these mental states, for instance, attention, knowledge, belief, and individual intention. Consequently, psychologists, neuroscientists, cognitive scientists, and scholars of artificial intelligence, tend to concur on the same concepts. When these mental states lose their individual status and become collective phenomena, then the terms used to refer to them are common attention, mutual belief, and collective intention. Here, however, consensus declines quite noticeably.

All the mental states mentioned will be considered not as entities in themselves, as absolutes, but only as structures that are necessary for communication to take place. Hence, I will not deal with them exhaustively. I will cover only those aspects that are pertinent to my theme. In particular, I will offer an original definition of two variants of these concepts, that is, of shared belief and of communicative intention, primitives that are indispensable to the theory of cognitive pragmatics.

2.1   Cooperation

Let us consider the following poem by Sawaki Kodo:

The darkness of the shade of the pine trees,
Depends
On the moonlight.

Does this poem have only one meaning? Despite the vast amount of critical material available to comment on the poem, explain it and interpret it (see Deshimaru 1977), everybody is free to take it as he or she wishes, choosing from among the many levels of comprehension possible. Every reader becomes a sort of coauthor of the poem—though it cannot be denied that Sawaki has placed precise constraints on interpretation by selecting certain signs and not others, constructing lines of a certain length, and so on. Nevertheless, while still respecting the words of the poem, different readers—with different life histories, different personalities, different cultures—construct different meanings, all of which are compatible with the same set of words, written once only for all the interpretations that have been and will be given. Furthermore, the English speaker is now reading a transliteration into Latin alphabet, in which the original Japanese ideograms are lost. Each ideogram is composed of elementary signs that often have more than one meaning. Despite the fact that the Japanese reader selects a specific interpretation of the graphological sign, he may nevertheless be influenced by the secondary meanings of the ideograms employed, thus maintaining an overall richness that the alphabetical translation cannot retain.

Sawaki's message lives anew each time we reread his poem; in addition, this meaning continually changes as the context in which the reader finds himself changes. The same applies to a painting, a film or a symphony. The spectator is the author's partner, to the point that he becomes a rightful coauthor of meaning. The importance of the original author lies in the fact that for each work, the author remains the fixed and stable element in each author–user pair. Picasso, Disney, and Mozart have thus guaranteed for themselves trillions and trillions of interactions, continuing to live each time a new partner takes up one of their works, recreating it, adding his own contribution to that of the artist. In literary criticism, an equivalent stance asserts that the work is created every time the reader engages with the original and apparently unchangeable text produced by the writer.

For an act to be fully communicative, there must be at least two actors and both must have the intention of generating the act together. The construction of meaning comes about the moment that the two agents pool their parts; *physical copresence*, that is, a sharing of the same spatio-temporal location, is not, however, essential.

In the case of ordinary face-to-face conversation, the two interlocutors do come into physical contact. This is the prototypical situation. But a conversation carried out on the phone, for example, where physical copresence is absent and a common space is not shared, remains a bona fide conversation. Obviously, talking to someone over the phone is different from talking to that person face to face: extralinguistic communication is virtually impossible in this type of situation, obliging the interlocutors to rely almost exclusively on verbal language, thereby losing much valuable information. No matter how reduced such a form of conversation may be, a telephone call nevertheless remains a valid form of communicative activity, one in which all the general rules of communication still hold.

Let us now modify the situation further, so that the second dimension of physical copresence is also eliminated—temporal copresence. If A telephones Sydney from Rome, she will notice that her voice reaches the ear of her interlocutor with a delay of a few tenths of a second, because of the great distance the sound has to travel. To avoid a confusing overlap of questions and answers, A and B will rapidly learn to lengthen the pauses indicating a change in conversational turn. This will give the receiver time to hear and reply without subverting turn-taking norms. Although a temporal delay is introduced between emission and reception of the message, we may assume that the agents still keep to the general scheme of conversation, even though certain small tactical modifications are made.

Two people who communicate electronically have even longer intervals between one message and another, and two people corresponding by post accept intervals that last for days. In these cases, too, messages take on life the moment they are received, and not when they are sent. A letter that gets lost cannot be considered to be a genuine message that has simply not been received, but an aborted attempt at communicating. Stated differently, there is no entity that may be accorded the status of a message right from the outset, independently, that is, of the activity of the person destined to receive it. Thus, when physical copresence is absent, an attempt at communicating takes place in a spatiotemporal dimension that is virtual, and it becomes real only when the addressee receives the message and considers it such, in other words when he recognizes its status as a communication act.

We may thus classify most of communication that takes place via the computer as virtual communication. In this case, the analysis of the context in which the communication takes place becomes a fundamental criterion. People who interact through the computer are no longer simply the users of a given system, but social actors in the real sense of the term. Whereas initially it was human beings who were forced to adapt to complex computer rules, now it is taken for granted that it is the objectives of the human users that must determine the conception and use of the manufactured product.

Meaning is constructed through the interaction of speaking and listening, or writing and reading. The meaning of a communicative event comes into being through the abstract contemporaneous execution of the two reciprocal activities. Spatial distance and temporal intervals are problems related to the channel along which the message is transmitted, not to the meaning of the message. A further point, however, is that the channel influences the content: the agents must take into consideration the constraints a given type of channel imposes upon the content to be conveyed. Adjusting the message to the channel is a process that is carried out automatically. Nevertheless, it should not be forgotten that becoming used to a genuinely innovative mode of communication is no simple matter. The custom of exchanging written messages is only two hundred years old, since prior to that time postal services were the exclusive preserve of the aristocracy and diplomacy. The telephone is so recent that many elderly people are still unable to use that instrument without encountering any difficulties. Electronic messages are still the privilege of a minority, even if this mode is expanding rapidly.

Each communicative interaction is an activity where the initiative alternates between the participants involved, and where the responsibility for the interaction is constantly shared between those participants. In the philosophy of language, in sociology, in linguistics, in psychology, in psychotherapy, the approach based on shared activity has gained methodologically ever stronger positions compared to the stance that views communication as a flow of subsequent moments of activity and passivity. What sense does the analysis of a couple kissing have if it is carried out from the standpoint of both individuals acting as independent parties and the physical, cognitive, and emotional aspects are investigated separately for each person? Whatever the result of analyzing each individual separately may be, it is highly improbable that the sum of the two analyses will add up to the phenomenon of kissing, both from the viewpoint of the behavior that may be recorded and from that of the private phenomenal correlates of the two people kissing.

In psychotherapy, a distinction is made between the two approaches, namely cooperation and manipulation. Some schools of psychotherapy are founded on the principle of consciousness raising, where the patient is made increasingly aware of his condition essentially thanks to his transference toward the analyst, or by means of the relationship with the psychotherapist. Differences between individual approaches apart, both within psychoanalysis and within cognitive psychotherapy, for a person to recover it is essential that he understand what has happened to him. It is only by deep comprehension and acceptance of what has been analyzed together with the therapist, and, consequently, by modifying the mental states that determine the patient's behavior, that the patient may abandon his pathological *habitus* and restructure his *modus vivendi* in order to achieve greater happiness. Using work carried out together with the therapist, and constructed together, the patient may then make his own autonomous choices in life.

Other schools have claimed that the patient's understanding his own problems is basically irrelevant to the process of recovery. Behavioral therapy (Wolpe 1969), suggestive therapy (Erickson 1982), directive therapy (Haley 1963), and family therapy (Gurman and Kniskern 1991) all assert that the patient's well-being corresponds to a different way of acting. In this view, the task of the therapist is to try to intervene directly with the behavior of the patient in order to interrupt his pathological habits, and to orient to what the therapist judges to be a more normal way of life. In this case, the therapist is not interested in working on the relationship with the patient, but in restructuring the latter's behavior in the quickest and most efficient manner possible.

The manipulative approach descends from the behaviorist paradigm, in which the only entity responsible for meaning is the source of the message. Consequently, detailed planning is necessary in order to achieve the maximum efficacy in penetrating the patient's mind, with the declared goal of directly changing his behavioral patterns. In place of a conversation, manipulative models evoke a lecture, in which listeners are suitably stimulated and reinforced. The source pays careful attention to the feedback obtained from the destination. However, the sole aim of such care is to work out whether the destination has understood the message. Naturally, all of this is evaluated on the basis of criteria established by the source.

On this approach, A remains the sole judge of the correctness of what has been said: B is the measure of the effectiveness of A's discourse. A assumes omniscience with regard to her own internal states, from her motivations to the linguistic choices she makes. Since this is a "black box" model, however, such internal states are never considered—only the input and the output may be scrutinized. Action is the domain of the speaker, being passive is the task of the listener; when turns change, the roles are inverted. What happens between one position and the other—comprehension, knowledge modification, conflict—is alien to the investigation.

The cooperative approach I am outlining in this book is far removed from the manipulative stance which has long dominated communication, and whose theoretical value is weak, contrasting starkly with the vastness of the applications it has given rise to. Suffice it to think of the hammering repetitiveness of advertising on television, where an extraordinary waste of means is repaid by a ridiculously small return on investment compared with what would be obtained if a technique that activated the viewer were employed. Instead, the viewer is reduced to a nauseated pulp. It is a social disgrace that advertising companies have not yet realized that behaviorism was buried almost fifty years ago and so insist on treating us worse than Skinner (1969) treated the pigeons he was conditioning. At least the birds received water and maize without being subjected to TV ads.

Seen from the cooperative standpoint, successes and failures are to be distributed equally between participants as a whole. Later we will see that the listener becomes equally responsible for what has been said the moment he commits himself to correcting the mistaken assumptions made by the speaker concerning what is supposedly shared by the two participants.

The most common form of communication, conversation, should be treated as a dynamic mode of interaction. The contribution of each agent takes on meaning within the global structure of the conversation itself. Dialogical exchange must not be reduced to a rigidly sequential analysis of the individual speech acts of which the conversation is composed, and in which each agent alternates between being active and passive. The opposite is true: each participant is constantly active, no matter whether she is speaking or listening, whether she is writing the message or reading it.

When one analyzes a single speech act in isolation, as happened and still happens in traditional linguistic and psycholinguistic approaches, one should at least be aware that the operation is artificial. One should not suppose that this procedure leads one to the heart of the matter—always assuming, that is, that such researchers are interested in communication, and not merely in syntax and lexicon, and declare their intent to be such. Later in this chapter we too will take into consideration private mental states, states that are necessarily individual: beliefs, knowledge, intentions, motivations, and the like. But when communication is taking place the mental states of all the participants are active contemporaneously, not sequentially. By the same token, two lovers who kiss have their own lips, hormones, and desires, but when they kiss, these dimensions fuse into an indissoluble single process.

Thus, if it is epistemologically correct to employ basic concepts whose roots lie in individuality, it should nevertheless be borne in mind that in natural conditions interaction implies a common activity that must be faithfully reconstructed in all its complexity, after having been subdivided into its constituent parts. On the other hand, while recognizing that the complexity of communication cannot be reduced to the actions of the individual participants, one must not forgo the analysis of the private part of a common activity.

Things are easier when communication is used in good faith to realize cooperation, with actors sharing the same objective. To tell the truth, this is the situation that has produced the best analyses in the literature. The numerous examples range from two women who must move a piano (Grosz and Sidner 1990) to a ballet company rehearsing a choreography (Searle 1990). Can we still speak of cooperation when the participants have differing objectives in the speech event? Can we still speak of cooperation when two people are quarreling? Let us take the following exchange from Edmond Rostand's comedy, *Cyrano de Bergerac* (1897):

Cyrano: But tell me, why are you staring at my nose?
The Nuisance: Me?
Cyrano: What's so strange about it?
The Nuisance: Your Lordship is wrong.
Cyrano: Is it squashy and hanging like a proboscis?
The Nuisance: I never . . .
Cyrano: Or is it a hook-nose, like an owl's?
The Nuisance: I . . .
Cyrano: Is there a wart at the tip?
The Nuisance: But . . .
Cyrano: Or is there a fly walking up and down it? So, what is that that is so extraordinary about my nose?
The Nuisance: Oh!
Cyrano: Is it really so phenomenal?
The Nuisance: I certainly did not look at it!
Cyrano: And why didn't you look at it?
The Nuisance: I had . . .
Cyrano: So you find it disgusting.
The Nuisance: My Lord . . .
Cyrano: Does it have an unhealthy look, perhaps?
The Nuisance: My Lord!
Cyrano: An obscene shape?
The Nuisance: No, not at all!
Cyrano: So why that critical look? Does it seem too large, perhaps?
The Nuisance: No, quite the contrary. I find it small, very small, minute!
Cyrano: What? Are you making fun of me? My nose is small?   (1)

Note how conversational structure is maintained, respecting relevance, the question-answer format, and turn-taking. The disagreement between the two quarrelers may be compared to a duel, a duel to the death perhaps. Nevertheless it respects given conventions. The opposite view focuses attention on each single, observable action, in which each quarreler offends the other without expecting any cooperation whatsoever. If we move to a higher level of generalization, however, from that of the single act to that of the overall orchestration of a quarrel, then we find that each single utterance aiming at the individual's own advantage merges into a coordinated, cohesive global framework.

In his treatise *The Duel* (1986), the historian Victor Kiernan illustrates how the duel was the staging of a ritual that was as formal as a religious ceremony: two men faced each other, alone and opposite each other, but both were subject to the judgment and control of representatives of their own society. At least two seconds were present as witnesses to the behavior of their respective dueler. The seconds also acted as advisors, observers, and directors. The main task of the seconds was to ensure the procedure was respected, and that both contenders had the same chance of victory, agreeing on time, place, weapon, and other pertinent conditions, and guaranteeing that neither of the contenders obtained unfair advantages or went against the rules. Swords had to be the same length, pistols had to be loaded in the same way, neither of the duelers was to have the sun in his eyes. The duel was part of a rigid code of honor that each dueler constantly adhered to, even in situations of the gravest danger. For the rest of his life, the dueler's reputation would depend on that trial. Indeed, there is no doubt whatsoever that a man educated to act courteously with another person who is trying to kill him is quite capable of acting civilly in all circumstances.

Naturally, cooperation may always be violated, as when two drivers quarrel, and each insults the other without heeding in the least what the other person is saying. This situation may be compared to that of an aggressor suddenly knifing her victim. When a participant's role is reduced to that of a mere object, then we can no longer classify this event as cooperative communication. Such cases are indeed rare, precisely because it is extremely difficult for a human being not to pay attention to what other humans are saying to her.

Even in cases of violence, aggressiveness is usually ritualized, thereby allowing the agent to maintain a positive image of herself even while she is violating a social norm. A cogent example is the aggressive rites engaged in by adolescents, in which even the most surprisingly illegal behavior—surprising to the alien adult—takes place in accordance with rules that the adolescent members of the group are fully cognizant of.

Michael Tomasello and his collaborators propose that human beings, and only human beings, are biologically adapted for participating in collaborative activities involving shared goals and socially coordinated plans of action, a notion similar to that of the behavior game which I shall explain in the next chapter. Interactions of this type require not only an understanding of the goal, intentions, and perceptions of the other persons, but also, as a crucial addition, a motivation to share these things in interaction with others (Tomasello et al. 2005). Tomasello integrates his multifaceted experience from comparative, evolutionary, and developmental psychology, to offer evidence that human beings possess a social capacity that gives them the motivation and the cognitive skills to feel, experience, and act together with others: what he calls *shared* (or "*we*") *intentionality*.

2.1.1 Conversational and Behavioral Cooperation

In developing his concept of cooperation, Grice considered extreme cases of success and failure. Success occurs when the interlocutor understands the speaker's wish and accommodates it. Failure occurs when the interlocutor does not understand the speaker's wish or when he has no intention of accommodating the latter's desires and thus interrupts the conversation. This stance has one great advantage: it is clear. However, it does not take into account other, intermediate positions. To deal with these other possibilities, we must subdivide cooperation into behavioral and conversational cooperation.

Consider the following conversations:

A: It's Thursday tomorrow. Can you take the children to school?
B: Of course I can.   (2)

A: It's Thursday tomorrow. Can you take the children to school?
B: I'm sorry, I have to be at the University by eight.   (3)

From a strictly linguistic point of view, both exchanges are cooperative, since B's replies are relevant to A's questions. Totally noncooperative answers do not appear, as, instead, would be the case if B were to answer:

B: "What a beautiful moon this evening."   (4)

However, there is one level at which (2B) is cooperative in a way that (3B) is not. (2B) complies with the perlocutionary intent expressed by A, which does not refer simply to the abstract information regarding B's commitments, but is, to be precise, a request to take the children to school. Following the distinction introduced by Airenti, Bara, and Colombetti (1984), we may state that although both conversations exhibit *conversational cooperation*, only (2B) also exhibits *behavioral cooperation*.

Behavioral and conversational cooperation are modeled respectively on the assumption of the existence of behavior games on the one hand, and a set of conversational rules on the other hand, which we will call, by analogy, the *conversation game*: both will be explained in chapter 3.

2.2   Mental States

Human beings possess, at any given time, a series of mental states. These may be both emotional and cognitive, and both of these may be either conscious or unconscious. Here we will deal only with those states that are relevant for an understanding of the process of communication, that is, states that are causally relevant in interactions between humans. I omit some states on the assumption that they do not constitute primitive notions that form part of the process of the production and comprehension of communication acts. We will now analyze the following states: attention, belief, knowledge, and consciousness. Volitional primitives— intentions, goals, plans, and communicative intentions—are dealt with in section 2.3, while motivation is treated in section 4.6.

2.2.1   Common Attention

For communication to be possible, all the participants must pay conscious attention. Participants must not focus their attention only on what is happening in the interaction, but must also be sure that every participant is indeed paying attention too. We thus encounter the most important feature of conversation for the first time in this book: participants must continually confirm and be confirmed of the fact that they are interacting.

In the literature this prerequisite is defined as *conditions of contact*. What this term is intended to convey is the fact that the initial prerequisite for communication to be established is that there exist an agreement that the agents are all paying attention to what is happening. Herbert Clark (1992) has made an in-depth analysis of the contact conditions in our culture. He has insisted on the fact that gaze is the most important means for coming into contact with others. We usually prepare the ground for communicating by seeking and maintaining eye contact with others. Interrupting eye contact or not maintaining such contact for a significant length of time that would guarantee that the encounter is not a casual one is tantamount to signaling that one is not willing to start up a conversation.

In section 6.2, we will see that establishing eye contact is innate in infants and is already active at the age of one month. Human beings are animals with a strong predisposition to communication. This is borne out by the fact that all the prerequisites for this activity are wired into the brain, and are there ready to be used.

Eye contact is obviously not the only way contact may be established. Acoustics is a frequent alternative, above all when the agents involved cannot see each other for some reason. Consider the opening sequence of a telephone conversation:

A: Hello?
B: Good morning. This is Karl. Is that the Engels home?
A: Yes.
B: May I speak to Friedrich, please?   (5)

If the acoustic contact conditions were unacceptable, one of the two inter-locutors would already have started complaining, interrupting the stan-dard opening procedure.

Once contact conditions have been established, communication may proceed. Both participants know that from now on everything that happens will be treated as shared knowledge, whether they refer to acts they execute themselves or whether they refer to acts carried out by other parties. Once the attention of both agents has been explicitly activated and focused onto what is happening between the two parties, each agent will assume that the other will keep track of:

1. What is said or done by A and B. For example, B will have to remember the meaning of what A has said to him and accept it as shared, if A has said something to him, or of what A has showed him, if A has showed him something.

2. What has been said or done by C, D, or other participants, provided this is a communication act that involves A or B directly or indirectly, or that this becomes especially important while A and B are interacting. For instance, both will have to remember that a passerby has asked one of them how to get to the station; or both must remember and take as shared the fact that a gentleman on a motorbike crashed into a bus while both of them were paying attention to what was happening in the street.

3. What has happened during the interaction, even if this was not the consequence of actions carried out by them or by others, provided both A and B were paying attention to what was happening around them. For example, both participants will have to remember that lightning struck a pole right in front of them.

2.2.2   Shared Belief

The concepts of knowledge and belief are closely connected in the litera-ture on pragmatics. Such concepts are standardly formalized as predicates or modal operators. Traditionally, belief is employed as a primitive. The properties of a belief are defined by a set of axioms derived from the theory of logic developed by Jaakko Hintikka (1962, 1966). The main problem encountered by Hintkka's approach is what is termed *omniscient logic*: an alleged consequence of the framework is that subjects must believe all of the logical consequences of each of their beliefs. The problem of omniscience has been partially solved by Kurt Konolige (1985); his model allows a subject to be attributed an incomplete set of inferential rules. Nevertheless, the model still presupposes that a subject always executes all the inferences she is capable of carrying out.

Now human subjects are a far cry from Hintikka's ideal subjects, for humans can believe in a given state of affairs but may then not derive the necessary logical consequences for a variety of reasons. First of all, humans may not possess any form of mental logic that enables them to derive the logical consequences from a set of beliefs without making any mistakes. This has been convincingly demonstrated by the polemic that brought into conflict mental logic (Rips 1994) and mental models (Johnson-Laird 1983, 2006). Mental model theorists maintain that human beings possess deductive competence that is based on their capacity to represent situations through the employment of mental models. Thought consists in a set of procedures that build and modify such models, achieving results that may be correct but are sometimes systematically wrong. Logic is a human invention. It perfects natural reasoning capacities through the process of formalization. Logic does not consist, therefore, in the activation of innate neural circuits. If this were not so, it would be difficult to explain why we so often make mistakes when we have to solve deductive problems.

The second major difference between human and ideal subjects is that humans typically exhibit inconsistencies in their belief systems. Such inconsistencies allow local contradictions. Furthermore, humans may be aware of such contradictions, but in cases such as these they are more likely to ignore the contradictions. For example, a person may fervently believe in the general truth that that all men are equal, though he maintains a racist attitude in a specific subdomain.

Other interesting versions of belief systems are those advanced by Hector Levesque (1984), whose approach makes the distinction between explicit and implicit beliefs, and by Fagin and Halpern (1987), who attempt to formalize the notion of *awareness*. Unfortunately, these models also run into the problem of omniscience, if only in a weak form. This systematic failure (gauged in terms of modeling human behavior) of theories that are based on the idealization of the human subject and that ignore their biological constraints suggests that any approach based on strict logic either leads to postulating people with an unnatural competence in deriving the consequences of their own beliefs, or—if the theory is excessively weakened—it will no longer be able to guarantee reasoning capacities as powerful as those possessed by humans.

In any case, no theory of logic dealing with mental states has succeeded in formalizing all the primitives required to model communication. I will therefore refrain from attempting to develop a general logic of mental states. I will concentrate, instead, on rules of inference that are specific to communication (see chapter 4) in order to understand how humans generate and comprehend speech acts in conversation. Such rules enable an actor to carry out two operations: (a) to make plausible inferences in order to recognize her partner's mental states, and (b) to take decisions on how to continue contributing to the conversation.

We too may take Hintikka as our point of departure and assume that *belief* is a primitive mental state. *Knowledge,* by contrast, is a derived concept, that is, a sort of abbreviation of *true beliefs* about the world. It should be noted that the condition described in the formula:

$$\text{KNOW}_x\, p \equiv p \wedge \text{BEL}_x\, p \tag{6}$$

does not consist exclusively of a mental state, for the formula also contains an assertion about the objective state of the world. The symbol "$\wedge$" corresponds to the conjunction "and." Formula (6) expresses the concept that the fact that a person knows a certain thing p is the same as saying that that person believes in p, and that p is true of the world.

Furthermore, the KNOW operator (knowledge) may also be employed within the scope of an operator that expresses a mental state, as in:

$$\text{BEL}_x\, \text{KNOW}_y\, p \equiv \text{BEL}_x\, (p \wedge \text{BEL}_y\, p) \equiv \text{BEL}_x\, p \wedge \text{BEL}_x\, \text{BEL}_y\, p \tag{7}$$

In this case, the global formula describes a mental state, because the reference to an objective state of affairs in the world is embedded within a mental state of belief. Formula (7) expresses the concept that if a person believes that another person knows a certain thing p, then not only does she think that the other person believes p, but she too is convinced that p is true.

Employed in this way, KNOW has a deictic interpretation. This corresponds to the evaluation of the belief held by another person compared with one's own beliefs (Miller and Johnson-Laird 1976). The function of an operator identifying a fact of this type is to distinguish between situations in which A believes that B believes in something that A is objectively certain is true, and situations in which A believes that B believes in something that A is not sure of, or that she even holds to be false. In the former case, we may apply the KNOW operator, embedding it in a belief BEL, to obtain situations of the type:

Desdemona believes that Iago knows that she is faithful to Othello.

Othello believes that Iago knows that Desdemona is unfaithful. (8)

In both cases, the actors are subjectively certain of the propositional content of their beliefs, and they evaluate their partner's belief on the basis of their own. And indeed, Desdemona is certain of her own faithfulness, while Othello is equally sure of her infidelity. From a subjective standpoint, which is the one we are making every effort to keep to, the fact of whether the contents of a belief are true or false is, at this point, irrelevant. Both Desdemona and Othello are offering deictic and not absolute interpretations of the beliefs they respectively ascribe to Iago. The two utterances represented in (8) contradict each other, even though it is of course impossible for Iago to believe in two incompatible states of affairs. The crux of the tragedy lies in the fact that Iago has managed to make both Othello and Desdemona believe that he agrees with each of them.

The opposite case is that in which actress A believes that her interlocutor B is convinced of a certain thing that she, instead, believes to be false.

Desdemona believes that Othello thinks she has been unfaithful to him.

Cyrano de Bergerac believes that his precious Roxanne thinks that the handsome cadet from Gascoigne Christian de Neuvillette is the author of the passionate declarations of love addressed to her. (9)

Naturally, Desdemona knows she has been faithful to Othello, just as Cyrano knows he is the real author of the letters which Christian only puts his signature to, but both are fully aware of the mistaken beliefs their blinded interlocutors hold, which will unfortunately lead to both their unhappy deaths.

To introduce the concept of shared beliefs—a concept that is indispensable when we are dealing with mental states in communication—I must first differentiate between three types of beliefs: *individual*, *common* (also called *mutual*), and *shared*. I will do so in an intuitive fashion, allowing myself a certain definitional leeway. (Those interested in a more formal treatment of the problem, and a precise correspondence between logical and psychological terminology, may consult Colombetti 1999.)

In all the cases examined so far, the agents believed a certain thing, or believed that the other agents believed a certain thing, but in a totally autonomous fashion, with no connection existing between the agents themselves. We will call this type of belief *individual belief*.

Often, however, in a given context, all the agents have the same individual beliefs: all agents generally share knowledge of their surrounding environment, or a certain amount of knowledge that is culturally transmitted. For instance, A may share with B a love of opera, and, with all pacifists, the opinion that all atomic weapons should be banned, and, with all humans, the evidence that we are born of a mother and a father. Much human interaction is based on this type of belief, which is spread over a more or less wide group of people, and which we will call *common belief* or *mutual belief.*

Clark (1996) speaks of *common ground*, meaning the sum of knowledge, beliefs, and suppositions that two or more people share. Common ground enables us to identify a series of cultural communities, which may be classified according to the type of beliefs a community shares. A cultural community is a group of people who possess profound knowledge that other cultural communities do not possess. Hepatologists do not all live together in a large hepatological village: what makes a community of these people is the set of shared beliefs, practices, terminology, conventions, values, habits, and knowledge concerning the liver and its diseases. Egyptians are experts on Egypt, Catholics on Catholicism, mechanics on cars, philatelists on postage stamps, socialists on socialism, cocaine addicts on cocaine, teenagers on adolescence, and so on. Each type of expert knowledge consists of facts, procedures, norms, and assumptions that the members of the community assume they can take for granted in other members. Knowledge is ranked: some information is of central importance, and must necessarily form part of each member's repertoire, whereas other information is only peripheral.

However, having common beliefs is not a sufficient condition enabling communication to take place. Suppose that a person is in a foreign country whose language she does not know, and she wishes to convey her mental state to other interlocutors: she will not employ a gesture whose meaning she is familiar with unless she thinks the other participants are also cognizant with its meaning. There is no point in making a gesture that only she is familiar with. At the outside, everyone present might happen to know the gesture at an individual level, and yet never use it because they are not aware that all the others are also aware of the meaning it conveys. The conclusion, therefore, is that in order to communicate, in addition to possessing common beliefs, each participant must also be aware of the fact that all the other participants possess those very same common beliefs.

I define a *shared belief* as that belief which is not only common to all the participants engaged in the speech event, but of which each participant is aware is possessed by all the other participants. From a psychological standpoint, shared belief has a crucial feature: it is subjective, and not objective, as is common belief. In actual fact, no one can ever be certain that another person has knowledge of a certain type: she may at most assume that he has it, and may be convinced that they share it. To be certain, or to have true knowledge as Hintikka would say, she should in some way be able to observe the mental states of others in some direct manner, and not simply infer them from circumstances. In theory, I might pretend to share with others the belief that the earth is round, but be privately convinced that it is flat, without anyone ever suspecting what is really going on in my mind. Taking up a subjective position where shared belief is concerned means, fundamentally, assuming that each agent has a space of shared beliefs that contains all the beliefs the agent herself is convinced she shares with a given partner, or with a group of people, or with humanity in its entirety.

Schiffer (1972) defines mutual belief as a sequence of potentially infinite individual beliefs, one embedded in another. Formula (10) represents the original definition:

Mutual Knowledge$_{xy}$ p = KNOW$_x$ p and KNOW$_y$ p and

$\qquad$ KNOW$_x$ KNOW$_y$ p and

$\qquad$ KNOW$_y$ KNOW$_x$ p and

$\qquad$ KNOW$_x$ KNOW$_y$ KNOW$_x$ p and

$\qquad$ KNOW$_y$ KNOW$_x$ KNOW$_y$ p and

$\qquad$ (*et cetera ad infinitum*) $\hspace{3cm}$ (10)

There follows a more intuitive translation of the same formula, which clarifies the fact that a mutual belief derives from an individual belief.

A believes that p.

B believes that p.

A believes that B believes that p.

B believes that A believes that p.

A believes that B believes that A believes that p.

B believes that A believes that B believes that p.

. . . and so forth, potentially *ad infinitum*.

Hence, A and B possess the mutual belief that p. $\hspace{2cm}$ (11)

Clark has pointed out that Schiffer's formula *ad infinitum* is cognitively implausible: in order to conclude that a given belief is definitely common, all the interlocutors should commit themselves to carrying out the series of inferences set out in (11) every time. Even if we conceded that we stop after a reasonably short time, for example at the third or fourth level, the most banal conversation would still become a strenuous undertaking for adults, and virtually impossible for children under the age of ten: there are too many embeddings, and these require cognitive resources unavailable under a certain age.

The solution proposed by Airenti, Bara, and Colombetti (1993a) is to assume that each shared belief consists of two correlated primitives. The assumption that a shared belief is also a primitive is intuitively justified by the ease with which human beings deal with shared information right from their earliest years of life, an ease that rules out the need for making complicated inferences in order to identify the shared information contained in any utterance whatsoever. If I ask my daughter Helen what the hamster is doing in the bathtub, she will take it as shared information that the starting point of the communication is that the hamster is in the tub, without requiring to infer this through a lengthy and cumbersome process whose final consequence is my assertion.

The formal connection between belief and shared belief is established by the so-called *fixpoint axiom* (Harman 1977), which captures the circularity of mutual belief:

$$\text{SH}_{xy}\, p \equiv \text{BEL}_x\, (p \wedge \text{SH}_{yx}\, p) \tag{12}$$

where SH_{xy} means that both the agents x and y reciprocally hold the belief that p. What formula (12) expresses is that when actress A takes p as shared by B and herself, this means that on the one hand she herself takes p as being true, and that on the other hand she believes that B also takes p as being shared by both of them. Circularity derives from the fact that sharedness is present on both sides of the formula, both in the *definiens* and in the *definiendum*.

By distributing belief BEL_x on the conjunction, infinite implications of the following type may be obtained from formula (12):

$$\text{SH}_{xy}\, p \supset \text{BEL}_x\, p$$

$$\text{SH}_{xy}\, p \supset \text{BEL}_x\, \text{BEL}_y\, p$$

$$\text{SH}_{xy}\, p \supset \text{BEL}_x\, \text{BEL}_y\, \text{BEL}_x\, p$$

$$\text{SH}_{xy}\, p \supset \ldots \tag{13}$$

The symbol "$\supset$" corresponds to the concept "implies." Formula (13) expresses the possibility of generating a theoretically infinite sequence of individual beliefs, starting from a shared belief. The following constitutes a more intuitive translation:

Since in A's opinion, she and B share the belief that p, this implies that:

A believes that p.

A believes that B believes that p.

A believes that B believes that A believes that p.

. . . and so on, potentially *ad infinitum*. (14)

One important difference between mutual belief (10) and shared belief (12) is that the former is *objectively* common to both interlocutors. This means that both A and B really do believe that p, and both should therefore possess the same mental state corresponding to the belief that p.

Shared belief, on the contrary, assumes a subjective viewpoint, since no agent can ever be sure that all the other participants possess the same beliefs she holds. Hence, shared belief always expresses the standpoint of one of the interlocutors. A may take a certain fact as shared by both B and herself, but this assumption is subjective, one that does not necessarily correspond to the real mental states possessed by B. No one can open another person's brain and look inside in order to check out what beliefs the other person actually does hold. And as we shall see in chapter 5, subjective assumptions regarding sharedness play an important part in nonstandard communication, especially in cases of deceit.

It should be noted that formula (13) enacts the opposite procedure of Schiffer's formula (10): we start from a shared belief in order to infer, when necessary, individual beliefs; Schiffer, instead, starts from individual beliefs in order to establish mutual belief.

In my model, all the inference rules employed in the two stages of comprehension—that is to say, in comprehending an expression act and in comprehending speaker meaning—locate both the antecedent and the consequent within the operator SH_{xy}, where x is the subject whose mental processes are represented by the rules, and y is her partner. We may thus state that the inference is drawn within the *space of beliefs shared by x and y*. This space is a central feature of the model, because one of the essential conditions of communication is that each agent maintain her space of shared beliefs, thereby enabling her to update her knowledge of the participants as the interaction proceeds.

2.2.3 Consciousness

An (unconscious) widespread prejudice exists on the subject of conscious-ness. This has permeated our culture since Sigmund Freud published his revolutionary and immensely influential *Die Traumdeutung* (*The Interpreta-tion of Dreams*) in 1899. With the publication of this book, it was virtually taken for granted that the unconscious is a kind of deep water in which is submerged knowledge that is inaccessible to consciousness, and which is even capable of influencing behavior. According to the Freudian model, the passage from the unconscious to the conscious is tantamount to light-ing a lamp in a dark room: everything remains just as it was, with the only difference being that now we may see what was not perceptible previously. Thus, for instance, once the reasons that impeded the recognition of a repressed desire have been eliminated, that desire emerges in consciousness for what it is.

Cognitive science takes a different view. Awareness of something has to be constructed; it is not an immanent property of a mental state. Some-thing that was previously unconscious cannot be rendered as something conscious without modifying its meaning in some way: it is not a question of transporting a static part of knowledge from one state (darkness) into another (light), but of interpretation, of a transformation of one thing into another. In cognitive terms, the passage from an unconscious mental state into a conscious mental state alters the knowledge content, forcing some-thing into a given type of interpretative framework—one that is typically serial—when prior to that it was represented in a totally different fashion, one that is typically parallel (Marcel 1983a,b). Searle (1992) has refined our analytical tools further by pointing out that many cognitive processes, such as those that enact our syntactic capacities, are neither conscious or unconscious. Rather, they are *nonconscious*, inasmuch as they are realized exclusively at the neural level, without any further mental processing.

2.3 Intentionality

The concept of intentionality has two fundamental meanings. These two meanings must be borne in mind and kept distinct. The first concerns the fact that an intention always refers to something; it is always directed at a person, an object, or an event. Both actions and mental states that are characterized by intentionality necessarily possess a focus on which the actor concentrates her perspective. The actor thus orients her action or thought toward that focus. I will call this first meaning the *direction* of the intention.

The second meaning refers to the fact that intentionality may also be characterized by *deliberateness*. This means that an action or a mental state that is intentional may include a nucleus that is wanted, decided on, selected, pursued, and so on. This nucleus of deliberateness is not necessarily always present, because not all of a person's intentions are actually formed and realized as a result of the choice made. The philosopher Michael Bratman (1990) has clarified what the nucleus of deliberateness consists of, with an example that has become famous and which is based on the distinction between strategic bombers and terror bombers.

During a war, it may be decided to bomb only military targets (typical of strategic bombing), or to strike civilian targets too, as is the case with terror bombing. The intention behind terror bombing—to strike houses, schools, and hospitals in order to terrorize the civilian population—is explicit and deliberate. By contrast, the explicit and deliberate intention of strategic bombing is to strike only those locations that are of military interest. It may happen, of course, that such military installations are situated near houses, schools, and hospitals. These latter buildings will therefore run the risk of being bombed too. The strategic bomber may therefore kill civilians as a collateral effect of his bombing action. He does not, however, possess the deliberate intention to do so. For both bombers, the act of dropping bombs is one that is both directed (that is, directed at an explicit objective) and deliberate (that is, consciously decided on and pursued). But whereas terror bombing aims at the deliberate killing of civilians as a means of winning the war, strategic bombing does not involve the deliberate killing of civilians, in the sense that it is an accepted but not desired consequence of the action of bombing military targets.

The key concept is that our actions always have a set of consequences: some of these are desirable; in addition, sometimes these consequences may constitute the deep reasons that drive us to taking that course of action. Other effects, instead, are accepted as being inevitably tied to the preestablished objective, but we judge them as being irrelevant or even harmful to our deeper purposes. If a person likes the taste of garlic, she will deliberately ask for it to be one of the ingredients in the dishes she eats. The desirable consequences of eating garlic are its properties of being anticholesterol and antivampire. The irrelevant consequences are the smell and the color it gives to the food. The negative consequences are its cost and bad breath.

Bearing in mind direction and deliberateness, we may now discuss its relationship to awareness. Figure 2.1 sums up the distinctions I am introducing. The clearest notion, (1), is that of an action that is fully

1 *Directed, deliberate, conscious intentional action*

Fully intentional action (Napoleon intends to defeat Wellington at Waterloo).
Stable intention (Napoleon works out a battle plan which aims at engaging
the British and the Prussians separately).
Deliberate effects (In the case of victory, Napoleon counts on being able to
thrash out a new continental peace treaty).

2 *Directed, nondeliberate, conscious action*

Intended action (while Napoleon is examining his troops on parade before
the battle, he sits straight-backed on his horse).
Accepted effects (given his intention to win the battle, Napoleon accepts the
fact that one of the consequences will be that thousands of French soldiers
will die at Waterloo).

3 *Nonintentional, conscious action*

Stereotyped behaviours, determined by nondirected mental states and
emotions (Napoleon always keeps a hand on his abdomen), or influenced
by emotional tones which cannot be connected to precise causes, such as
free anxiety or depressive mood (on Saint Helen, Napoleon is in poor health,
sluggish, taciturn).

4 *Directed, deliberate and unconscious intentional action*

Impossible case (even though it should be remembered that according to
Freud the Id is capable of desiring and deciding).

5 *Directed, nondeliberate, and unconscious action*

Unconscious goals realized in a parasitical fashion compared to the conscious
action plan (before the battle, Napoleon retains the brave and confident
marshal Ney for a long time by his side).
Parapraxis (when the Prussian troops commanded by Blücher arrive,
Napoleon drops the telescope handed to him by his attendant, almost as if
he had canceled them out from the field of battle by not recognizing them).
The difference consists in the fact that in the former case unconscious goals
do not interfere with conscious goals, while in the case of parapraxis,
unconscious goals hinder the realization of conscious goals.

6 *Nonintentional, unconscious action: mental states at the neural level*

These are actions which lie beyond the sphere of consciousness; hence calling
them unconscious it is not technically correct.
Automatic and physiological actions (Napoleon walking properly and digesting
a light breakfast at dawn).
Neural states (the neural activity which lies at the basis of all the actions
examined, from creating the battle plan to Napoleon's anguish following
his defeat).

Action

Conscious

Unconscious

Figure 2.1
The relationship between intentionality and consciousness.

intentional, conscious, and deliberate: the subject wishes to realize a given objective, which may refer only to herself (I wish to achieve peace of mind), or to the external world (I want to achieve world peace). The intention need not be verbalized: little children have intentions and are conscious of them, even though they may be unable to express their desires in explicit terms. The fact that an intention is deliberate means that an action plan may be generated in order to realize that intention. This is exactly what happens in the case of conscious intentions. I retire to a Zen monastery, or I join the peace corps in Africa. A conscious intention has a plannable course of action as its counterpart.

I will now introduce another dichotomy, connected on this occasion to the time when the intention is activated, and which is akin to the distinction introduced by Searle (1983) between *prior intention* and *intention-in-action*. To indicate the stability of the former type of intention over time, we could call it "stable" intention, pitting it against intention-in-action, which is transitory and sometimes extremely similar to what may be called "reflexive thought." A prior intention, one that is necessarily deliberate, underlies all action plans, whereas an intention-in-action activates the goals and subgoals that are specific to the realization of the objective. Continuing our previous example, a prior intention, which lies at the basis of the entire action plan, is that of retiring to a Zen monastery, whereas intentions in action are those that realize the specific actions necessary to ensure the plan is brought to a successful conclusion: looking for a suitable Zen monastery, finding a Zen master, leaving one's current job, and so on.

An intention-in-action is often automatic and not the result of deliberate, conscious thought, as when we apply the brakes because a careless pedestrian has suddenly stepped off the curb: perhaps we go too far if we say that we have decided to apply the pedal, but there is no doubt that we are aware of what we have done.

Can it be argued that there exists a third type of intention, one that may be considered unconscious? It is difficult to deny that humans often act on the basis of motives or desires of which they are unaware. Clinical literature abounds with convincing examples of directed behavior, which is triggered by motives that the person only comes to understand after great and sincere effort on her part and on the part of her therapist. The life of each and every individual is full of unrecognized negative feelings (e.g., rage, fear)—which manifest themselves in involuntarily aggressive acts toward the detested object—as well as of unrecognized affection, which also manifests itself in inexplicable emotions and positive tendencies toward the beloved object. Here again, it is often the stranger who is the first to recognize the desires that the person denies she has. How long this state will last depends on the person's degree of self-awareness: those who do not know themselves may go through the whole of life never understanding their deep emotions.

By definition, an unconscious intention cannot generate a deliberate action, because if this were so, it would be immediately recognized for what it is. This is possible in a sense in psychoanalysis: the Freudian Id is capable of deciding on a course of action without the Ego gaining awareness of it. But such a vision of the mind as being formed by different *homunculi* each of whom leads his own independent life and is in constant battle with the others is a far cry from the standpoint we are assuming in this book. My own position is, therefore, that an unconscious action that is fully intentional (i.e., directed and deliberate) does not exist. For this reason, case 4 in figure 2.1 is impossible.

My thesis is that an unconscious, nondeliberate intention may exist. This operates as a parasite living off the generation of a conscious course of action (case 5 in figure 2.1). Whereas conscious intention may generate action plans directly, unconscious intention is an opportunist, taking advantage of a course of action by exploiting possible modifications in order to ensure that the goal—which is not consciously recognized—is realized without implementing a specific action whose purpose is the realization of this unconscious goal. When prior intention is unconscious, it may facilitate the building of an action plan whose objective is conscious, or, on the contrary, it may obstruct its realization. For instance, my goal of going to the opera house to see *Rigoletto* may be made easier by my knowing that that fascinating woman Silvia will also be going (and here we may suppose that I am unconsciously attracted by her and that equally unconsciously I wish to meet her). Contrariwise, this goal may be impeded by the presence of Silvia's fiancé (whom I abhor, again unconsciously, and whose presence with her would unconsciously make me feel ill at ease).

If the unconscious goal is consistent with the conscious objective, it becomes a facilitator whose presence it is almost impossible to detect. If, instead, the unconscious goal moves in the opposite direction of the conscious objective, then in blocking the conscious objective it may manifest itself in such a way as to become recognizable.

Moving on now to intention-in-action, if this is unconscious, it acts as a modifier of the action that is being carried out in compliance with a conscious intention. For instance, in leaning forward to shake hands with a detestable colleague, I may involuntarily jolt his glasses, causing them to fall. If, however, I have planned my act of destruction, it can no longer be classified as an unconscious desire. Behavioral dysfunctions and para-praxis are excellent exemplifications of unconscious intentions-in-action. The *parapraxis* is provoked by an unconscious desire, which is achieved by means of an action that is incongruous with the conscious and deliberate action plan. For example, Freud (1901) reports the case of a lady who had forgotten to try on her wedding dress, remembering only at eight o'clock at night on the eve of the wedding, when the dressmaker had given up all hope of seeing her customer. This detail was of itself sufficient to demonstrate the fact that the bride was far from happy at the thought of having to wear a wedding dress, and was trying desperately to forget that painful ceremony. As was easily foreseeable, the lady later divorced.

The interesting point is that the only way of subjectively uncovering an unconscious desire is through behavior, hence, through an observable effect, rather than through introspective analysis. If the action—which the unconscious desire is exploiting in a parasitical mode—is not carried out, the corresponding intention is lost. That desire will never reach the level of consciousness, even if a few neurons will remain dissatisfied. Furthermore, even if the unconscious desire manages to transform itself into a modification of the previously planned action, it will never reach consciousness unless the action so modified is subsequently attributed intentionality proper.

The key to such awareness lies in recognizing the incongruity of one's behavior with one's conscious intentions: the person must attribute "as-if" intentionality to the unconscious antecedent of her behavior. Stated differently, unconscious desire is reconstructed after the fact. It is a useful method of providing a full and clear explanation of past behavior. I will cite another of Freud's cases from the same source. A lady has spent an evening out with her husband and two male friends, one of whom is her lover. The friends escort the married couple back home, taking their leave on the doorstep. The lady bows toward one of the men and extends her hand, uttering courteous words of circumstance. She then takes hold of her lover's arm, turns toward her husband, and is about to take leave of him in the same fashion as she took leave of the first gentleman. The husband takes the situation as a joke, removes his hat and says with exaggerated courtesy: "Let me kiss your hand, dear lady." Frightened by these words, the lady abandons her lover's arm, sighing: "That this should happen to me!" The husband believed his wife would never be unfaithful to him, and had often sworn that if that were ever to happen, then more than one life would be in danger. He therefore had severe internal constraints that prevented him from noting the challenge his wife's error represented.

Another category is that of stereotyped behavior, or behavior connected to conscious but unintentional mental states, in other words, states that have not been deliberately selected and are not directed. Examples of this type include a state of anxiety or a state of endogenous depression. In these cases, the person is perfectly aware that she is in a state of anxiety or depression, but she is unable to identify any reason for being in this state: consciousness of the state exists, but there is no directed and deliberate intentionality. The person's behavior is influenced by such mental states well beyond her will.

2.3.1 Communicative Intention

Let us now examine what happens when instead of speaking of action in general we focus our attention on communication acts. One fundamental difference between actions pure and simple and communication acts is that the latter are always carried out together with someone: communication does not come about in isolation or in complete autonomy. Thus, though we may speak of a single agent when we refer to actions in general, when we enter the domain of communicative interaction we must always have at least one actor (A) and one partner (B) to whom the act is directed. Other agents (C, D, etc.) may participate as audience to the communicative event.

I define *communicative intention* as the intention to communicate something, plus the intention that that intention to communicate that particular something be recognized as such. To be more precise, A possesses a communicative intention that p, with regard to B—that is to say: A intends to communicate that p to B—when A intends the following two facts to be shared by both A and B:

1. that p
2. that A intends to communicate that p to B

As I explained in section 1.1, making information achieve the status of sharedness does not mean one has communicated it. The necessary condition for real communication to take place is that such information be intentionally and explicitly proposed to the interlocutor. Grice points out that communicating includes not only the speaker's first-order intention I_1, that of achieving a certain effect on the interlocutor, but also the second-order intention I_2, namely, that the first-order intention I_1 be recognized as such by the interlocutor.

For example, by wearing my King's College tie, I make the fact that I belong to the teaching staff of that institution shared, but it cannot be asserted that I communicated this particular fact. The first-order intention I_1, namely, that of letting others know where I teach, has been satisfied, but the second-order intention I_2, namely, that other people recognize that I desire to communicate this fact, has not been satisfied. It would have been satisfied had I openly declared:

I teach at King's College, Cambridge. (15)

In this case, listeners would gain awareness not only of the specific fact, but also of my open desire that they become aware of that fact. The philosopher Peter Strawson (1964) has, however, drawn attention to the fact that if we wish to speak of open communication, not even the second-order intention I_2 is sufficient; a third-order intention I_3 is also required. I_3 ensures that I_2 is recognized for what it is. Though logically sound, Strawson's examples are rather complicated, so much that they even irritated Grice himself, and we need not go into their details here.

But at this point, Airenti, Bara, and Colombetti (1993a) have demonstrated that if an nth-order intention I_n is required in the definition of communication, then the actor might not posses the nth+1-order intention I_{n+1}. In this case the interactive situation would not be fully open, because part of the situation would not be intended by the actor as having to be recognized, but would be a part she intends to keep private.

From a technical standpoint, this sets up two alternatives: either an infinite hierarchy of intentions is postulated, or a circular definition of communication is furnished by employing the notion of shared belief that was introduced earlier in this chapter. Formally, communicative intention may thus be defined as follows:

$$\text{CINT}_{xy}\, p \equiv \text{INT}_x\, \text{SH}_{yx}\, (p \wedge \text{CINT}_{xy}\, p) \tag{16}$$

What formula (16) means is that X has the communicative intention that p toward Y (in symbols, $\text{CINT}_{xy}\, p$) when X intends (INT_x) that the following two facts be shared by Y and herself (SH_{yx}): that p, and that she intended to communicate to Y that p ($\text{CINT}_{xy}\, p$).

All of this may be translated into more acceptable English as follows. A intends to communicate a certain thing to B. A concurrently desires that

B take as shared between the two not only the specific content she wishes to convey, but also the fact that she actually did wish to convey that content to him.

Consider again an example. Aeneas is hesitating between his loved one and his imperial mission. Mercury delivers to the hero Jupiter's order to leave Carthage immediately, before Dido, who is furious because her lover has abandoned her, can burn his ships:

Set sail: that is all. (17)

Jupiter not only wants Aeneas to take the high seas at once, but that he do so as a sign of his submission to fate. Aeneas must therefore depart not simply as an act of convenience, but, more importantly, as an act of conscious obedience to divine will.

Similar to shared belief, communicative intention is also a primitive in pragmatics. This means that it implies, but is not reducible to, an infinite number of finite embeddings of intentions and shared beliefs. The following logical implications may be derived from formula (16):

$\text{CINT}_{xy}\, p \supset \text{INT}_x\, \text{SH}_{yx}\, p$

$\text{CINT}_{xy}\, p \supset \text{INT}_x\, \text{SH}_{yx}\, \text{INT}_x\, \text{SH}_{yx}\, p$

$\text{CINT}_{xy}\, p \supset \text{INT}_x\, \text{SH}_{yx}\, \text{INT}_x\, \text{SH}_{yx}\, \text{INT}_x\, \text{SH}_{yx}\, p$

$\text{CINT}_{xy}\, p \supset \ldots$

Formula (16) means that given the fact that A intends to communicate a certain thing to B, we may infer that A also intends that her original intention to communicate that particular thing be recognized. If need be, this includes the further inference that A wishes B to recognize her intention of letting B know that she really did intend him to become aware of her intention to communicate to him that particular message. And so on, until the cognitive resources possessed by both manage to make sense of the sequence of embeddings.

In figure 2.2, I apply to communication the distinctions I have discussed with regard to the consciousness and intentionality of actions.

1. Deliberate and conscious communication acts

Communication The first case is that of communication proper, which must possess both characteristics, that of intentionality as well as that of consciousness. In actual fact, in order for communicative intentionality to be successful, two conditions must be respected: the specific content of the communication (that *p*) must be recognized by the interlocutor, and the

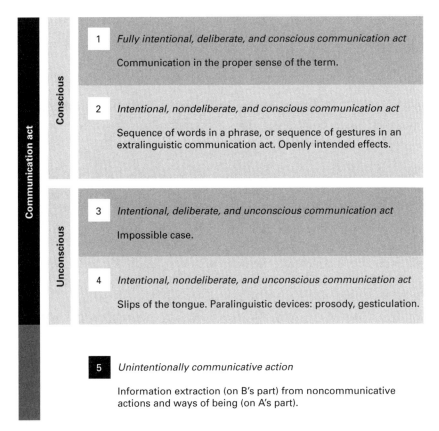

1 *Fully intentional, deliberate, and conscious communication act*

Communication in the proper sense of the term.

2 *Intentional, nondeliberate, and conscious communication act*

Sequence of words in a phrase, or sequence of gestures in an extralinguistic communication act. Openly intended effects.

3 *Intentional, deliberate, and unconscious communication act*

Impossible case.

4 *Intentional, nondeliberate, and unconscious communication act*

Slips of the tongue. Paralinguistic devices: prosody, gesticulation.

5 *Unintentionally communicative action*

Information extraction (on B's part) from noncommunicative actions and ways of being (on A's part).

Figure 2.2
The relationship between intentionality and consciousness in communication acts.

intention to communicate that specific content must also be recognized. This second condition renders communicative intention a mental state that is necessarily a conscious one. In fact, A cannot possess the intention that B recognize a certain thing without A being openly aware of her own intention. Communication is based on communicative intention; communication must therefore also possess the quality of consciousness.

2. Intentional, nondeliberate, and conscious communication acts

Sequence of words or of gestures   If intentionality is not deliberate, but we are nevertheless conscious of what we are doing, then the result is a typical case of a sequence of words in an utterance, or a sequence of movements in a complex action. Normally, a person is fully aware of what she is saying.

However, she does not plan her sentences in advance. She generates them on the spot, with a sequence of words that are composed spontaneously in order to achieve the specific communicative goal. This is a kind of communicative intention-in-action: conscious, goal-directed, but not deliberate. In some cases the words might have been planned in advance, for instance if it is supposed that the words will become historic phrases, or that they might be recorded. This is certainly the case when we write a particularly important letter, or when we draft a contract.

Openly intended effects Tackled from the standpoint of communicative intentionality, we are in a position to deal with the problem left open by Bratman, that of where to stop the chain of nondeliberate intentions. In other words, up to what point can we consider the effects, the effects of the effects, and so on, as being comprehended? What is it that guarantees the inductive chain of inferences and presuppositions? A calculation of the presuppositions and inferences in the true sense of that mathematical term is certainly not what provides this guarantee. Strictly speaking, we are entitled to consider as fully comprehended only those effects that both the agents consider to be obvious, evident, and certain with regard to the action the interlocutors are deciding on together.

Realistically, I believe the solution lies in hypothesizing a gradient of expressiveness that is mutually comprehended. In concrete terms, I will take as openly intended, even when this occurs in a nondeliberate manner, only those effects that occur first and that both agents consider evident and certain with regard to the interaction they are engaged in. From this point on, attributing communicative intention becomes an arbitrary process, and cannot be considered as taking place by default. At most, if the comprehension is achieved of certain nondeliberate effects occurring after the first, immediate effects, this will be attributable to the workings of a given context. Such caution is necessary—bearing in mind the old Chinese proverb that the beating of a butterfly's wings here will cause an earthquake at the antipodes—in order to avoid the case of a highly perspicacious actor saying that she has seen a butterfly beat its wings with the intention of communicating the message that there will be an earthquake at the antipodes. The converse consequence is equally important: the listener is not free to interpret what the speaker has said as he pleases.

3. Intentional, deliberate, and unconscious communication acts

Impossible case Whereas procedures and mental acts may be either conscious or unconscious, communicative intentions are governed by a special constraint, that is, they are always necessarily conscious. One direct consequence of this fact is that there can exist no mental state that is both communicatively intentional and unconscious at the same time. If I intend communicating something to someone, I must be fully conscious of the fact.

4. Intentional, nondeliberate, and unconscious communication acts

Slips of the tongue   The fourth possibility is that of a nondeliberate, unconscious communicative intentionality. As I pointed out for action in general, this too is a case where intentions are made manifest only when they modify behavior in such a way as to render it incongruous. If they influence behavior in a way that is acceptable in relation to the primary conscious intent, then these intentions cannot be recognized. The clearest case is that of the *slip of the tongue*. Freud (1901) identifies two types of lapses, only one of which is of interest to us here. The first type is triggered off by interference from a preceding or succeeding part of the conversation regarding the utterance that has been made. For instance, when talking about sculpture, saying "Milo by Venus" instead of "Venus by Milo."

The second and more interesting type, instead, is brought about by drives external to the conversation, which manifest themselves through a slip of the tongue. For example, a man may address his partner as "mommy," if she reminds him of his mother at that point in time, or if she has activated a schema that is identical to one of those he usually uses when interacting with his mother. In uttering the word "mommy" the speaker is aware of what he has said, he has proffered those sounds conveying that meaning in a voluntary manner, and he may even understand why he committed that slip. Notwithstanding these considerations, he did not fully intend to call his partner "mommy," nor did he explicitly wish to make her understand that he believed she was like his mother.

Times of war produce numerous slips of the tongue, which are not very difficult to understand (Freud 1901).

"What regiment is your son with?" a lady was asked.
She replied: "With the 42nd Murderers" ["Mörder"—instead of "Mörser," "mortars"].   (18)

Paralinguistic features   Paralinguistic devices in speech should actually be considered as fluctuating in the periphery of consciousness. Agents participating in a social event are not normally aware of the tone of voice or the type of gesture they use. They may easily gain awareness, however, because, for instance, the interlocutor points this out to them, or because they themselves suddenly begin paying attention to secondary behavioral traits that are usually beyond consciousness. It will thus be advisable to consider paralinguistic devices as occupying a peripheral position with respect to consciousness. These devices could also become deliberate, and therefore turn out to be fully communicative, if they were decided on before the production of the utterance and the interlocutor were made to recognize their status as such. For example, A may deliberately raise her tone of voice to make B understand how angry she is with him, and B may, on the contrary, cry by ostentatiously exhibiting his tears to A.

5. Unintentionally communicative actions and modes of being

Information extraction   As I stated in the first chapter, if there is no intention to communicate, then there is no communication, only extraction of information. An observer who is interested in doing so may extract information from anything, even if the context does not justify him thinking that A had intended to communicate something to him. In general, information extraction consists of attributing meaning to the actions of others, and only the observational powers of the perceiver can guarantee a sensible interpretation of what is perceived. It is no coincidence that it is an ability that is almost diagnostic by nature, and which should therefore be taken up in a chapter on clinical pragmatics, to clarify the meaning of symptoms.

The able doctor deduces important conclusions on the basis of signs that only an expert knows how to decode. We must not, however, forget the frequency of inductive errors. For example, people who are jealous continually suffer from sensations of betrayal, though it may well not be the case that their beloved really is being unfaithful to them. In the throes of a delirium caused by jealousy, partners beyond suspicion are accused of immoral behavior on the basis of clues that a neutral observer would find totally unrealistic, but which the person suffering from delusions believes are absolutely valid.

The distinctions we have made have been developed within a cognitive approach to mental processes. That is, it is the people who are interacting who establish, within the privacy of their own mental states, whether or not they are communicating something intentionally, or if they are letting information seep out without explicitly admitting that this is so. The entire process, then, must take into account the fact that the different types of intentionality are complicated further by the level of awareness at which they are enacted.

2.3.2 Action Plans

Traditionally, both in psychology (Miller, Galanter, and Pribram 1960) and in artificial intelligence (Wilensky 1983), a *plan* is seen as a set of hierarchical goals, connected to actions whose execution will lead to the realization of those goals. In the sphere of communication, where it is important to infer other people's plans so that we may better understand what the other person wants to convey and what that person wants us to do, it is more useful to adopt a definition that underscores the mental states of the agents rather than real actions. We will therefore follow Martha Pollack's (1992) lead, according to which a plan is a configuration of beliefs—concerning the executability of the actions implied—and of intentions to carry out the actions referred to.

A plan may be analyzed at different levels of detail. The more detailed the level at which the analysis is carried out, the greater the number of steps that are made explicit and the smaller the part that is left indeterminate. For instance, when Emma Bovary decides to flee with Rodolphe, her plan consists quite simply in discovering whether her lover is a willing partner, and to go anywhere, provided it is with him. When the plan takes shape, they decide to go to Genoa via Marseilles, in a private carriage which Rodolphe will hire in Paris. Madame Bovary takes not an iota of interest in how to handle husband and daughter nor in how to organize their flight in concrete terms. As the fatal day draws near, these actions are also decided on, thereby becoming an integral part of the action plan. Thus Emma buys a trunk which is not too heavy and a lined cloak (Flaubert 1856).

Building a plan is cognitively taxing and time-consuming. Hence human beings always tend to employ ready-made plans in order to conserve their energy. Furthermore, a ready-made plan means that it has already been put to use on some previous occasion, thereby guaranteeing the plan has some probability of concrete success. Turning, finally, to communication, a structured plan is often socially shared by all those people who belong to the same culture. This offers the dual advantage not only of rendering the agent's intentions immediately comprehensible to all the interlocutors, but also of clarifying what sequence of actions will be executed.

In addition to ready-made plans and plans to be constructed, a further distinction should also be borne in mind: that between individual plans and interpersonal plans. An *individual plan* concerns only the planner herself. When Dante decides to start writing *The Divine Comedy*, he does not involve anyone else directly in the writing of the work, even though the work will later modify the lives of many people. I will dwell no further on this type of plan, because the second type is of far greater importance in communication. An *interpersonal plan* includes actions that must be performed not only by the planner herself, but also by one or more partners. Emma and Rodolphe; Othello, Iago and Desdemona; Churchill, Hitler, Roosevelt, and Stalin; they all intertwine their own actions with those of other actors.

An early intuition regarding this type of plan may be traced back to the concept of *script* introduced by Roger Schank and Robert Abelson (1977): a sequence of stereotyped actions that define a familiar situation, one that comprises both individual and interpersonal plans. The concept of script is in its turn based on that of *frame*, a data structure used in artificial intelligence for the representation of stereotyped knowledge (Minsky 1975, 1986). A script defines the scenes that one can reasonably expect will take place in a given situation: in the example the authors illustrate most fully, the restaurant script, we find scenes describing the customer entering the restaurant, ordering, waiting as the cook prepares the food, then eating, and paying the cashier.

One alternative that is of interest because it is not tied to ready-made, immediately available fixed schemes is that of *shared plans*, as defined by Barbara Grosz and Candace Sidner (1990). A shared plan is a collaborative procedure between two people, where each agent mutually believes that:

1. she will play her part in the shared action;
2. she will play her part if and only if the other agent also plays his part.

A shared plan does not presuppose a list of fixed actions. Instead, it is subject to continual negotiation on the part of the agents, the prime goal being that of ensuring mutual comprehension. Grosz and Sidner wish to explain the flow of the conversation, which they consider is a shared plan that must be developed together by both agents. Neither of the participants has any expectation with regard to her partner, over and above those that may derive from general principles of rationality and of universal knowledge about the world.

The concepts of shared plan and cooperation help to define who a person is in relation to others, thereby establishing the agents' reciprocal range of action. Every time the action of an actor crosses paths with that of others—even in the limited case when the others only have the power of preventing her from making a certain move—the actor will be obliged (a) to acknowledge the roles played by the other actors and (b) to ensure that her own role is acknowledged. For example, queuing correctly obliges a person to stand openly and visibly in line, ostensibly acknowledging that the people in front of her constitute a queue with an objective to fulfill—and not a casual, elongated conglomeration of individuals with nothing in common—while at the same time being herself recognizable by the others as one of the people in the queue.

By indicating in some manner that one is a certain kind of person, one signals to others what the appropriate kind of behavior is in one's regard. By interweaving reciprocal signals, we obtain a network of reciprocal expectations that are far more complex than the simplistic scripts developed by Schank and Abelson. Declaring who we are, on the one hand, induces others to treat us in the pertinent fashion; on the other hand, in order for our declaration to be a felicitous communication act, we must really be treated in a manner appropriate to the declaration made.

Actions proper and all the other modes of being and of manifesting oneself that make a certain type of person—a doctor, a traffic policeman, a teacher—visible and recognizable by others are not simply indicators of being that kind of person, as the sociologist Erving Goffman (1959) reductively asserts. That is, they are not signals that may be detached from actually being that type of person, or from doing the things that type of person does. Rather, the modes of acting and manifesting oneself are essential and structural constituents of that type of person. In order to be a certain kind of person, it is mandatory and binding that other people produce responses that empower that person to be and act in accordance with who that person is. If the doctor is not treated as a doctor—by the rest of the world: by colleagues, paramedics, patients, the public—if she is not allowed to perform those actions that a doctor performs—examining, diagnosing, prescribing—something essential that makes that person a doctor is missing. A person may also try to be a great seducer, but if no one believes the person is a seducer, if no one allows him- or herself to be seduced, then it is impossible to retain that role.

Of course, one may exhibit external signs, such as the white overall from the pocket of which appears a stethoscope—in an attempt to deceive others or oneself. However, there are some things that one must normally know how to do, and ways of behaving that are extremely difficult for a layperson to imitate. In actual fact, part of the training period consists precisely in learning how a professional behaves both in specific work situations and in those other situations where she must be acknowledged for what she is, even though no explicit declarations may be made regarding her status. In this sense, at a discotheque one may pretend one is a surgeon—or even the opposite, a great dancer in an operating theater—but one cannot keep up the role when one is required to perform those actions appropriate to the role declared. In such circumstances, the mock surgeon had better avoid the hospital and the alleged dancer the ballroom.

What one does to render evident that one is a certain type of person is correlated with how much others are able to comprehend in recognizing a particular kind of person. Obviously, what makes the difference is the type of audience: criminals wish to be recognized as criminals by other criminals, but they desire that such recognition on the part of the police be delayed as long as possible. The ethnomethodologists Lawrence Wieder and Stephen Pratt (1990) have demonstrated that the ability to recognize members of a category one wishes to be recognized as belonging to, is one of the criteria for being recognized as a member of that given category. Being a Native American who can be recognized as such by other Native Americans is one of these cases. One feature that unmasks a bogus Native American is his incapacity to recognize the subtle differences between a person who pretends to be a Native American and a real Native American. For instance, a real Native American does not talk to strangers, whether they be Native American or not. This means that if someone opens his mouth, he is not a Native American. Furthermore, if someone does not realize that the person who has spoken is not a real Native American, this will mean that he too is not a real Native American.

We may here introduce the crucial difference that separates "acting as," which is a sort of "as-if" exhibition, from "being a," where all the features of a given role have been interiorized and emerge in that person's behavior. The first is the product of exhibitionism aimed at deceiving. The second expresses a genuine way of being through observable behavior. The clearest example is the difference being "acting the fool" and "being a fool." Only real fools can achieve a depth of stupidity that is the essential trait of their state.

3   Behavior Games and Conversation Games

The idea that "the entire process of using words" may be seen as a kind of game was first introduced by Ludwig Wittgenstein (1953, part I, remark 7) with his original notion of *language game*. The aim of using the word "game" is to underline the fact that speaking a language is part of an activity, a "way of life." Establishing such a broad meaning for his use of the term enabled Wittgenstein to scrutinize a whole series of games that may be played out through the use of language, demonstrating its great flexibility. Here are a few examples of phenomena that Wittgenstein considers to be language games:

Ordering and acting on orders.

Acting in the theater.

Singing in a circle.

Asking, thanking, swearing, greeting, praying.

Showing a child objects and naming those objects.   (1)

The idea that one should focus on language *use* instead of language *form* is one that is definitely revolutionary and that still maintains its validity more than fifty years later. Its very power, however, has long prevented scholars from making an important distinction between the concept of a game as the means by which interaction is regulated, which I will call a *behavior game*, and the idea of a game as governing the structure of conversation, which I will call a *conversation game*.

With regard to the latter concept, Mann, Moore, and Levin (1977) introduced the concept of *dialogue game*, without, however, really developing the important intuition they had of explaining communicative interaction in terms of mental states. The term itself had been taken from Carlson (1962), who defines dialogue games as cooperative activities for exchanging information. The rules of this type of game define when it is appropriate for a player to ask a question, furnish an answer, and so on. Dialogue games are thus seen as a sort of grammar specifying which moves are appropriate in a given context. As games, Carlson's notion of dialogue game differs from my concept of conversation game, inasmuch as the basic function of the latter concept is to explain cooperation in conversation in terms of the inferences made by participants. If truth be told, the idea of a grammar of conversation has turned out to be less productive as a research strategy than a line of inquiry based on joint commitment to the common enterprise of playing together. The concept that a game regulates people's behavior in their interactions with each other has been researched by a long list of philosophers,, economists, mathematicians, sociologists, students of law, anthropologists, linguists and psychologists. But the intentions of this vast array of scholars are so different that an attempt to trace a simple thread that links them all would turn out to be an exercise in erudition and nothing more. In this domain, the most exhaustive fresco has been attempted by the historian Johan Huizinga (1939), who has recounted the importance of games in the various cultural aspects of human history: in law, in war, in art, and in philosophy.

The term "game" is inevitably associated with children and calls to mind the juvenile activity that remains present in adult life. I would like to retain—and not eliminate—that playful aura for a variety of reasons. First and foremost, it is through play that little ones of every species, and in particular social mammals, learn the rudiments of adult behavior, in a context that is pleasant, open, and not dangerous. This stricture is equally applicable to the offspring of lions, monkeys, and human beings. In learning to play, one learns the rules governing the life of the group, and one tests one's capacities to obtain food, find a partner, and survive. But games are not simply an apprenticeship training one to face life: in the higher mammals games are a self-perpetuating activity, in which adults participate wholeheartedly for the sole pleasure of an interactive activity that is a reward in itself. Thus, the group games played by dolphins or the numerous social activities engaged in by primates undoubtedly have many points in common with the games played by humans, which I will describe later.

Games are thus one way of learning to become an autonomous member in a cooperative society, a quality that may be goal-directed or may be a goal in itself. Without a shadow of doubt, games are precious to the life of an individual and for the continuation of the society to which that individual belongs. In addition, they also constitute a means of self-gratification. This should not surprise us if we consider the fact that games represents a normal mode of interaction with the people who love and care for us when we are very young. We will now examine the main types of interaction, from the most conventional to the least structured.

3.1 Behavior Games

In conversation we must make a clear distinction between communicative competence and interaction schemas. Communicative competence is a general characteristic of the mind, whereas stereotypical interaction schemas are culture-bound. Indeed, the latter may pertain to a small group of individuals, or even two people. The idea that will be developed in this chapter is that communicative competence may be viewed in formal terms as a metalevel property that controls first-level inferences; such inferences are carried out on shared representations of stereotypical interaction schemas.

Consider the following concrete example:

A: Tomorrow's Thursday. Will you coordinate the exam supervision?
B: Actually, the Vice Chancellor has fixed a meeting for 9 A.M.   (2)

In every standard context, B's reply would be taken as a justification for refusing to carry out A's request. As stated earlier, B cooperates conversationally but not behaviorally. The intuitive concept of a behavior game allows us to explain conversation (2), for it enables us to assert that, through her request, A is proposing that she and B play the behavior game:

PEDAGOGICAL DUTIES
X is responsible for running the departmental activities from Monday to Wednesday;

Y is responsible for running the departmental activities from Thursday to Saturday.   (3)

With his reply, Y rejects X's proposal, justifying himself by explaining he has a duty that takes priority over examinations. X thus takes Y's reply as concurrently constituting a counterrequest on Y's part to take over his exam session. The point is that in order to cooperate, at least at the level of conversation, both agents must share the behavior game PEDAGOGICAL DUTIES. In real terms, mutual knowledge of game (3) is exploited to achieve conversational cooperation, even if Y fails to execute the moves foreseen by X, and, therefore, behavioral cooperation is not achieved.

The reason for introducing behavior games is that the literal meaning of an utterance is only the departure point for its comprehension. "Why is she saying this to me?" and "What does she want from me?" are the real questions requiring an answer. If someone sitting in the reader's office says to him:

"I'd like a coffee." (4)

it is obvious that she is proposing a game such as HOSPITALITY, and the rules of that particular game place the encumbrance of providing coffee on the host. And indeed, either the host does produce coffee or else he is obliged to explain why he has not deigned to satisfy the indirect request. If the same assertion were to be uttered in a context in which the reader is not the person responsible for the pleasurable aspects of the situation, for example in the course of taking a walk in the park with a colleague, then that utterance will be interpreted as a proposal to play a different behavior game, for instance GOING TO THE CAFE. However, if a stranger pops his head round the reader's office door and utters (4), then the poor reader will be utterly at a loss as to how to interpret that utterance. In real terms, either the reader is able to find a behavior game that will enable him to interpret the statement, in which case he will know what the stranger expects of him, or else he will be nonplussed.

Although the semantic meaning of expression (4) is immediately comprehensible, the effects the speaker wishes to activate in the hearer must be induced. In the case just mentioned, there is no context that enables both the reader and the stranger to identify a behavior game known to both parties that may be connected to the utterance: hence the failure to understand.

A behavior game is that structure which enable actors to coordinate their interpersonal actions, and which actors employ to select the real meaning of an utterance among the many meanings that utterance might in theory convey.

3.1.1 The Structure of a Behavior Game

For two actors to cooperate at the level of behavior, they must operate on the basis of a plan that is shared at least in part. Following Airenti, Bara, and Colombetti (1993a), I will call a *behavior game* between X and Y an action plan that is shared by X and Y. The shared knowledge required for two actors to be able to interact in the same game may be a combination of tacit and explicit. As we shall see later, the two actors may have an explicit representation of the game, or they may have a tacit representation that is sufficient to enable them to direct their actions. Stated differently, for a game be playable, it must be represented in the actor's memory; the actor need not, however, be fully aware of the game (see, e.g., game (7) below).

Plans have to be seen as trees of intentions, where the leaves may represent both precise intentions to carry out a given action, and stable intentions, depending on context. Unless clarity requires it, when illustrating a game, I will limit myself to describing the prescribed actions, leaving implicit the fact that what is always being referred to is the intention to carry out an action and not the actual execution of that action. Thus, I exclude from my treatment problems connected with the realization of actions, such as motor control, concrete physical possibilities, and so forth.

In addition to actions, behavior games include *validity conditions* that specify the conditions under which the game may be played. Validity conditions may be viewed as an extension of the *felicity conditions* that Austin (1962) invoked to guarantee the success of performatives. The essential features of validity conditions, which do not apply only to performatives but to any move of the game, are time and place. However, some games may impose other conditions connected to the mental states of the participants, or constrained by the actions to be executed. Such conditions include manner and effect. With regard to manner, think for instance of a formal dinner party, where the point is to behave in a polite manner, adequately using covers and conversation, independently of what is being served, and of how much one likes it. With regard to effect, think of pursuing the goal of avoiding your adolescent daughter being not arrested by the police officer she has just insulted, a situation where anything may be taken into consideration; limits of time, money, or dignity do not apply to the parent's interaction with the officer: the only point is to obtain her release.

Finally, a game is playable only if the relationship between the participants allows it. In some cases, if the game has wide social applicability, as is the case with asking someone the time, then the participants need not even be acquainted. In other cases, participants must be members of the same group. For example, only two freemasons who have both recognized their common status as freemasons may discuss topics reserved to those belonging to that lodge. At the extreme of this type of case we have games that may be played only by two specific players and by no one else. This is the case, for example, with games played by parent and child, or by a married couple.

[NAME OF THE GAME]

Relationship between the players (X, Y, Z)

Validity conditions

time ....
place ....
others ....

Moves in the game

X does something
Y does something
Z does something
...

Figure 3.1
Structure of the behavior game.

The *relationship* is therefore the set of behavior games that two people may play together. We will take this subject up in section 3.1.6.

The structure of a behavior game is shown in figure 3.1. The first thing to note is that each agent has her own subjective, and not objective, vision of the game, since the entire process is based on the notion of shared knowledge, this latter notion also being subjective and not objective. In our notation, then, beside the name of each game there should appear the perspective of each player: G (A, B) represents game G viewed from A's standpoint, while G (B, A), instead, represents the same game, G, viewed from B's standpoint.

We will now examine some examples to clarify the concept of behavior game. The first instantiation is one that is widely applicable, the game that allows us to ask a stranger the way.

ASKING THE WAY
Relationship between the players

no conditions

Validity conditions

time: no conditions
place: no conditions

Moves in the game

    X asks Y for some information
    Y gives the requested information
    X thanks Y.   (5)

To tell the truth, to assert that there are no limiting conditions is an exaggeration, because the standard constraints governing conversation still apply: the actors must speak the same language, they must have established contact, and so forth. I do not assert them explicitly because they are default conditions and they are not binding. For instance, although it is normally true that two agents must speak the same language, consider the case in which A is an Italian in Japan, she does not speak Japanese, and the address is written on a piece of paper in ideograms she cannot herself read.

Nor are contact conditions absolutes. A could write a letter to B asking him how to reach a place whose location is known to B since B has been therefore before.

Now let us examine a less general behavior game, linked to two specific players created by Sir Arthur Conan Doyle (1887), Sherlock Holmes and his biographer, Doctor Watson:

SOLVING AN ENIGMA
Relationship between the players

    friends, but Holmes being recognized as having superior intelligence

Validity conditions

    time: no conditions
    place: the scene of the crime, or in the apartment at 221b, Baker Street, London

Moves in the game

    Holmes asks Watson for the solution
    Watson offers an incorrect solution
    Holmes illustrates some of the shortcomings in Watson's reasoning
    Watson challenges Holmes to find the solution to the enigma
    Holmes deduces the correct solution
    Watson expresses his admiration
    Holmes concludes with: "Elementary, Watson."   (6)

Assigning games a declarative knowledge structure means that we can talk about them, mentioning them if needs be. This does not imply, however, that the actors in a game must be aware of the structure of the game, of the moves, or of the motivations that induce them to play the game. In other words, players may have, but need not have, an explicit representation of the games they play.

All the games we have considered so far are readily accessible to the players' conscious knowledge. It is, however, worthwhile illustrating one type that is not so automatically accessible. Let us consider the game that the ethologist and psychoanalyst John Bowlby (1973) calls the "anxious attachment-care mode" between mother and child. According to his description, when a mother is anxious and hyperprotective, a child between the age of two and five responds with an excessive fear of strangers and a great difficulty in exploring the environment, which is detrimental to his development. This confirms the overly careful mother's view that her son is incapable of fending for himself and that there is a continued need for her to protect him. Each time the small child detaches himself in any way from the mother, this creates anxiety in the mother; the child, in his turn, becomes anxious because of his mother's anxiety.

Leaving aside the deep reasons for this affective style of caring, such reciprocal interaction predisposes the child to a phobic personality structure. This makes the child see the environment menacingly unpredictable, thereby giving rise to intense fear and the sensation that he is unable to face the environment alone. Both the mother and the child, when he has become an adult, could, by means of a successful psychotherapy, gain awareness of the nature of the game, discussing the game openly between themselves. But such awareness is unnecessary for playing the game. This is demonstrated by the fact that the child was a protagonist in the game when he was young, at an age at which it was totally impossible for him to represent the game consciously.

I now schematize the structure I have just outlined in order to provide an instantiation of a behavior game that is not necessarily conscious:

DIFFICULT DETACHMENT
Relationship between the players

Hyperprotective mother/dependent child

Validity conditions

time: no conditions
place: any place from which only one of the actors leaves

Moves in the game

> the mother behaves in an anxious and hyperprotective manner
> the child behaves in a nonindependent manner
> the mother feels anxious about the child's lack of independence
> the child feels anxious over any detachment from the mother
> the mother feels anxious over any detachment from the child.   (7)

What I am formalizing here and calling behavior games are socially ubiquitous structures. Even if the only really significant debt is to Wittgenstein and his notion of language game which I outlined at the beginning of the present chapter, two other writers are worth noting. In sociology, Goffman (1959) has bequeathed detailed, accurate, and finely drawn descriptions of numerous social games. He provides us with clear photographic representations of what happens between people and between groups of people. But his representations leave us, at the end of this descriptive banquet, rather full and somewhat indifferent, given the lack of introspection into what is happening to the actors, all soulless puppets, bereft of motivations calling to action.

The psychotherapist Eric Berne (1964, 1970) is the exact opposite. He describes those everyday neuroses common to all of us as constraining behavioral schemas depending on an individual's personality. Berne is a highly intuitive and expert therapist, as well as a brilliant writer. But he too becomes difficult to digest when he claims the world can be explained with his simplified version of psychoanalysis, where the child, the adult, and the parent take the place of their more dignified counterparts—more dignified on a lexical level, too—the Id, the Ego, and the Superego. When, however, he forgoes making impossible comparisons, Berne is capable of making us understand the reasons for the games we play—both personal and sexual games—better than anyone else.

3.1.2 Types of Game

Among the various criteria that may be used to classify the different types of behavior games, I will, in the first instance, privilege an extensional criterion. I will consider games as having essentially an equivalent structure, differing with regard to the number of people capable of playing them.

There are three main types of games:

Cultural games: these are common to an entire culture, affecting a large number of people.

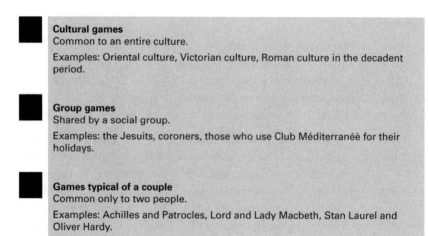

Figure 3.2
Game types.

Group games: these are shared by a more or less restricted number of people forming a given group.
Couple games: these are shared by only two people.

We will now examine these three types singly, bearing in mind that a classification of this nature is not based on rigid, watertight distinctions (figure 3.2).

Cultural Games   "Culture" as I intend it refers to large-scale phenomena that may vary from *the civilized world* to *Western culture*, from the *Mitteleuropa tradition* to the *Parisian style*. What this means is that if two people belonging to the same culture find themselves in a given situation and a specific game is enacted, both know reciprocally what they expect the other to do.

Naturally, the more the game is widespread, the more the expected behavior approximates to a social norm. As such, it may be taught explicitly as well as through experience. Examples range from asking someone for directions to the multiplicity of rites laid down by books on etiquette. That such rules change from one country to another is something the traveler is well aware of: saying one is sorry is as obligatory in the West as it is forbidden in Japan, for in the latter country excusing oneself would be interpreted as a refusal to take responsibility for one's actions. Studies on intercultural communication (Piller 2010) and on linguistic anthropology (Duranti 1997) have shown that culture affects the different pragmatic possibilities of realizing interaction. Also due to the influence of cross-cultural psychology (Berry, Poortinga, and Pandej 1997), this approach has caused the weakening of the thesis of universality and a greater attention to an ethnocentric dimension. As examples we can think here of the deployment of compliments and expressions of thanks. These are rigidly defined by each culture, but their workings are far from obvious. Table manners vary from belching at the end of the meal to serving oneself to each dish twice and twice only (the first time to be courteous, the second time to show one has appreciated the food); common courtesy may be exhibited through the norm that any proposal must be rejected the first time it is made, or by expressing the hope that the interlocutor is asking something out of the ordinary so that one may show one is fully available to the proposal being made. Under the reign of the absolute monarch Louis XIII, this was the court style popularized by the three musketeers, always ready to any excess in risking their lives to prove fidelity to the king and mutual friendship (Dumas 1844). The more difficult was the request to accomplish, the more clear became the proof of courtesy and respect.

Turning to paralinguistic features, over and above gender differences, which show that girls speak two to three times as fast as boys, on average Italians speak more quickly than French, who in their turn speak more quickly than Swiss. In their turn, Africans speak in a higher tone of voice than the Europeans, so that an interethnic conversation may give rise to both parties, though for opposite reasons, a sensation of irritation or of unease.

Extralinguistic behavior has been studied extensively in most of its aspects. Proxemics imposes what is culturally considered the proper distance between two speakers in a wide variety of interactional types. Distances are shorter for Southerners compared to Northerners. With regard to eye gaze, La France and Mayo (1976) have shown that in North America, rules differ for white people and blacks. Blacks look at their interlocutors when they are speaking, but not when they are listening. Whites do the opposite: the listener fixes the speaker, while the speaker looks at the listener only sporadically, fixing her gaze on him only when she is about to terminate her turn at talking. Thus, in an interethnic conversation between black and white, eye contact will be rare and brief if the white is talking while it will be practically uninterrupted if the black is speaking.

Cultural games are tied to the lifespan of the culture itself. The descriptions Gibbon (1994) provides us of political and social life in Rome during the period of decadence differ from those handed down to us by Julius Caesar (58–52 B.C.) when the Roman Empire was at its apotheosis.

According to cultural psychologists, common ground between people consists in large part of a repertoire that is "in the mind" because it has been put there by the communities into which the individual was born, has lived in, and in which he now lives (Tomasello 2009).

Let us examine the game of an invitation to supper as a paradigmatic case in order to observe cultural variations over time. On the occasion of a formal invitation to supper, at the beginning of the eighteenth century in Europe, the guest turned up without bringing anything. He was, however, obliged to send a bunch of flowers the following day with a thank-you note for the lady of the house. Gradually, as the years pass, the game is modified, until the guest is permitted to send the flowers the day of the meal itself, thereby saving the host the worry of having to buy them—for it is taken for granted that flowers there must be—and therefore reserving himself the pleasure of seeing the flowers laid out in the dining room. One further step in the evolution of the game occurs when the guest actually brings the flowers with him, or an equivalent act of homage: a box of *marrons glacés* or some similar superfluity. The game has fallen into mercantile decadence in recent years, since the guest now brings with him something to be consumed during dinner itself, such as a bottle of wine. For a person socialized into the original version of the game, we are now verging on an insult, for the insinuation is that the host is incapable of providing all that is necessary herself.

In order to formalize my transfer to the University of Turin at a social level, the Dean of the Faculty of Psychology invited my wife and myself to dinner together with a number of future colleagues. I thought it would be appropriate to celebrate the occasion with a bottle of the most exclusive champagne, produced in only a few bottles by my uncle Paul. However, the bottle was put carefully aside, despite my insistence that it should be drunk that evening. The dean had decided on other wines, and he had no intention of tolerating infractions of etiquette, not even in the name of Paul Bara. Social class is equally important, as Charles Dickens and Marcel Proust demonstrate when they write about the various social classes in Victorian England and in *fin de siècle* France in order to show their differing rituals.

Group Games   In the case of a group game, the game is shared by a more or less restricted circle of people, and these people have normally shared the experience of structuring the game themselves. Examples of groups of this nature include *Harvard Law School graduates, the Sicilian mafia,* and *Vietnam war veterans*. According to Mario Puzo (1969), if a person asks a mafia boss for help, he must be extremely careful not to offer anything in exchange in an overt or direct fashion. One case he recounts is that of the Italian immigrant who goes and asks the Godfather to avenge his daughter, for she has been raped by two young men who have managed to avoid any legal punishment thanks to their politically influential parents. When he asks how much he has to pay in order that justice be done, don Corleone—for cinema lovers, an unforgettable Marlon Brando—replies:

"Whatever have I done that you should treat me with such disrespect?"

(8)

His turn to play will come, but the time and the move itself will be decided by the Godfather himself. Years later, in the dead of the night, a phone call will inform him how to repay the favor he received.

Light Aviation Squadrons (i.e., Italian reconnaissance planes and helicopters, where I served for an adventurous year as medical lieutenant) are a mix of daring in the air and fanatical prudence on the ground, as is wont for people who must entrust their lives to a mechanical means to carry out missions that may sometimes be extremely risky. While the officers (the pilots) pride themselves on offering everything—from an *aperitif* to dinner—to their mechanics, the game becomes more complex among the officers themselves. The lower-ranking officer is obliged to the higher-ranking officer. The latter will have to recompense the former once in a while in a spectacular fashion by spending a sum that is conspicuously far higher than that spent by the lower-ranking officer. The higher the ranks involved, the more the game tends toward a sort of potlatch, that ritual by which a person's material goods are destroyed in order to gain social status. An interesting exception occurs when a pilot from another base comes to visit: his share of the costs are borne completely by his colleagues, independently of rank.

Mutatis mutandis, the same game is played in academia. Here the survival of a professor visiting another university is guaranteed by the costs he incurs being borne by the professors hosting him. The visitor will return the favor if and when his hosts pay a return visit to his own university. This kind of game enables the participants to travel at almost zero cost, and is extremely pleasing from a human standpoint, for it forges extremely important links—based on bread and salt—between people who formerly knew each other only superficially.

Group games may be taught explicitly, even though they are usually acquired through imitation, often without the participant's really being aware of what one is able to accomplish effortlessly. One particularly interesting case is that of a group whose members wish to recognize each other without being recognized by outsiders. Marilyn Murphy (1991) explains the strategies used by a lesbian in order to recognize another lesbian without revealing her own identity: in addition to her look—particular attention being paid to her shoes, which must be low-heeled and comfortable—outlines how a lesbian walks (first the heel, not the toe), sits (knees over 25 cms. apart), looks at another woman (maintaining eye contact without one's gaze slipping away), moves her body ("as if the various parts of the body belonged to her, and not as if they had been borrowed from the proprietor and woe betide her if she got a scratch on them!").

Couple Games   Couple games are played by two people and are valid only for those two particular people. The game played by a couple may be extended into a group game. Typically, two friends, two colleagues, or a married couple may create the new game's structure.

Groups personalize cultural games, whereas couples personalize both cultural games and group games, constructing recognizable variants. For instance, the way two friends greet each other may turn into a playful insult instead of the usual exchange of well-wishes. It makes use of exactly the same mechanism by which a dialect of a subgroup is formed from the national standard language.

One might ask if wider games exist than those described above, a kind of set of universal games, applicable to humankind as a whole. There certainly exist behavioral schemas common to all human beings—think, for example, of a mother protecting her young who is looking for care—but to be such they must be genetically determined, hardwired into our brain right from birth. It is precisely for this reason that behaviors of this type do not come within our definition of a game. A game remains a structure that must be learned, one that may be negotiated and rejected. For this reason, if some behavioral pattern is innate, it cannot be considered a behavior game. Of course, any specific action, innate or learned, may be utilized as a move within a game.

As we will see in section 3.1.6, it is the set of relationships between players that defines the games that may be played by them.

3.1.3 Playing a Game

An actor will play a game provided two conditions come about: that the game be playable, and that the actor is interested in playing the game. This dual constraint is even more obvious if we first consider an action plan that requires no human participation, with the exception of the subject herself.

If the reader is suddenly seized at this very moment by the desire to have a cup of tea, he will have to take into consideration the only concrete possibility available, namely that he will have to make the tea himself. Does he have a kettle, some water, and an acceptable brand of tea? If one of the necessary elements is missing, this will block the action, at least until a viable alternative is found. For example, if there is no tea, he might be happy to make do with coffee, or else he might decide to procure himself some tea by means of a subplan, such as going out to buy some. Furthermore, the actor must be in a position to carry out the actions detailed in the subplan. If, for instance, he were laid up in bed, he would be unable to carry out even the simplest of required actions, such as pouring water into the kettle.

We have asked ourselves whether the action plan can be realized. Apparently, the intention would seem to create no problem. It only needs a small complication, however, to show that the situation is not as simple as it seems. In actual fact, the intention must be measured against other intentions active in the system, both short-term and long-term intentions. For instance, the reader might for some reason wish to finish reading this chapter as quickly as possible, a reason that will prevent him from causing the interruption required to make the tea. Or his intention may be incompatible with another, long-term intention. For example, a preoccupation with his health will limit the reader's intake of caffeine if he has already reached the given limit for daily tea-drinking.

The intention—any intention—comes into conflict with other intentions active in the system, and a hierarchy of intentions is always maintained; otherwise the normal flow of global behavior would be continually disturbed and interrupted by a pathological, infantile will incapable of resisting any temptation whatsoever. If we now extend what we have been saying to games involving several participants, then the observations made in relation to action plans for single participants applies equally to all participants in an action plan: is the game playable, and is everyone motivated to play it? Motivation will be dealt with in section 4.6. We will now deal with the playability of the game.

Validity conditions fall into three categories, two of which are fixed (time and place) and one of which is open-ended, to enable the insertion of any conditions that are specific to that game. We deal with the three categories in turn.

Time   Behavior games may not be enacted at just any time. Concepts such as "office hours," "opening times," and "service" specifically tie an agent's availability to preestablished times. A clerk will accept a duty, a baker will sell bread, a taxi driver will take a passenger to her destination, only if their respective requests are made within the timetable in which the contract obliges them to act. Outside official hours they will feel no obligation to furnish any service.

In other cases, temporal conditions are less rigid. At home, one may normally dine at seven, but the occasional delay of a few minutes will modify neither the game nor one's willingness to play that game. Finally, there are games such as (5) and (7) that do not set any time restraints, though they may be preferentially activated at certain times rather than at others.

Place   Games provide for an activation situation within which the prescribed moves may be made. In this sense, Austin (1962) observes that inappropriate circumstances render the execution of performative utterances infelicitous. A performative utterance has been defined in section 1.3 as an utterance that does not merely describe something, or that does not restrict itself to describing something. Rather, it is one that *does* something. Since behavioral games include complete Austinian performative procedures, a single performative utterance is the equivalent of a move in a behavior game.

The appropriate circumstances thus have a crucial effect on behavior games, as an example from Austin himself will illustrate. If an agent utters the words:

"I hereby take this man as my legitimate spouse."   (9)

not during a wedding ceremony in the registry office or in church, but on the beach or at the theater, her utterance will not produce the effect of her being married. Thus, transferring the precept to behavior games, if an actor attempts to activate a game in an inappropriate context, her intent will fail. For instance, a passerby cannot get into a taxi driver's cab when he is not on duty and say to him:

"Take me to the airport, quick!"   (10)

and expect the driver to take her where she wants to go.

A game that does not adhere to a performative procedure will have less stringent place constraints, in the sense that failure will not be an automatic consequence. Nevertheless, a preferred place will retain its importance. One cogent example is the psychotherapeutic setting, by which is meant the space within which the psychotherapist carries out his work together with the patient. A standard minimal setting consists of two armchairs, or of an armchair and a divan, placed in the position most congenial to the psychotherapist. The most common positions are the two interactants facing each other or the psychotherapist sitting behind the patient. The setting is considered to be fundamental for the efficacy of the session, inasmuch as it defines the relationship, effectively underlying what is said and what is not said, so much so that even expert therapists find it laborious to work when they are not in their favorite setting. Psychotherapy becomes difficult when performed outside the formal setting, because the psychotherapeutic relationship, which is so different from ordinary interaction, can no longer be taken for granted.

Often, constraints of time and place exist simultaneously, and both of them establish the validity conditions of the game. For instance, a teacher cannot give a lesson whenever she feels like it: there is a school timetable that obliges both teacher and students to be in a given classroom (place) at a specific moment (time). Thus, if a teacher holds her lesson in room 39 from nine to eleven on Wednesday mornings, she cannot move the lesson to another time or place, unless she comes to an agreement on this with the students.

Typically, it is professional games that lay down more complex validity conditions, integrating time and place. A lawyer will see her clients in her office or in court, at a preestablished time. She is not obliged to offer legal advice sitting under an umbrella at the beach. Even if she were to provide an answer to a specific query, she would not feel professionally committed to her answer, since the person advancing the request would not be occupying the role of a genuine client. Hence, a chat on the beach would not be considered as the execution of one's professional duties. The lawyer would not present a bill. This laxity is counterbalanced by the fact that she would be subject neither to professional secrecy nor to any form of responsibility were an error to occur.

An exceptional situation in which a professional person may override time and place constraints may certainly be imagined. Nevertheless, the contract must be formalized. For example, the private detective Nero Wolfe requests that the destitute daughter of his Greek shoe-shiner, suspected of murder, pay him the sum of one dollar as a retainer. Once he has been legally hired, Nero may protect her from the vexations of foolish Inspector Kramer and from the threat posed by the real killer who, in the meantime, has also murdered the honest shoe-shine man (Stout 1963).

Those professions that are not regulated by any form of constraint stand out by contrast. In such cases, professionals are obliged to operate at any moment, at any time. A policeman, for example, is never off duty. He must enforce the law in any circumstance. This particular condition allows him, in certain countries, to carry a firearm even when he is not officially on duty, whereas a security guard is not allowed to do so. Doctors are another category who must intervene whenever the necessity to do so arises. In an emergency, they have no option but to act, whether they like it or not. Doctors are bound by a special constraint that is unknown in other professions: they must intervene even if no prior contract has been established between themselves and the patient. However, this particular condition operates only in special circumstances. In her own private practice, the doctor may refuse to accept someone as a patient.

Other Conditions Some games may establish other validity conditions, related to specific aspects of the games themselves. For example, some games set out conditions for the client. The person wishing to hire a car must have a driver's license and a credit card. Other games lay down conditions the professional must fulfill. To be a doctor, the person must have taken and passed the necessary examinations of the state in which she wishes to work. Other games establish further conditions concerning the relationship between the players. Officers may impart orders to subalterns, but not to other people, and conversely soldiers must obey their superior officers but not others.

However, given the fact that any form of stereotyped interaction may constitute a game, there are, in principle, no limits to the validity conditions that a game may lay down.

3.1.4 Moves in a Game

Once the validity conditions are guaranteed, a game must be negotiated, that is, it must be proposed and accepted by all those who commit themselves to taking part in it. Once the game has begun, it will be played by the participants for the entire course of its logical lifespan, until it reaches its natural conclusion.

Bidding Bidding may take the form of a communication act or of a behavioral act corresponding to the first significant move in the game. The communication act mentions the game itself, either by name or as a metonym, that is, by referring to any of the constituent parts of the game, for instance by mentioning one of the validity conditions or one of the moves.

Of course, the game may be introduced by means of an indirect speech act. For example, the actor may refer to the desire her partner has expressed to play the game suggested. Applying rules of courtesy, it is common to propose a game in an indirect fashion, thereby allowing everyone to save face in case agreement is not reached.

Figure 3.3 presents possible opening moves in what is the classic of sadistic games, that introduced by the Marquis de Sade (1791). In this game, Justine, a virtuous and ingenuous maid, is abducted, taken to an out-of-the-way castle, and entrusted to a very beautiful young woman devoted to vice, who then ties and whips her in front of the libertine while the latter dines with some philosopher friends. The philosophers will then instruct her as to why virtue does not render one happy and will then proceed to profane her in all possible manners.

Carassa and Colombetti (2009) clarify that often by bidding a game the actor provides the partner with an affordance, that is, an opportunity for action. She does not necessarily know the reasons the partner may have for accepting or rejecting her proposal; what she knows, relying on common background, is that he will be able to perceive an affordance of the type she is offering him.

Once the game has been opened, it remains active until it is formally closed. Generally, it is the players themselves who indicate that the game

---

THE MISFORTUNES OF VIRTUE

Communication act

    by name
        [I would propose to whip someone, over dessert.]
        [Why don't we whip the poor innocent child this evening?]
        [I have organized dinner with whipping this evening.]

    as a metonym
        [Haven't we abducted anyone today?]
        [Please prepare the silk rope.]
        [Is the whip ready?]

Behavioral act

    [The libertine gives each guest an elegant whip.]
    [The virtuous maid is brought into the room together with the aperitifs.]
    [The virtuous maid is tied by the lustful young woman.]

Figure 3.3
Types of bidding moves.

they priorly agreed to play is to continue through their behavior. Not all the moves made need be attributed to the game, but when games continue for a long time, the players ensure they periodically confirm the meaning to be attributed to their actions.

On special, highly ritualized occasions, such as a degree ceremony or a court hearing, there might be a figure such as a chairman, a chancellor or a clerk who must officially declare the meeting open and closed, but this is the exception and not the rule. In such cases, however, it is the person in authority who establishes the execution of the opening move, and the other participants may in no way interrupt the procedure, if this is carried out in the correct fashion and in the appropriate circumstances. Similarly, it is the wielder of authority who decides when the game is to come to an end. Here too, the other participants may not appeal against the decision taken by the authorities.

In a less rigid, less formal game, the closing of the game may become an object of discussion. In principle, all the participants should agree that the objectives of the game have been realized, and that the statutory moves have been made, so that everyone may consider herself satisfied, or, at least, has nothing to complain of with regard to the way the game has been carried out.

In the case of competitive games, the participants must be satisfied with the way the procedures have been carried out, seeing that both parties cannot be satisfied with the results. The concept of "knowing how to lose" refers to respecting "fair play" even in defeat. This concept is greatly valued in highly competitive environments, where interpersonal relationships must survive both victory and defeat. My daughter Helen bursts into tears every time she loses at cards, taking offense in equal proportion at fate and at the winner: at ten years of age she has not yet developed the concept of making do with the happiness provided by the procedure, given that it is difficult to always be happy at the result.

A serious challenge leveled against closure implies that a player does not accept the game as terminated. The player could launch the accusation that the rules have not been respected during the game or that closing the game at that point breaks the rules. The discussion of the consequences of this type of event will be taken up in the next section.

Moves A behavior game specifies the moves that constitute that game, at the highest level of detail possible in order to avoid obliging the actors to employ one sole mode of execution.

For instance, in the game illustrated in figure 3.3, it is vital that there be a virtuous maiden playing the part of the victim. It does not matter how the maiden is acquired. She might be abducted from a convent, or sold by unscrupulous parents, or circumvented by a cynical seducer.

Broadly speaking, participants must agree as to whether a specific realization of a move may be held valid with respect to the context and the players' goals. If a move in the game lays down that something must be done that will please one's partner, then the action chosen by the actor will depend on what she believes will make her partner happy on that given occasion. A Havana cigar, a bottle of port, two tickets to the concert or to Polynesia: anything will do, provided it is appropriate to the situation.

Some games that are particularly idiosyncratic or highly institutionalized may, on the contrary, require the execution of a specific move whose procedure is described down to the smallest detail. When the Pope grants an audience, nothing is left to improvisation. Every behavioral act is specified in advance in all its features. The same normative precision would be completely out of place in meeting a person who, despite being very important, does not occupy an almost divine role.

3.1.5 Breaking Off a Game

Having begun a game does not necessarily mean one has to finish that game. Nevertheless, an actor who withdraws from a game is subject to social sanctions whose severity is proportionate to the importance the game has for the community. *Breaking off a game* does not include a person's desire not to play that game in the first place, an option that is always open to a person. Instead, the term refers to an actor beginning a game and then withdrawing when it is her turn to make a given move. For example, in Dostoyevsky's *The Player* (1866), nothing obliges Aleksei to begin his morbid relationship with roulette. He is not, however, allowed to leave Rulettenburg and return to Russia without paying his debts, despite the fact that capricious Paulette—the person responsible for the unfortunate lover's manic attachment to roulette—has finally recognized she too is in love and is now willing to return Aleksei's love.

Sometimes it is the law that guarantees a contract will be respected. Hiring a contractor will incur legal sanctions if the purchaser does not respect the payment dates she committed herself to honoring. Indeed, if it turns out that there was no free choice, then the contract is considered null and void because it is vitiated. If an actor is forced to take part in a game, then she cannot be expected to honor the rules. The virtuous maiden forced to play the game MISFORTUNES OF VIRTUE is in fact allowed to try to escape her terrible fate; that's why she is tied.

In other cases, it is the social group that penalizes the individual who does not respect the rules by attempting to avoid the commitments taken on.

Rigid contracts are coercive and precise, leaving little to interpretation, because the moves are described in detail. Sanctions are equally clear and unavoidable, for the very reason that ignorance is no excuse, and mistakes in good faith virtually impossible. The etiquette of the Chinese Imperial Court establishes only one form of sanction for any infraction: decapitation. Modern civilizations are more flexible, limiting themselves to blander forms of penalization. These generally aim at marginalizing those who attempt to live as social parasites by exploiting cooperation when it is other people's turn and abstaining when it is one's own turn.

Elastic games are flexible and open, leaving actors free to create their own moves, provided the spirit of the game is respected. Before official sanctions are imposed, bad faith must be proven, that is, a precise and conscious intention to avoid fulfilling one's obligations. The uncontrollable explosion in the number of lawsuits in contemporary society is directly correlated with the flexibility of social games, since these offer margins of discretionary choice between what is licit and what is illicit, which was simply not allowed in earlier times. Cultures that are more rigid from the standpoint of behavioral norms oblige their members to interact in much more stereotyped fashions. Nevertheless, they simplify relationships, for they lay down behavioral pathways that are fairly stable.

Human beings prefer one type of game rather than another because of their personalities and because of their experiences during crucial periods of their lives. Personal preferences do not, however, have an ethical base. In absolute terms, nothing renders one type of game better than another. Individual choices must not be confused with the well-being of humanity. When the sexual liberation movement of the 1960s swept away, among other things, the rigidity of behavioral schemes permeated by courtship rituals, it certainly brought a breath of fresh air to mutual seduction rites. The price paid for such new freedom to act was an equally new form of confusion, which this time affected males more than females, for the former were now obliged to be both rigid and tender, whereas it had earlier been females who had been rigidly constrained by behavioral norms.

Complete paralysis lies ready to entrap us as soon as the new moralists manage to prohibit through legal enactments that ambiguity which is essential in the initial phase of sexual selection. The United States is in the vanguard of this delirium, for their legislation requires the partner's reiterated and explicit consent before any even vaguely erotic act may be carried out, such as a kiss or a caress. If implicit consent is necessary in order to impede violence, the consequence of explicit consent is that of blocking sexuality. Indeed, one has the sensation that a vigorous attempt is underway to replace Eros (mostly a social activity) with an obsession with sport or with food (mostly individual activities).

The group will never forgive an actor who breaks off the game when that actor plays the role of the guarantor of the game. In such cases, in addition to the standard sanctions, further penalization is added by the confraternity that cannot tolerate weakness within its own group. Thus, the doctor who kills her patient creates a greater shock than a normal assassin, and corruption seems more despicable in a judge than in a politician. Nonrespect for the game one has committed oneself to playing is, in any case, a sign of noncooperation that renders successive interactions more difficult. Since the assumption of reciprocal cooperation is not an act of absolute faith, but a tie that gradually gains strength as positive experiences accumulate, breaking off an important game has lasting negative consequences.

The essence of social penalization is being considered untrustworthy. This is why in many cultures "losing one's honor" is so often associated with death, either at one's own hand or at the hand of another. The punishment for not having kept one's word is therefore always significant, and correlated with the value that the given commitment has in that cultural context. In the Senji era in Japan between the seventeenth and eighteenth centuries, when a military ideology reigned supreme, there was only one possible remedy for a samurai who lost face if he wanted to recover his dignity: ritual suicide, which took the form called seppuku.

From an evolutionistic point of view, the cooperative style typical of human beings obliges the group to discourage free-riders, those who benefit from participating in mutualistic endeavors without doing their part. In addition to the bad reputation that a free rider earns for himself, and which makes him a second-choice partner for the others, the honest members of the group are ready to sacrifice a part of their resources for the satisfaction of seeing him punished. Tomasello (2009) claims that both norms of cooperation and conformity are cemented by guilt and shame ("I judge myself badly before others do, if I misbehave"). I doubt that critical self-judgment be a universal human trait, but together with ill fame and threats of punishment it definitely strengthens social norms and institutional respect.

The case of the actor who one presumes knows the rules of the game but who in actual fact is incapable of playing that game is quite another matter. In this type of situation we speak of *failure*, distinguishing between a lack of knowledge and the inability to carry out the preestablished procedures. The latter topic will be dealt with in section 5.3. We now turn to the former topic. Stated succinctly, knowledge failure occurs when the actor does not know what move is expected of her and carries out a move that is either wrong or inappropriate. It should be added that an actor does not necessarily realize that her behavior is inadequate. Her partners might also wish to protect her from realizing her knowledge failure in order to avoid the embarrassment that would ensue. According to anecdotal fantasy concerning the Royal family of Great Britain, when the Ugandan dictator Idi Amin, having regrettably been invited to dinner at Buckingham Palace, happily drank water perfumed with rose petals in which he was supposed to clean his fingers, Queen Elizabeth drew the finger bowl to her lips, an act instantly imitated by all the guests.

It may be no easy task for the actor to distinguish between failure and breaking off, if the partner is behaving in an ambiguous way. When Turiddu appears in the *Cavalleria rusticana* (Verga's boring drama written in 1884, and Mascagni's enthralling opera composed in 1890), shortly before paying with his life for his irresponsible flirtation, he leaves Santuzza in a state of uncertainty as to whether her bitter jealousy is well founded or not, as to whether Turiddu has been unfaithful or if he is simply guilty of guileless neglect. At first, Santuzza is uncertain as to whether the bond of matrimony has been broken. When she gains that certainty, she ensures vengeance is wreaked upon Turiddu.

3.1.6 The Relationship between the Players

For two players to be in a position to play a game, the first issue to be cleared up is whether the nature of the relationship between them is of the type that will enable them to interact through engaging in that particular game. One static definition of the relationship between two people consists in listing the types of games they mutually recognize they may play together.

Cultural games are open to all those who share the same culture: it is generally sufficient that both people speak the same language to ensure that they can both adequately play a game of this type. We might even go so far as to affirm that it is sufficient to occupy the same spatiotemporal coordinates to guarantee the playability of the more general types of cultural games.

For group games to constitute part of the games two players may engage in together, both partners must recognize the condition that they belong to the same group. Indeed, the initial stage of an encounter between two strangers is usually devoted to determining whether there are groups that both people belong to:

Are we by chance both linguists, or vegetarians, or supporters of Milan Football Club, or card-carrying members of the Republican party, or opera fanatics, or ex-convicts, or both divorced?   (11)

The set of groups the two people are both members of defines the type of games that will be mutually recognized, even though it does not automatically follow that a game that is known will have to be played. Group membership always creates some degree of reciprocity among people. This explains why it is at times easier to hide the fact that one belongs to a certain group than to explain that one has little desire to play a given game. Abroad, for instance, one may sometimes avoid declaring one's nationality when a group of one's countrymen are behaving in a manner one does not wish to be associated with. Thus, when I was in Japan, I steered clear of making my nationality known to a conformist group of Italians dining in a high-class restaurant, to avoid becoming involved in the usual, boring eulogy of spaghetti, reputedly far superior to sushi.

Furthermore, as we have already seen, acquaintance with a game does not imply that both people will wish to engage in that game with each other. This emerges in an even starker fashion when we consider games played by couples, which are connected to two specific individuals. We may be willing to accept physical contact with a friend though we find such behavior in others intolerable.

A more dynamic way of defining relationships is also to identify those games that may presumably be played by two individuals who have never engaged in those specific games together previously. This is tantamount—for each actor—to asking themselves the question:

Would the other presumably be interested in playing game G with me, if I made the proposal?   (12)

Of course, a certain reply to that question can only be had when the proposal is actually made, or when the opening move is executed. However, to minimize the number of possible refusals—and the consequent reciprocal loss of face—each actor will attempt to predict the presumable reactions of the other party. For example, it may be difficult for a clerk to decide whether or not to invite her boss to her son's wedding: he might accept against his will, or worse still, refuse, causing serious embarrassment to both parties. Only simulation of the other will enable an actor to establish what course to take. But rather than trying to guess the inscrutable mental processes of other people, what every person does is to ask themselves a more precise version of the previous question:

What is the nature of the relationship between myself and the other person?   (13)

In the most complex cases, and given the proviso that one is capable of making subtle distinctions, one may ask oneself:

How does the other person view our relationship?   (14)

The difference between the two questions lies in the fact that in (13) the actor assumes that the relationship between herself and the other is objective and absolute, whereas in (14) she realizes that there may be differences in the way each person sees her or his relationships with others. The dynamic definition of relationship, seen as one of the constituent features of the category "games playable with others," is subjective by nature. The static definition may be considered objective, inasmuch as a knowledgeable observer could establish whether a specific game has been played by that particular couple, or if it belongs to their shared culture. Strictly speaking, however, objectivity in this sphere is a chimera, for people forget, they construct their memories, they reinterpret events, and so on.

The relationship thus becomes the generator of constraints and affordances, starting from games that have been played or that unquestionably belong to the sphere of common culture, to arrive at those games that may potentially be played, but whose execution depends on the reciprocal perception of the two actors. Thus, in asking the other person something, the actor implies that she believes that both parties consider the relationship such that it justifies the question she has just asked.

Bateson (1979) was the first to observe that each communication comes about at two levels: one is the level at which the informational content travels, and the other is the level at which the relational message is conveyed. The nonverbal part of the interaction is that part which Bateson holds is assigned to conveying the relational component of the message. For example, let us suppose that A says to B:

"Please shut the door."   (15)

The tone and the other paralinguistic features of the utterance will clarify to B how A construes their relationship, whether as one between two equals or as one in which there is an asymmetry of power.

The intuition is both excellent and correct. Nevertheless, there is no reason why one should assign the communication of the relational component exclusively to the extralinguistic part of the message. The interaction as a whole predicates simultaneously, through all its aspects, both the specific informational content and the relational content. Although it is undoubtedly true that the tone of voice may transform an insult into a plea, it cannot be stated that it is always the extralinguistic component that defines the relational aspect. To demonstrate the point, let us examine what happens in *Salammbô* (Flaubert 1863), when the prisoner Spendius says to the Libyan mercenary Mathos, who has just met Salammbô and who is already in love with her and wounded by a rival:

"You have freed me from prison: you are now my master! Order, and I will obey!"   (16)

From a conceptual standpoint, the utterance is highly informative as to how Spendius, who has been condemned to life imprisonment, sees his relationship with the warrior who has freed him: that of slave and master. Thus, maintaining the essence of the notion of two communicative levels, it is better to extend the possibility of communicating information about the nature of the relationship to both levels.

Every game is part of the relationship that each agent has with the other players, and the relationship is one of the principal elements that is taken into consideration when deciding whether to accept the offer to play a given game. It sometimes happens, therefore, to make a game playable, that the relationship between the players must be altered. For instance, a psychotherapist cannot meet her patient socially. Were both parties to desire to do so, then the therapeutic relationship would have to have been terminated some considerable time earlier.

In other cases, an actor may attempt to play a game in order to modify her relationship with the other participants. Thus, a snob may try to enroll in an exclusive club not so much because she is interested in the activities of that club, but because she wishes to have an egalitarian relationship with the other members.

Nor should it be forgotten that sometimes an utterance apparently directed to B by A has as its real destination some other participant(s), as happens when A talks to the sister-in-law so that the mother-in-law will get the message. In a case such as this, the same speech act will enable A to communicate something to B and something totally different to C and D. Once again, it will be the games that are being played by A and the other participants that will determine what A wished to convey—both conceptually and relationally—to each of them.

The relationship may also be the reason why an actor does *not* accept an invitation to take part in a game, which she would otherwise accept. In the case of (15), B might refuse to close the door not because closing it in particular goes against any of his objectives, but only because he wishes to show A that he has no intention of being considered a person who carries out A's requests. In a case of this type, one might take offense at the tone employed by the speaker, while the propositional content of the utterance could well be neutral or even positive.

For instance, in *The Woman and the Puppet* (Louÿs 1898), while Conchita declares she loves only Mateo, she continues to repulse his advances before their marriage, and once she has married him, she frenetically betrays him in order to make his erotic obsession even more violent, which is far more exciting for her than merely sexual intercourse. Their special relationship paradoxically prevents Conchita from carrying out an act that she ardently desires, as she will confess before dying at the hand of Mateo, who has been driven mad by jealousy and frustration.

3.2   Free Interactions

Since not all human interactions exhibit those stable features that characterize behavior games, let us now see what happens when the situation does not coincide with any shared game.

The most important situation of this type is the *noncooperative situation*, where cooperation is withheld. When a person was condemned to exile in ancient Greece, his fellow citizens no longer spoke to him, nor gave him hospitality. They even denied him food and water. Obviously, the conditions holding in situations in which no cooperation exists are so restricted that they do not allow a relationship to develop to any significant degree.

It should be noted that language is not the determining factor. Robinson Crusoe establishes an important relationship with Man Friday, even though neither knows a word of the other's language at the outset (Defoe 1719). Similarly, an anthropologist may successfully make contact with an unknown Amazonian tribe, although initially she does not speak their language. In this type of case, the anthropologist and the natives will have to find a game that is so general that it will enable both parties to consider it as shared. Naturally, if the communication is interrupted—perhaps because the natives turn out to be anthropophagous—the relationship will come to a sudden end.

A less dramatic and more common form of noncooperation compared to the anthropologist occurs when one finds it impossible to create even the most superficial of relationships with others because the latter have no interest whatsoever in establishing a relationship. In this case, shared games exist, but the reciprocal intention to activate those games does not.

A second possibility within the domain of reciprocal cooperation is that the actors share no common behavioral framework. This case steps beyond the normal bounds of cultural games to explore a new territory, as happens when, for instance, one undertakes a journey to a country whose culture is radically different. Imagine an Arab visiting Polynesia. In his books, James Clavell has described the difficulties Westerners encounter when interacting with Easterners, such as Japanese and Chinese. In *Shogun* (1975), ambitious John Blackthorne alternates between success and defeat in trade, love, and war, along the path of seeking acceptance by a Japanese society whose sixteenth-century culture is still intact. Accounts of culture conflict proper are quite dramatic. Suffice it to think of the genocide of the Native Americans. In his autobiography, the medicine man Black Elk, born into a glorious and noble tradition of life, has left us with a desolate portrait of his meetings with the uncomprehending civilization of the white man, from Buffalo Bill to Queen Victoria (Neihardt 1932). But even if one remains within one's own cultural tradition, one need only change social environment to find that one has left behind one's usual social games. When, for instance, one starts a new job, new activities must be undertaken with new colleagues. Sharing the same culture is definitely a help, but it is far from sufficient. Nevertheless, transferring one's activities from Florence to Paris is far less stressful than moving from London to Guatemala City.

Finally, no precise shared game can be played when two actors try to move from superficial rites to a deeper mutual knowledge, even though the two people are interested in each other. It is easier to court an old school friend than a person of a different generation. And this is nothing compared to the difficulties, narrated by Kipling, that a representative of the British Empire and a young Indian woman had to overcome in order to comprehend each other's feelings.

In the situations I have just described—and in similar situations where the actors are free to invent the procedural moves they wish to make—we speak of *free interactions*. Naturally, the principle of cooperation applies also in free interactions, otherwise no significant communication could take place. Furthermore, any behavior game the two actors might share can also be played in addition to the interaction the actors are currently engaged in. For instance, if two Bostonians do not share any games played by couples (they do not know each other, they come from different social backgrounds), nevertheless they still have contemporary American culture in common as well as a set of social games that are specific to the Bostonian context.

For free interaction to take place, the activity in which the actors are engaged must not be stereotyped. Indeed, an important part of the content must be novel. If A's car breaks down on the highway and B stops to help her, their interaction will be unstructured. The situation will be played according to the rules of the game of helping the needy, if B is a passerby amenable to this game. If, however, B is a state employee driving an official emergency vehicle, then the interaction between A and B will be regulated by a precise contract. When mutually known reference schemes do not exist, then shared planning becomes extremely important.

Thus, three basic possibilities exist: nonsocial situations, free interactions, and behavior games:

Nonsocial situations.   The agents are immersed in the same situation, but they neither engage in a social interaction nor communicate.
Free interactions.   Agents cooperate and communicate without preestablished behavioral schemes.
Behavior games.   Agents cooperate and communicate relying reciprocally on preestablished schemes.

3.2.1 Setting Up a Game
Some games are transmitted culturally, as are elementary politeness games, or they may be taught explicitly, as when a new employee is introduced to the duties she will have to carry out and to the people she will have to interact with in order to carry those tasks out. Other games, however, may be invented directly by the actors themselves. If they find themselves in a situation in which they cannot or do not wish to enact any stereotypical game, they may draw up an integrated plan of the actions to be executed.

If such integrated planning turns out to be a success, or useful to further development of the interaction, or if for any other reason the plan is worth remembering—among fellow soldiers a spectacular disaster may become a constant reference point—the plan may be used as the foundation for a behavior game. Reproducing the interaction on the basis of the previous experience, a structured scheme may be developed, which in its turn acquires the stability that will transform it into a behavior game. In inventing a game, the agents sometimes proceed to a higher level of abstraction compared to the game itself, discussing the reasons for the creation of the game, its features, the benefits expected. This metalevel is only possible if the mental representation of the game is explicit.

The vagueness of the confines between free interaction and a behavior game explain why games played by couples may seem strange, or even incomprehensible, to the outside observer. Nothing ties the actors, apart from their own creative limits and the fact that all the participants gain satisfactory profit from the interaction. Individual gain cannot be measured in economic terms. It is a psychological notion. What an actor considers adequate compensation is strictly personal. Hence a Sade will profit from making others suffer, while a Sacher-Masoch gains profit from suffering, and both are satisfied by their relationship, leaving the task of rationalizing the affair to the observer.

Games develop slowly; they reach a high level of stability; they are extremely resistant to change. Indeed exchanging one game for another seems a much simpler task than modifying the extant game. Simpler still is changing partners while maintaining more or less the same game. No matter what the situation, only the actors can intervene in a game. An observer, even the most authoritative of observers, remains, by definition, an outsider.

3.2.2 The Development of a Game

How does a game develop? How do children learn the typical structure of a game? These are crucial questions in the study of communication and in trying to understand how linguistic abilities develop. Naturally, the relationship with the mother is the first occasion the child has of coming into contact with a human being. Thus, it seems quite logical to seek in the mother–child relationship the basic emotional and cognitive structure that will become the subject's standard mode of affective and social interaction once the child has become an adult.

Jerome Bruner (1983) has analyzed and described the first structured interactions between mother and child in detail by introducing the notion of *format*. This is essentially a precursor of what I have called behavior games. Such initial modes of exchange between mother and child reflect the essence of cooperative interactions. In addition, they constitute both an extraordinarily efficacious environment for language acquisition and the cultural means by which the child learns the rules that regulate the culture in which the child is soon to become a protagonist.

Section 6.2 will deal with the development of communicative competence. Here I will simply show how the behavior game derives from the format. According to Bruner (1983), formats are stereotypical behavior structures. They are idealized and precisely defined. He holds that they are idealized because they are constitutive (the words of the game are potentially pure performatives) and self-sufficient (they have no functional value beyond the confines of the game itself). Furthermore, they are totally conventional, and they have no natural features (that is, they are made up of elements that are all invented and artificial, and they are kept together by rules that leave little scope for manipulation); their deep structure cannot be modified; a series of realization rules regulates the surface structure of the game. The format analyzed by Bruner is a variation on the game peek-a-boo. A puppet is moved in such a way as to appear from and disappear into a cloth cone mounted on a stick. The game was first played when Jonathan, the subject Bruner analyzed, was five months old.

In general, it may be observed that formats have a surface structure and a deep structure. The deep structure of the peek-a-boo format has two topical moments: the disappearance and the reappearance of the puppet. Surface structure is composed of a series of realization rules that govern the actual execution of the game. It allows alternatives such as the use of a screen and different objects that may appear or disappear, variations in time and in the actions that may take place between the disappearance and the reappearance of the puppet, variations in the utterances employed, changes in the causes of the puppet's disappearance, and so forth. There are no surprises in store in the deep structure. Quite the opposite. If participation and enjoyment are to reach the highest levels, then the deep structure of the format must be recognized. Surprise is achieved by varying the components of surface structure. For example, secondary features such as the accompanying utterances ("look!"; "here!"; "wow!") or the time lapses between actions may vary. Compared to behavior games, formats exhibit perfect correspondence between moves and their concrete realization.

Other points must be underscored, for they are identical in adult interactions. First of all, formats teach and expect the child to respect turn-taking rules. The child must take his turn at the right moment and furnish the appropriate contribution. Next, roles are interchangeable. One person hides the puppet while another is the spectator. But roles may vary from one occasion to the next. Initially, Jonathan plays the part of the spectator. But at the age of eight months, he begins to intervene directly, wanting to be the person who maneuvers the puppet, a goal he gradually manages to realize over the following months as his motor control improves. Finally, the format provides the opportunity to both parties to focus their attention on an ordered sequence of events. It therefore furnishes the child with the basic structure of conversation.

In learning to master a set of formats, the child learns the basic general forms of interaction, both those with adults and those with his peers. Such forms constitute the framework on which behavior games proper will later be built, so much so that the basic structures of the two phenomena are identical. The fact that the child plays the standard format in physical contact with his parents is important because it demonstrates that the original structure of the interaction is embodied, rooted in emotions and actions. In fact, the child may engage in this type of intellectual task only if he has an emotionally stable relationship with the interactants and trusts them. It is thus not pure chance that the 5- to 6-month-old child can learn a game such as peek-a-boo only with the stable members of his family.

For example, my daughter Simona began to structure a three-person format which we called "the lift" at the age of six months. The structure was as follows. I held Simona in my arms. I was standing next to my wife who was either standing next to me or lying down. I would slowly pass the baby over or down to my wife and then take her back up into my arms. When the child came into contact with her mother, she would laugh heartily, only to emit a form of lament, together with her mother, the moment I took her back into my arms and held her aloft. The structure was repeated varying times and positions. The child always took a fully active part. The lift, in an infinitely varied number of forms, remained a favorite of hers until the age of six, at which point she had become too heavy to lift and lower for the requisite number of times that would satisfy her.

Both in peek-a-boo played by Jonathan and his mother and in the lift played by Simona and her parents, it is the affective bond between child and close relatives that makes the creation and consolidation of such a structure possible. But if the affective bond is so important, then it should be possible to find interactional structures that are purely emotional. In order to explore this hypothesis, recourse must be had to studies on attachment. Since the literature in this field is extremely complex, I will closely follow the approach adopted by Bowlby (1988).

Attachment patterns generally begin to be investigated at the age of twelve months. A check is carried out at eighteen months. Their stability over time depends on the absence of change in the mother's attitude: if the mother does not change her behavior toward the child, the pattern becomes established. It is also important to note that the child usually develops a relational modality of one type with the mother and a relational modality of another type with the father. If the two modalities are identical, then the probability that the child will exhibit the same cognitive organization as an adult increases. If, instead, the parents have different approaches to caring for the child, then the degree of freedom the child will have will increase proportionally to the difference in style.

In terms of behavior games, if the child learns only one emotional game, this will be the only game she will have to draw inspiration from for the rest of her life. If she knows more than one, she will be able to move through life with greater freedom to maneuver. Style of attachment is the emotional counterpart to the cognitive format. Like the format, it constitutes the basic scheme by means of which one's entire life experience will be structured and interpreted. The attachment pattern influences the child's attitude toward herself, toward other people, and toward the world. In the remaining part of the book, I will concentrate mainly on the cognitive aspects of games, because these are the ones that are most involved in communication. Nevertheless, it is obvious that emotional aspects also play a fundamental role in communicative processes.

3.3   Conversation Game

A conversation game may be defined as a set of tasks that each participant in the conversation has to fulfill in a given sequence. Each task is characteristic of a phase in the generation/comprehension process that will be described in chapter 4. Furthermore, a conversation game specifies how the different phases have to be linked up both in standard and in non-standard cases.

In each phase, the task associated with that phase is carried out employing a set of inference rules called *base-level rules*. The conversation game may be epitomized as a set of *metarules* that define both the task to be carried out in each phase and which task is to be activated next. The concept of a rule is employed in formalizing an analytical description. Naturally, nothing of the sort exists in the brain. Everything is realized through neuronal activity.

In each phase, the metarule associated with that phase defines the task by means of a logical formula that is obtained from the application of the base-level rules. In addition, the metarule also establishes what must be done both when the task is completed and when it is not executed.

Thus it is the conversation game that establishes how a *dialogue* (a sequence of speech acts) is carried out. A dialogue is a highly structured activity involving at least two agents. The structure of real dialogues has been studied intensively by ethnomethodologists (Psathas 1979; Schenkein 1978; Turner 1974), who advocate that nonquantitative, ethnic methods must be employed in studying social interactions. Their work on how spontaneous conversations occur provides considerable data on how different types of dialogue evolve.

Dialogues exhibit both a global structure and a local structure. The *global structure* determines the flow of conversation. In particular, it determines the way in which the different phases of the conversation are connected sequentially. I define a *sequence* as a block of exchanges tied together by strong semantic and pragmatic coherence. The majority of interactions consist of three sections of utterances: an opening sequence, the body of the interaction, and a closing sequence. The most highly investigated case is that of the telephone conversation, where the global structure of the conversation is especially rigid (Schegloff 1972).

At a more detailed level of analysis, a dialogue may be considered as consisting of an alternation of *turns*, each of which is a sequence of speech acts uttered by the same actor. *Turn-taking*, which has been extensively studied by Sacks, Schegloff, and Jefferson (1978), is part of the *local structure* of a dialogue. Local structure also manages the relationship between speech acts within the same turn. A turn may thus be composed of more than one speech act, the set of these acts being characterized by coherence. A cogent illustration of such a turn is provided by the opening scene in Othello, in which Iago, together with Roderigo, a gentleman from Venice whose advances have already been rejected by Desdemona, goes to Brabanzio, the senator, to inform him that his daughter has fled with the Moor.

Iago: Awake, what ho, Brabanzio, thieves, thieves, thieves!
    Look to your house, your daughter, and your bags.
    Thieves, thieves!
Brabanzio: What is the reason of this terrible summons?
    What is the matter there?   (17)

In addition, local structure also manages relations between consecutive turns, the main concept here being *adjacency pairs*, which Schegloff and Sacks (1974) define as stereotyped sequences of interactions, such as greeting/greeting, offer/acceptance-refusal, question/answer, and so forth. For instance, if a turn conveys a question, then the adjacent turn should generally convey an answer, as in:

Romeo: Have not saints lips, and holy palmers, too?
Juliet: Ay, pilgrim, lips that they must use in prayer.   (18)

Alternatively, a sequence with a clarifying function may be embarked on to then be followed by the completion of the initial sequence:

Iago: Awake, what ho, Brabanzio, thieves, thieves, thieves!
   Look to your house, your daughter, and your bags.
   Thieves, thieves!
Brabanzio: What is the reason of this terrible summons?
   What is the matter there?
Roderigo: Signor, is all your family within?
Iago: Are your doors locked?
Brabanzio: Why, wherefore ask you this?
Iago: 'Swounds, sir, you're robbed. For shame, put on your gown.
   Your heart is burst, you have lost half your soul.
   Even now, now, very now, an old black ram
   Is tupping your white ewe.   (19)

Exchanges (18) and (19) both become ridiculous if one alters the rigid turn-taking structure of a dialogue, for example by inverting the order of the turns.

According to philosopher David Lewis (1969), a dialogue is a game of cooperation were both participants "win" if both understand the dialogue, and neither "wins" if one or both do not understand. In such a vein, the best treatment ever has been offered by Martin Pickering and Simon Garrod (2003), who propose a mechanistic psychology of dialogue, the *interactive alignment account*. They use the notion of *coordination* to mean that interlocutors are coordinated in a successful dialogue just as participants in any successful joint activity are coordinated (e.g., ballroom dancers, or lumberjacks using a two-handed saw). They distinguish coordination from alignment, which occurs at a particular level when interlocutors have the same representation at that level.

Pickering and Garrod (2003) argue that there must be parity between production and comprehension processes, which requires that the representations held by actor and partner be the same. Both interlocutors foreground the same information, and therefore tend to make the same additions to their situation model. Interlocutors align on implicit common ground, and in particular they draw on common ground as a means of repairing misalignment Their analysis is at an objective level: they assume a God's-eye perspective, to explain what happens during a conversation. In fact they succeed in efficaciously describing what happens, as this emerges from the recording of a dialogue. As I focus on the mental state of each agent, my description of the same conversational events is by necessity unlike theirs; notwithstanding these differences, I regard our two approaches as complementary.

Cognitive pragmatics views the global structure of dialogues as deriving from sharing the knowledge of an action plan. Consequently, the global structure of a dialogue does not derive from linguistic rules, but from behavior games. In sum, the behavior game governs the interaction as a whole, whereas the conversation game is responsible for the harmonious local development of the dialogue.

4 Generation and Comprehension of Communication Acts

I do not intend to analyze an elementary exchange in a dialogue in formal terms, but to explain the scheme of conversation in its entirety, since the latter is a special and fundamental case of communication among humans. As we saw in chapter 2, conversation is not so much a game of table-tennis, in which the agents alternatively exchange information, as a communal and simultaneous effort to build something together.

Awareness of this fact does not, however, exempt us from analyzing conversation down to its smallest unit, for a microscopic decomposition of the communal construction brings out the alternating nature of the dialogic structure, a structure that is also composed of intervals between the recognizable alternating turns. The construction of meaning takes place in parallel fashion, not consecutively. Analysis, however, has its own set of requirements, and decomposition into constituent units is just as useful as the reconstruction of the full complexity of the natural state of conversation.

The general scheme is as follows: the actor produces an utterance; the partner builds a representation of its meaning. The mental states of the partner pertaining to the topic of the conversation may be modified by comprehension of the utterance(s). The partner then plans the next move in the conversation, which he then generates. The rules proposed comprise a dyadic model of communication acts that range from comprehension to reaction, that is, from the reconstruction of the meaning intended by the speaker to the establishment of the high-level intentions required to generate the response.

Assuming that actor A produces an utterance addressed to partner B, we may distinguish five logically connected steps in B's mental processes:

Stage 1. Expression act, where A's mental state is reconstructed by B starting from the locutionary act.

Stage 2. Speaker meaning, where B reconstructs A's communicative intentions, including the case of indirect speech.

Stage 3. Communicative effect, which consists of two processes:

    (*a*) *attribution,* where B attributes to A private mental states such
        as beliefs and intentions; and

    (*b*) *adjustment,* where B's mental states concerning the topic of the
        conversation may be altered as a result of A's utterance.

Stage 4. Reaction, where B produces the intentions he will communicate in
his response.

Stage 5. Response, in which B produces an overt communicative response.

The linking together of these five stages is managed by the conversation
game: stated more formally, it is the equivalent of a set of metarules. The
standard sequence is that described, from stage 1 through to stage 5.
However, if any one of the first three stages fails to complete its task, the
normal chain is interrupted and the process moves directly on to the
response stage. This is due to the fact that the conversation game lays down
the rule that the partner will react to the actor's utterance, even when he
does not understand it. This he may do, for instance, by asking for clarification. The global outline of these five stages is sketched out in figure 4.1.

The execution of each task is governed by a set of base-level rules that
define which dominion-dependent inferences are to be employed to carry
out that task. These rules have different roles in the various processes. I
must stress that such rules are a convenient means for describing communicative interaction. This does not imply they actually exist in the mind
or in the brain.

Comprehending the expression act (stage 1) and speaker meaning (stage
2) are managed by a limited number of specialized rules. The reason for this
is that comprehension is a process that is shared and achieved by two
people, with the result that the actor must, in principle, be able to predict
how her partner will reconstruct the meaning of her utterance. Stated differently, since comprehension rules are constitutive of meaning, meaning's
construction is shared by all those who are taking part in the interaction.

In contrast to the two initial stages, the effect of the utterance on the
partner is a question of private mental processing. In this case, individual
motivation and general intelligence prevail over shared social norms.
This means that it is impossible to formulate an exhaustive set of rules for
stage 3.

Stage 4, the reaction stage, is again different. The task here consists in
planning a communication act whose starting point is the private motivations activated by the flow of the dialogue. It should therefore be possible

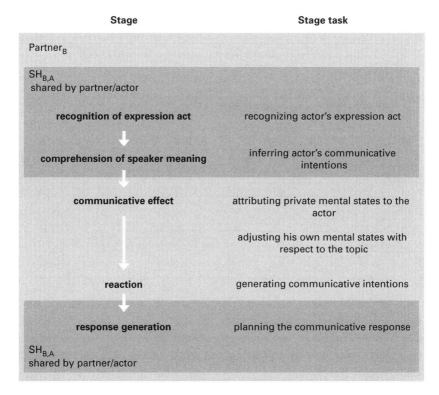

Stage	Stage task
Partner$_B$	
SH$_{B,A}$ shared by partner/actor	
recognition of expression act	recognizing actor's expression act
comprehension of speaker meaning	inferring actor's communicative intentions
communicative effect	attributing private mental states to the actor
	adjusting his own mental states with respect to the topic
reaction	generating communicative intentions
response generation	planning the communicative response
SH$_{B,A}$ shared by partner/actor	

Figure 4.1
The five stages of comprehension and generation of a communication act.
Source: Airenti, Bara, and Colombetti 1993a.

to identify a set of norms that describe cooperative interaction. Such norms are neither universal nor logically necessary. They depend on the specific culture the agents belong to and on the specific circumstances the dialogue takes place in: in our terms, on the behavior game that is being played. This being the case, I will not introduce base-level response rules, but will simply present a few paradigmatic examples. The task of defining cultural and situational taxonomies of the rules for stage 4 must be left to the scholars of ethnicity.

Finally, response generation (stage 5) is based on a highly specialized type of planning and on a set of shared and constitutive linguistic and extralinguistic rules. This stage will be discussed at a global level in this chapter.

Throughout the chapter I will have recourse to formal definitions. Their simplicity should ensure they are readily comprehensible. In any case, I will also provide a verbal description together with exemplifications. In the following sections, only metarules will be formally described. A formal definition of the corresponding rules is offered by Airenti, Bara, and Colombetti (1993a).

4.1 Recognizing the Expression Act

I define an *expression act* as the concrete realization of a communication act, overtly intended by actor A to be perceived by partner B as directed toward him. In the case of a speech act, the departure point of this stage is the analysis B carries out of the utterance emitted by A. This may be stated in terms of the corresponding locutionary act, with receiver B, propositional content p, and literal illocutionary force f. It should be remembered that the illocutionary force indicates how the utterance is to be interpreted, that is, what type of illocutionary act is being carried out by the actor in uttering the expression. The main types of literal illocutionary forces are:

Assertive: "Alphonse, you're a sadist."   (1)

Interrogative: "Leopold, are you a masochist?"   (2)

Directive: "Romeo, deny thy father and refuse thy name."   (3)

Taking propositional content as a primitive, I will not decompose it into lower-level constituents such as reference and predicate. What this means is that my theory of dialogue posits itself at the propositional level.

Even though a locutionary act is usually carried out in order to express a mental state of the actor, this is not the only possibility. For example, if A tries to improve her English by repeating the days of the week out loud, we cannot attribute any mental state to her other than that of uttering:

Sunday, Monday, Tuesday, Wednesday, Thursday, Friday, Saturday.   (4)

In this case, B cannot infer any mental state ascribable to A from the locutionary act beyond her intention to generate that specific locutionary act.

In the more usual case of the expressive use of an utterance, actor A expresses a mental state through producing a locutionary act, for example:

"Romeo, I love thee."   (5)

The standard inference that may be drawn from an expression act consists in attributing to the actor the mental state expressed, which represents the standard first step in comprehending speaker meaning.

Two points are worth noting. First, even if the interpretation is based to a large degree on language, the locutionary act is not necessarily a linguistic one. For instance, in many situations raising one's hand is the equivalent of uttering the expression "Hello!," and smiling may be the exact equivalent of expressing one's pleasure to someone dear to one. Second, both types of acts, precisely because they *are* acts, may be moves in a behavior game. The consequences of this point will be examined shortly. The conversation game at this stage sets the hearer the task of recognizing the actor's expression act. Once this has been recognized, the conversation games activates the process of recognizing speaker meaning. If the expression act is not recognized, then it falls to the conversation game to manage the situation by activating the reaction stage, where an appropriate response will be planned. The outline of metarule M1 which dominates this stage is presented in figure 4.2.

I make use of a few notations which are worth explaining. An action is represented by a formula like:

DO_A something.

This means that actor A does something. In some cases, A may do something to partner B, or perform an action dedicated to B. If the actor is bidding a game through an action, we may find:

DO_{AB} Game G.

As games are subjective structures (in the sense that they are always represented from the point of view of one of the participants), we'll find either Game G(A,B), if it is described from the point of view of A, or Game G(B,A), if from the point of view of B.

Expression act

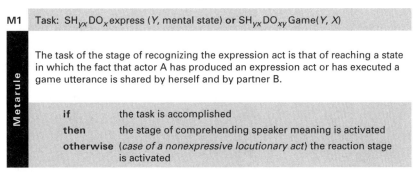

M1	Task: $SH_{yx} DO_x$ express (*Y*, mental state) **or** $SH_{yx} DO_{xy}$ Game(*Y, X*)

Metarule

The task of the stage of recognizing the expression act is that of reaching a state in which the fact that actor A has produced an expression act or has executed a game utterance is shared by herself and by partner B.

if	the task is accomplished
then	the stage of comprehending speaker meaning is activated
otherwise	(*case of a nonexpressive locutionary act*) the reaction stage is activated

Figure 4.2
Recognizing an expression act.

An interesting action A may perform is that of expressing a mental state to B, which will be represented as such:

DO_A express (B, mental state).

Sharedness (SH), intention (INT), and communicative intention (CINT) were introduced in chapter 2.

There is, however, one particular type of expression act that must receive separate treatment. Consider the following utterances:

I surrender.

Please stay.

I declare you man and wife.   (6)

These are all examples of performatives. Hence they do not exclusively express a mental state or an action that has a meaning independently of the utterance itself. Uttering "I surrender" corresponds to carrying out an illocutionary act that is part of a well-defined behavior game which we may presume is regulating some form of antagonistic conduct the two agents are engaged in. There is nothing intrinsically linguistic in this. This is demonstrated by the fact that the same action could have been carried out in a nonverbal fashion, for instance by waving a white flag.

I define a *game utterance* as an utterance whose associated illocution is completely defined by belonging to a behavior game. Although such utterances are generally linguistic in nature, they need not be. Nor are they necessarily performatives. For example, uttering:

Good evening.

Excuse me.

Pleased to meet you.   (7)

is tantamount to pronouncing game utterances. Let us examine "Pleased to meet you." Even though the sentence literally conveys a proposition, this proposition expresses no mental state. The actor is not literally expressing her pleasure at meeting B. Rather, she is participating with her partner in the behavior game of mutual introductions. It is precisely the irrelevance of propositional content that makes it possible to employ utterances whose propositional content is nil or has been forgotten by anyone who is not a philologist, "hello" and "goodbye" being cogent cases in point. In the same way, agents may use equivalent extralinguistic acts, such as shaking hands or kissing the other actor on the cheek.

The key point about expression acts does not consist in the psychological state denoted literally by the utterance, but in the game that is socially established and defines the use of the said utterance. Compare a speech act such as:

"I'm sorry."   (8)

with an utterance an actor might employ to really convey regret, such as:

"I must apologize for what happened the other evening."   (9)

The actor must avoid using idiomatic forms of expression if she wishes the hearer to take her seriously. In other words, if A intends to express her mental state, she cannot employ standardized game utterances. She must make use of utterances that mark the difference. This is not always an easy undertaking, but participants in an interaction can generally tell the difference between ritualism and essence.

4.2   Speaker Meaning

There are four basic steps in comprehending speaker meaning:

1. All inferences are drawn within shared beliefs.
2. The starting point is the propositional content of the expression act or the recognition of the game utterances, as recognized by B.
3. The result of the entire process is the recognition of the actor's communicative intentions.
4. In order to fully comprehend the communicative content of the utterance emitted by A, B must recognize which behavior game A is explicitly or implicitly referring to.

The task of this stage is to reconstruct all the relevant meanings the speaker intends to convey, starting from the propositional content of the expression act furnished by the preceding stage. The core of the process is sketched out in figure 4.3. In the model I am proposing, speaker meaning coincides with the set of communicative intentions conveyed by means of the utterance.

One crucial problem, and one my theory has in common with all computational models developed so far in the literature, is how to delimit the set of communicative intentions. Suppose, for example, that A and B are in the same room, and when B is about to go out A says to him:

"It's raining."   (10)

Speaker meaning

M 2	Task: $SH_{yx} CINT_{xy} INT_x DO_{xy} Game(Y, X)$

The task of the stage of comprehending speaker meaning is that of reaching a state in which the partner and the actor share the fact that the actor has communicated her intention to play a behavior game with her partner.

Metarule

if	the task is realized
then	the communicative effect stage is activated
otherwise	the reaction stage is activated

Figure 4.3
Comprehending speaker meaning.

What is A really communicating to B? The simplest hypothesis is that A is merely suggesting:

"Take an umbrella." (11)

Or, at a more general level:

"I advise you to take the relevant steps in order to avoid getting wet." (12)

But how many other things is A communicating to B?

With regard to the problem of delimiting the set of communicative intentions, two polar opposite positions may be adopted. The minimalist position consists in assuming that only the literal meaning is actually communicated, and that any consequence that the partner derives from this literal meaning is to be considered a private inference, one that is not overtly intended by the actor. This stance is so cautious that it does away with all possible difficulties. However, such excessive conservatism prevents us from dealing in an adequate manner with the private deductions the interlocutors may safely derive from literal meaning. Let us suppose that B draws the following private inference from (9):

This is not a real thunderstorm. Quite obviously, A is not used to our climate. (13)

Since (13) is clearly not based on mutual knowledge but on knowledge possessed only by B, the epistemic status of (13) differs from that of (11) and (12), which, on the contrary, are based on knowledge shared by both interlocutors. The minimalist position is thus unable to make a distinction between two different types of inferences that it is useful to be able to distinguish.

At the other extreme we find the maximalist position. This states that any inference the partner draws on the basis of mutual knowledge must be taken as overtly intended by the actor. The weak point of this second stance is that the inferences that may be drawn on the basis of common knowledge are infinite. Consider the following set of inferences sparked off by utterance (10):

The sun is not shining.

Rain wets the surface it comes into contact with.

It is healthier to be dry than wet.

Umbrellas and raincoats help one to avoid getting drenched.

The roads are wet.

The number of traffic accidents will increase.   (14)

The infinite number of inferences possible renders the maximalist position untenable in a cognitive model, for the latter type of model must succeed in accounting for the necessarily finite number of inferences a human being will draw.

To escape from this impasse, we may assert that the actor communicates only what may be derived from the literal meaning of her utterance, through inferences that are conversationally relevant. Sperber and Wilson (1986, 1995) contend that the concept of relevance is the most fundamental characteristic of all communication. One cannot object to the thesis that relevance guides inferencing processes; how the principle is actually realized is, however, open to debate. According to Sperber and Wilson, relevance is to be defined in terms of general properties of human deductive processes. In contrast, I define relevance in terms of cognitive structures that are specific to communication.

I will now outline the reasons behind this second stance. If we assume that inferences are made possible by the operation of base-level inferencing rules, then the correct place to establish whether an inference is relevant or not is the metalevel, because it is the metalevel that establishes which base-level rules are to be activated. We must therefore formulate metarules that are capable of driving the inferential process in such a way that all and only those conversational inferences that are relevant may be derived by the partner.

Viewed in terms of my theory, an utterance is relevant when it manifests the intention of an actor to participate in a behavior game together with a partner. Hence, the partner's inferential chain must end in a mental state which is equivalent to:

$$SH_{BA} \ CINT_{AB} \ INT_A \ DO_{AB} \ G(B,A) \hspace{3cm} (15)$$

The meaning of formula (15) is that, from partner B's point of view, A having communicated that she intended to play game G is taken as shared. For instance, through utterance (9) A is expressing her desire to reestablish her relationship with B.

This applies both when actor A announces that she intends to play a given game and when either she or her partner makes a move during the game. In the former case, the mental state (15) conveys a *behavioral bid*, which I define as the proposal to initiate a game. In the latter case, when the game is already underway, agents implicitly admit their awareness of being engaged in the game itself. We may therefore assume that the partner possesses a mental state that may be represented as follows:

$$SH_{BA} \ DO_{AB} \ G(B,A) \hspace{4cm} (16)$$

(16) means that B believes both A and B believe they are engaged in game G. An intuitive translation of conditions (15) and (16) expressing B's mental states is as follows:

A has communicated to me that she wishes to play game G with me.

$$(15b)$$

We are still playing game G. $\hspace{5cm}$ (16b)

In any case, the metalevel must select an inferential chain that reaches state (15), in which B may take A's request to activate game G as shared. I am not here arguing that the rules and metarules exist ontologically. What I am claiming, in contrast, is that the neuronal structure of the brain realizes something that may be represented by those rules and metarules.

The heuristics to be employed in order to identify the game being played should exploit the knowledge represented in behavior games. One sensible procedure would be to try to interpret an utterance employing a bidirectional strategy, approaching the problem both from the expression act and from the game in progress—if a game is indeed being played—or else from the small number of games possible, given the validity conditions that have been satisfied.

Starting from the validity conditions means selecting not a possible game, but the one most probable among all those possible. Thus, the most restrictive validity conditions must be considered first. Then the conditions must be gradually broadened to include the most general, as attempt after attempt fails. The heuristics should first contemplate games played by couples, then group games, and finally cultural games.

> **1**   **Game move**
> The dialogue takes place within the game being played.
>
> 1a. A linguistic or extralinguistic expression act
> 1b. A game utterance
> 1c. An action which the game legitimates is carried out directly

> **2**   **Proposal to play a game**
> The dialogue is used to mention the game, by referring to:
>
> 2a. Actions which the game has made provisions for
> 2b. Relevant features of the game (name of the game, actor's role, partner's role, validity conditions)

Figure 4.4
Openings in a behavior game.

If, instead, our starting point is the expression act, then it is the base level that must try to reach state (15), namely that state in which B takes it as shared that A has manifested her intention to participate in a behavior game. In this case, a wide variety of options are available to bid in a behavior game. These are listed in figure 4.4.

A first distinction must be made between cases falling under 1, in which the utterances are proffered out as moves in a behavior game, and cases falling under 2, in which the function of an utterance is to offer to play a behavior game. These two cases correspond respectively to situations in which the dialogue takes place within the game being played, with the utterance therefore constituting a move in the game, and to situations in which the dialogue is employed to mention a game one wishes to engage in.

In cases of type 1, any legitimate move in a game may be made. Such moves may be expressive and achieved through linguistic or extralinguistic means, or they may be game-specific utterances and actions.

In cases of type 2, the actor mentions a game, thereby proposing the playing of that game before actually making any game-specific move. The actor expresses a mental state that refers to the game by mentioning the moves in the game, or by referring to some feature of that game.

4.2.1   Indirect Speech Acts
One of the tasks of comprehension of speaker meaning is to make sense of those utterances that speech act theory classifies as indirect speech acts.

To avoid misunderstandings, I will here use traditional terminology. I will thus define an *indirect illocutionary act* as an illocutionary act whose meaning is conveyed through mediation, that is, through the execution of another illocutionary act. In cases such as these, the speaker carries out a *primary* illocutionary act through uttering a *secondary*, and literal, illocutionary act. In full reciprocity, the hearer understands both what the speaker said literally (*secondary* illocutionary act) and that other meaning that was conveyed in an indirect fashion (*primary* illocutionary act).

A few examples will clarify what I mean. Let us suppose that when two people take their leave after a meeting A wishes to express to B her desire that he telephone her the following day. Naturally, A may express this desire in manifold ways. Let us examine some of the more usual linguistic means employed:

Can you phone me?

Can *you* phone me?

Could you please phone me?

You remember my phone number, don't you?

Why don't you phone me?

Do you want me to give you a quarter for the telephone?

No suffering from amnesia, please.

It would be better if you called.

Let's hope your little finger doesn't get paralyzed when you have to phone.

Now repeat after me: 0—2—8—6—3—0—0—3.   (17)

This list, which the reader may easily add to, contains a series of questions whose apparent aim is to check B's ability to use the telephone, and a second set of assertions that range from wishing B good health to ordering him to repeat a series of numbers out loud. The interlocutor has no difficulty in comprehending all the utterances in (17). Each utterance is complete in itself and makes sense. Each utterance will be taken in this context as a precise request on A's part that B telephone her.

It is as well to note immediately that all the utterances in (17) may be given a literal answer, such as:

Of course.

Oh, yes.

Certainly.

Of course I do. I've got it written down!

Fine.

There's no need.

Certainly not.

Yes, all right.

Let's hope not.

Ok: 0—2—8—6—3—0—0—3.   (18)

But none of the literal answers in (18) commits B to making a telephone call as requested, just as none of the utterances in (17) contained the following direct and explicit request:

A: "Please phone me."   (19)

How does the hearer manage to comprehend the speaker's intention, rendering all the forms in (17) equivalent in practical terms to (19), over and beyond the syntactic and paralinguistic differences? It should further be noted that from the speaker's standpoint the only adequate response both to (17) and to (19) is the action of phoning. A would be satisfied with no other type of response. A would interpret the utterances in (18) as expressing promises of a future action, despite the fact that none of these utterances has the direct and explicit meaning conveyed by the form:

B: "I promise to phone you."   (20)

We will classify the forms in (17) as indirect speech acts where the primary illocutionary act is A's request that B telephone her. Over and beyond the difference in literal forms, what also distinguishes the indirect speech act in (17) from the direct speech act in (19) is that (17) also expresses a secondary illocutionary act, corresponding to the literal form of the various utterances.

The same analysis applies to B's replies. The respective forms of (18) constitute indirect speech acts in which the primary illocutionary act is the promise that B will telephone A. Here too, the major difference between the indirect speech acts conveyed by the forms in (18) and the direct speech act conveyed by (20) lies in the fact that (18) also contains a secondary speech act, corresponding to the literal meaning of the various utterances.

The problem we now have to face is how interlocutors manage to understand each other, overcoming the difficulties set them by indirect forms, a problem rendered even more interesting by the fact that indirect speech acts greatly outnumber direct speech acts in natural conversation. Four types of explanation exist, in addition to that advanced in this book. They will be referred to respectively as solutions achieved by means of *idiomatic expressions, inferential chains, contextual analysis, conventional and nonconventional indirect speech acts*, and, finally, my own proposal, *simple and complex indirect speech acts*.

Indirect Speech Acts as Idiomatic Expressions This approach attempts to provide an exquisitely linguistic solution to the problem of indirect speech acts. Sadock (1974) claims that indirect speech acts are idiomatic expressions that are semantically equivalent to direct speech acts. They are acquired and employed as such by the users of a given language. In concrete terms, just as "A miss is as good as a mile" is an idiomatic expression transmitting the message "If you fail, then it makes no difference if you only just failed; you failed and that's all there is to it," so the indirect forms in (17) have an equivalent meaning to:

"With these words, I am asking you to telephone me."   (21)

There area numerous formal objections to this theory (see Levinson 1983). I will make two that are based, first and foremost, on common sense, but which are nevertheless unanswerable. The first is the infinite number of indirect speech acts that may be produced to convey the same message. However, an utterance whose recognized status is that of being an idiomatic expression must be learned and used as such, and must have a highly restricted number of variants, if this status is indeed to be recognized by all the users of that language. The second objection is that speech acts that seem to fall under the heading of indirect speech acts may, at times, be used as direct speech acts, thus retaining their literal meaning. For instance, normally the utterance:

"Can you write your name?"   (22)

would be taken as a request to write one's name in the space provided. In the context of a neurological examination, however, question (22) would retain its literal force, conveying the meaning of checking the hearer's capacity to write his own name. A dysgraphic patient could, in fact, reply:

"My name is no problem, but any other word causes me great difficulty."
                                                                                                            (23)

Finally, we should note that the theory of idiomatic expression cannot explain the case where two possible interpretations may be placed on an indirect speech act, as in the following utterance, a case that presents no difficulty to the natural speaker (to contextualize, the setting is that of husband and wife getting ready for an evening out):

A: Do you know what time it is?
B: Don't rush me!
A: No, it's not that—my watch has stopped.   (24)

We may therefore conclude that this theory is inadequate and move on.

Indirect Speech Acts Solved through Inferencing   There are various inferencing theories: from the earliest, advanced by Gordon and Lakoff (1971), to the most recent, proposed by Sperber and Wilson (1986, 1995). I will analyze the theory advanced by Searle (1975), which may be held as validly reflecting the essence of the other theories extant in this field. Searle tackles the problem by trying to answer the question of how a speaker can say something and mean something (secondary illocutionary act) while at the same time wanting to say something else (primary illocutionary act). The basic idea is that the hearer carries out a series of inferences that enables him to recover the primary intention of the speaker, starting from literal speaker meaning. Searle (1975) lists ten different inferential steps required to solve even the simplest indirect speech act, the details of which we need not go into here.

An inferencing chain certainly enables speakers to work out indirect speech acts in principle. What is unconvincing about this approach is the assumption that comprehension of an indirect speech act comes about only after the hearer's failure to interpret the secondary illocutionary act.

A second criticism is developmental in nature. Children have already mastered indirect speech acts by about the age of three, that is, at least three or four years before they are capable of carrying out the type of logical inferences that supporters of this theory claim are used in the process of comprehension. This aspect will be dealt with in depth in section 6.1. What is of interest here is the unanswerable objection that derives from the way reasoning abilities emerge: how can a result be obtained that presupposes the use inferencing capacities that have yet to be developed? It is highly probable—or better, certain—that the result is obtained in some other way.

Indirect Speech Acts Solved through Contextual Analysis   This third approach constitutes a radical solution to the problem. This theory, developed principally by Gerald Gazdar (1979), denies that utterances have any literal force. Consequently, the initial definition of an indirect speech act vanishes into thin air: if utterances do not have a semantically autonomous literal meaning, then a distinction between direct and indirect illocutionary acts can no longer be made. The basic idea is that the context allows the hearer to arrive at the speaker's meaning, without having to go through an utterance meaning that is independent of the context in which it was emitted.

The comprehension of any type of speech act is entrusted to how the force of an act is expressed through the linguistic forms realizing that act in a given context. This type of theory was introduced in order to account for general pragmatic phenomena, relegating semantics to a position of secondary importance. Analyzing this theory in detail would take us well beyond the scope of this work. Hence I will discuss it only in relation to the problem of indirect speech acts.

Eliminating literal illocutionary force is a radical move, one that is difficult to give general support to: of course, what people remember is the meaning behind an utterance; but they also remember the form, hence the literal meaning of an utterance. When what has really been said is challenged, the interlocutors fall back both onto syntactic form and onto the paralinguistic features of emission in order to establish what was really intended. If example (23) may be explained by a change in context from an office to the neurologist's surgery, example (24), where the context remains unaltered, presents difficulties for this theory which are unanswerable. Let us complicate the situation even further and suppose that the husband, who believed his wife was trying to make him hurry up while she only wished to know the time, begs her pardon over the misunderstanding.

A: Do you know what time it is?
B: Don't rush me!
A: No, it's not that—my watch has stopped.
B: Sorry, but official banquets make me terribly anxious.   (25)

Contextual analysis offers no means of accounting for what has taken place. B should not be able to recognize the double meaning—or indirect meaning, to use classic terminology—unless he remembers the literal form of A's initial utterance.

Conventional and Nonconventional Indirect Speech Acts The psychologist Raymond Gibbs (1994) has drawn from each of the theories examined so far, showing how in a series of cases an indirect idiomatic speech act is equivalent to a direct speech act. Gibbs prefers to speak of *conventional* indirect speech acts when the context allows the hearer to grasp intended speaker meaning immediately, and of *nonconventional* indirect speech acts when the hearer must make a series of inferences to comprehend speaker meaning.

Conventional indirect speech acts are essentially based on what Gibbs terms the *obstacle hypothesis* (following Francik and Clark 1985): the speaker tends to formulate an utterance to deal with the greatest potential obstacle that the hearer can meet in satisfying the speaker's own request. Given that both interactants share sufficient knowledge of the context, the fact that the speaker mentions the most salient potential obstacle consti-tutes a powerful signal for the hearer as to what request has actually been made of him. This type of case illustrates the importance of metonymic thought in pragmatics: people use one aspect they have understood very well about something in place of a global something, or instead of another aspect, as in saying "Hollywood hated *Pulp Fiction*" for "The major film companies did not like Tarantino's kind of movie."

Gibbs has carried out a great deal of work on developmental psychology, noting how children use and comprehend direct speech acts and conven-tional indirect speech acts in exactly the same way. The criticism to be made of his proposal, which is nevertheless intuitively very appealing, is that it is difficult to establish how each context indicates a specific obstacle that can then define what will be considered conventional.

Simple and Complex Indirect Speech Acts   The problem of recognizing indirect speech acts does not exist in cognitive pragmatics, since there is no primi-tive notion of nonliteral speech act. The key point for the partner is always that of recognizing the opening bid in a behavior game, in whatever form that move is expressed. Once the game has been identified, inferring what move the actor is asking her partner to make presents no extra difficulties whatsoever for indirect speech acts compared to direct speech acts.

The corresponding issue in my approach for the problem of indirect speech acts is the degree of complexity of the chain that connects the expression act to the opening of the behavior game. Classic cases of indi-rect speech acts do not necessarily correspond to the longer inferential chains in working out indirect speech acts. In any case, all possible cases may be solved in my model without having to hypothesize any additional rule or knowledge structure: when an utterance is produced, the behavior game it refers to must be identified.

We may thus distinguish between *simple* and *complex* indirect speech acts. *Simple* indirect speech acts are those that refer the interlocutor directly to the game of which the utterance constitutes a move. As with Gibbs's conventional indirect speech acts, they are to be considered as being of the same cognitive difficulty as direct speech acts.

Complex indirect speech acts are those that oblige the interlocutor to effect a series of inferences before he can manage to attribute the utterance the value of a move in a specific behavior game. Whereas Gibbs bases his definition on social and contextual criteria that make an indirect utterance conventional, my distinction is based on whether the inferential process required to proceed from the utterance to the game, whatever utterance is used, is simple or complex.

In brief, the idea is that the locutionary act is always necessary as the starting point, but is not enough, even in those cases that are classically defined as direct speech acts. My expression act is *de facto* the unavoidable departure point for the reconstruction of speaker meaning, through the identification of a valid behavior game.

As a consequence of maintaining the literality of the expression act as the starting point, the objections raised against the theory of idiomatic forms and the theory of context cannot be advanced against my own theory. In addition, since my theory does not require the stage in which a failure is involved, it also avoids the most serious criticisms leveled at inferential chain theories. What still needs to be explained, especially in a developmental framework, is the complexity of the inferences to be made. In section 6.2, I will demonstrate how even small children can deal with complex inferential logical chains by starting from behavior games instead of starting from the semantic meaning of utterances.

The classic explanation of the ubiquity and frequency of indirect speech acts, shared by all scholars, from Brown to Lakoff to Levinson, lies in the fact that they are an efficacious tool of politeness, avoiding any form of imposition—at a surface level—on the interlocutor. This is not, however, the only means available for achieving politeness. Chinese provides a different option, one that is equally effective. Chinese tends not to employ indirect speech acts, since they are considered tortuous and disrespectful of other people's capacities, which are questioned by utterances such as (22). The Chinese speaker prefers to address the partner with forms praising the capacities to be activated, placing the pleader herself in a position of inferiority, and then employing direct, explicit forms, translatable as:

Thou that canst all, pass me the salt.

Oh man of a thousand abilities, shut the window properly.

Oh most generous and rich Lady, give a poor woman the money she needs to satisfy her basic needs.

Oh powerful Lord, this humble person implores you to respect the rules of this household.   (26)

The interesting fact about the theory based on games is that direct and indirect realizations of courtesy forms are both handled in the same way, that is, by recognizing the game underlying the specific utterances employed. Westerners and Chinese are required to distinguish the surface means of the game they are referring to and to reply to the game, not to the form. The powerful Lord in (26) may be reduced to a state of groveling by the humble man if the former does not abide by the latter's rules, just as would happen if an employee were to ignore the courteous request made by the director in the following utterance:

"Mr Noble, would you mind checking the books again before the inland revenue inspection tomorrow morning?"   (27)

The distinction between what one wants from another person and the means by which one's request is actually realized is important, and cognitive pragmatics seems to account for the difference in a more satisfactory fashion than other approaches.

4.3 Communicative Effect

Consistent with what has been discussed so far, I will consider as relevant to communication only those effects on the partner that are both intended and overtly communicated by a partner. In every communicative situation, an actor expects her partner to furnish a reply to all the communicative intentions expressed. Hence if the partner is to cooperate in communication he must process all the intentions communicated by A. In addition, he must take a stand on every one of those intentions. In particular, B must decide whether or not to take part in the game proposed by A.

I define the *communicative effect* on the partner as the entire set of mental states acquired or modified as a result of the communicative intentions expressed by the actor. This does not necessarily mean, however, that the effect on the partner will be that desired by the actor. One further condition is that these mental states really have been brought about by the corresponding communicative intention. For example, the fact that someone tries to convince me of something must constitute one of the reasons why I believe that something. If this specific condition is not respected, then it cannot be stated that the desired effect has been achieved.

Analogously, if a person had already intended to do something and then another person asks him to do precisely that, then it cannot be asserted that the carrying out of the afore-referred-to act constitutes proof that the speaker's desired communicative intention has been realized. The fact that someone asks me to do something must be one of reasons why I do that thing. If a driver breaks a traffic law and is stopped by a policeman and if she then asks the policeman to report her, it cannot be claimed that the policeman was induced into reporting her by her order. He would have reported her anyway.

There is a different type of case, one in which the actor does not call on the trust of her partner directly, but prefers to employ what evidence may be available in the environment, as in:

"Oh look, it's stopped raining!"   (28)

Here the actor induces her partner to look outside as a measure intended to convince him that it really has stopped raining. If the actor's intention is met, as shown by the partner's reaction, I consider this a case where communicative intention has been realized. One important feature of this stage is that, contrary to the two preceding stages, it is not a recognition stage. In actual fact, while comprehending both the expression act and speaker meaning implies the deployment of shared knowledge, the realization of the communicative effect is based on private knowledge and individual motivations. For instance, understanding that someone is asking us for a loan is based on shared social and linguistic knowledge. Deciding whether or not to grant that loan is something totally different, for it is based on entirely private motives. The actor cannot insert the appropriate motives into her interlocutors' heads. Rather, she must exploit other people's motivations to try to obtain the results she is aiming at.

One consequence of what I have been saying is that in order to maximize her chances of realizing her communicative intention, the actor must found her strategy on a model of her partner. The more precise the model is, the greater the chances of achieving the communicative effect. When the actor's request is banal, the previous point is of minor importance. The situation changes, however, when the commitment requested of the partner is high. To convince an assistant to devote many hours' work to a barren and boring task, the actor may have to have recourse to politeness, authority, blackmail, a challenge, a promise. What the best method is will depend on the assistant's personality and motivations. It will probably not depend on the syntactic structure of the utterance the actor chooses to employ.

At the point at which we cross over from speaker meaning into communicative effect, the inferential chain leaves the domain of shared beliefs and enters the domain of private mental states. The use of default rules in the domain of shared beliefs is justified by the fact that to ensure she will be understood, the actor must ascertain that each deviation from communicative standards must remain within the domain of shared beliefs. This authorizes the partner to consider every communication act as standard unless there is shared evidence to the contrary. The same assumption cannot be made of the communicative effect because we are not describing a recognition process here, but the causal process that modifies the partner's beliefs and private intentions.

For example, if an actor has communicated a belief to her partner, and her partner has reason to assume that the actor is sincere, then the partner will attribute the belief that has been communicated as also belonging to the actor. Stated differently, the partner will assume that the actor believes what she has communicated to him. This inference is treated as a logical implication, where the actor's sincerity is considered a collateral condition (see section 4.3.1). Note that a collateral condition may, however, be established by any reasoning process, including default inferences.

Even if communicative effect is based on private knowledge, it may be described by the following general framework:

1. The input is the actor's set of communicative intentions as recognized by the partner.

2. The output is the partner's set of mental states connected to the types of communicative intentions conveyed by the actor.

3. The process consists of an inferential chain that is made possible by collateral conditions that are, in their turn, established by the partner on the basis of both his knowledge and private motivations, and of the mental states he attributes to the actor.

We may now distinguish between the two basic processes in the communicative effect stage: *attribution* and *adjustment*. In the process of *attribution* the partner infers the private mental states of the actor, which, despite the fact that they are not communicated explicitly, are nevertheless important to adjustment.

In the process of *adjustment*, the partner's mental states with regard to a domain may be modified as a consequence of the utterance emitted by the actor. Such modifications come about on the basis both of the communicative intentions recognized, and of private mental states such as motivations, emotions, and beliefs, including those concerning the mental states attributed to the actor.

I will now outline the model of communicative effect proceeding backward from the predefined task of this conversational metalevel. The conversation game leads the partner to set himself the question as to whether he wishes to abide by the actor's intentions. The most important aspect is that the partner must decide whether or not to take part in the behavior game the actor proposed through the opening move.

Metarule M3 (figure 4.5) requires that the adjustment process be carried out, and the adjustment process in its turn requires that the relevant attributions be carried out.

The adjustment process is based on one of three possible subtasks. Let us analyze them separately, linking them to one of the following possible

Communicative effect

M3 — The task of the communicative effect stage is to comply with one of three possible subtasks in order to activate the reaction stage.

▶ **Subtask 1:**

If partner B takes it as shared that actor A has conveyed to him her intention to play a behavior game with him, then he too intends to play that game.
"If Laura asks me to go to the Opera with her, then I'll go."

▶ **Subtask 2:**

If the partner takes it as shared that the actor has asked him to do something, then he will do it.
"If Simona asks me to give her a kiss, then I'll kiss her."

▶ **Subtask 3:**

If the partner takes it as shared that the actor has communicated something to him, then he believes in that something.
"If Helen says she loves me, then I believe her."

Metarule

> **if** one of the three subtasks is successful
> **or if** all three fail
> **then** the reaction stage is activated

Figure 4.5
Communicative effect.

intentions of the actor: (1) that the two agents take part together in a behavior game; (2) that the partner carries out a given action; (3) that the partner shares one of the actor's beliefs. Any subtask, if successful, activates the reaction stage.

1   The Communicative Intention to Play a Behavior Game   To this end, the partner may use a motivation or a derived intention. In the former case, the relevant motivation is applied in the situation in which the partner is willing to play a specific game every time that game is proposed. The game must already have been agreed on by the parties. For this rule to apply, the partner must possess the following private beliefs:

a. that the actor really does intend to play that game;
b. that the game's validity conditions apply; and
c. that both the actor and the partner can play their respective roles in the behavior game.

Whereas the second and third conditions refer to beliefs about the state of the world, the first condition is a mental state that the partner attributes to the actor. The attribution process is founded on what the actor has communicated and on the independent knowledge the partner possess of the actor. Considerations of the *correctness* of the actor may lead the partner to assume that the opening bid is sufficient evidence to attribute the actor with the actual intention of playing the game. In other cases, the partner's knowledge of the actor's motivations allows him to attribute her the intention of playing the game. The same intention may also be derived from the reconstruction of the actor's plan. Yet another case is that in which the intention to participate in a game is not generated directly by a motivation but is derived through some planning rule from some stable, preexisting intention.

2   The Communicative Intention That the Partner Perform an Action   The normal case corresponds to the situation where the partner has neither a motivation nor an intention derived from a private plan to perform the requested action. For instance, when a person is asked for as glass of water, there is no reason to assume that he already had an independent intention to offer it. Rather, the action will be a consequence of the decision to play some kind of politeness game. In general, it is the decision to play the proposed game that generates the intention to perform the requested action, when it is a move of that game. Much more complex cases may of course occur, and these will be dealt with later.

3   The Communicative Intention That the Partner Share a Belief No problem arises if the partner already holds those beliefs. If the opposite is true, then the conversational metalevel obliges the partner to decide whether he wishes to adopt that belief or not. I will not treat the multifaceted problem of belief revision here, but will limit the discussion to the communication act. There are two types of reasons why a partner may believe in a fact: reliability of the source of information and positive evidence.

Reliability is based on two distinct aspects: sincerity and informedness (see section 4.3.1). Assuming the actor's *sincerity* means that the partner attributes to her the belief that she communicatively wishes to share with him. If he actually does not think that she believes what she is saying, then he will not be convinced by her words. To bridge the gap between attributing the actor a belief and accepting that belief, it is, however, necessary to assume that the actor is not only sincere, but also *well informed*. For instance, if granny warns you not to drink fizzy drinks because they are bad for your health, then you will be inclined to believe she is sincerely interested in your health. But to be convinced of what she says, you will undoubtedly want to obtain the highly qualified opinion of a physician.

Positive evidence also has a role to play in inducing the partner to carry out an action, as in the following example:

"Come by our house this evening and I'll introduce you to Diana, that divorced friend of mine I told you about."   (29)

Positive evidence may also be offered independently by A's declarations, as was the case in (28).

4.3.1   Basic Concepts Relating to Communicative Effect

In the model of communicative effect advanced by Airenti, Bara, and Colombetti (1993a), six concepts are particularly relevant. Four refer to the process of attributing the actor a mental state: *correctness, motivation, having a plan,* and *sincerity.* The first three are involved in attributing intention, while the fourth is involved in attributing beliefs. The other two concepts are involved in the process of adjustment: *ability* and *informedness.* To assume that the actor is capable of playing her part in the game proposed is an essential precondition in the partner's decision as to whether or not to participate in the game. Assuming informedness has a similar function in the partner's decision to participate as that of a belief conveyed by the actor.

There is, however, a clear difference between the three concepts of ability, motivation, and the possession of a plan, and the three remaining concepts of correctness, sincerity, and informedness, with regard to their respective logical roles in the process of bringing about a communicative effect. As we have already seen, the actor's abilities are taken into consideration when evaluating her game bid, but they are insufficient to motivate her partner to play. For analogous reasons, an actor's motivation and possession of a plan are necessary but not sufficient preconditions.

By contrast, correctness, sincerity, and informedness are sufficient to generate in the partner the effects associated with these features. Stated differently, it is a contradiction for a partner to say that an actor is correct if she has no intention of doing what she says, or to say that an actor is sincere if she does not believe what she says, or that she is well informed when she does not know the truth. Hence, correctness, sincerity, and informedness are not qualities permanently possessed by the actor, but established at each encounter, case by case. Since mental states cannot be observed, the partner can never be absolutely certain. He must, instead, assume these qualities, sometimes through analysis, sometimes by default, on the basis of hypotheses justified by his knowledge of the actor, of the situation, and of the topic domain. For example, a person may believe Hilary is a sincere person, except when she is talking about her marriage.

The perspicuity of these concepts is demonstrated by the use made of them in the planning stage. The effective communicator tends to corroborate her arguments by presenting evidence aiming to show she is correct ("Ask around—I always keep my word"), motivated ("This job has been my lifetime's desire"), has a plan ("The idea is to help each other in the two committees"), is sincere ("I prefer to tell the truth, even when it's not particularly pleasant"), capable ("We can go out tonight, I've got my father's car"), and well informed ("I read about it in last Friday's *Financial Times*").

4.3.2 Games and Moves

We have seen that behavior games shared by agents are represented at a level of abstraction that does not normally specify the details of the concrete actions implied in the statutory moves. For instance, a game such as EVENING TOGETHER does not specify whether the agents will go to dinner, to the theater, for a walk, or do some other activity. Furthermore, as with all human mental states, even those connected to the representation of games are subjective, not objective. In other terms, the typical representation that agent A has of a game is G(A,B), which does not necessarily correspond with the representation held by her partner B, whose representation is, instead, rendered by G(B,A). The inversion of the order in which the

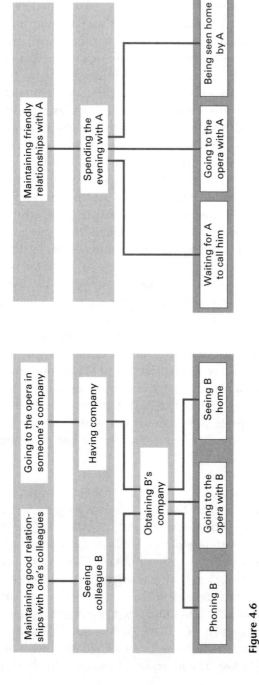

Figure 4.6

Two behavior games compatible at the behavioral level.

participants appear is intended to show that there exists no single, objective game G known to all the participants. Rather, each participant has her or his own subjective view of game G.

In addition, the game may be opened by a concrete bid such as:

"Let's go to the Metropolitan this evening."   (30)

The partner must recognize the proposed action as the specification of an abstract move represented in the game. B's recognition may also be faulty, thereby causing an incorrect reconstruction of the bid: B is convinced that the game proposed is α whereas A intended to open game β. Such a misunderstanding may never come to light if the game proposed by the actor and the game understood by the partner are *compatible* at a behavioral level, that is to say, if both games share a number of moves at a given level of detail. A case of this type is illustrated in figure 4.6.

However, unless the two games are identical at the level in which they concretely come into being, the misunderstanding will come to light if a break in the interaction occurs, for this will reveal their failure to communicate. Nevertheless, not all linguistic and social ambiguities are to be avoided at all costs: the execution of joint actions that each agent may interpret in different ways may be useful in softening the interaction. In general, if a move is compatible with more than one game, then agents are free to clarify which of the possible games they were actually referring to, or to leave a wider range of options open, postponing possible clarification to a later stage.

For example, when two people begin exploring the possibility of mutual courtship, both may find it convenient to keep up a certain degree of ambiguity on what meaning to attribute both to the socially neutral invitation—to the cinema or to an exhibition—and to the acceptance of that invitation:

"Would you like to go to the cinema one of these evenings?"   (31)

Only after the agents have got to know each other better can they decide if going out together is to be counted as a first move in getting to know each other better, or whether it constituted the final act in simply going somewhere together, without any further, deeper commitment. All this, then, occurs without exposing oneself to risks of losing face, as would happen if the nature of the game were openly declared from the outset.

Moves that are compatible with more than one game may therefore contain the seeds of their own communicative failure. They may also contain the opposite possibility, that of an ambiguity that both agents perceive perfectly and exploit. The intermediate case is also significant: one of the two agents may be aware of the ambiguity while the other agent is not. In this third case the agent who is conscious of the ambiguity has the option of deciding whether to clarify what game is being played or not. This case borders on deceit, and if the misunderstanding were to be later revealed, then the interlocutor would be left with an impression that could not be proved, namely, that he had been duped.

One example of this type is flirting. B understands perfectly well that A's invitation to dinner is a move in the seduction game. Nevertheless, he pretends he interprets it differently, counting on the fact that A is highly unlikely to make her own goals explicit. Imagine how the coarseness of an explicit offer would immediately make the offer totally unacceptable, transforming it into material for a comic film, as in the following utterance:

A: "First come to my place for dinner and then let's get straight into bed."   (32)

But if the speaker's intention has been clearly conveyed—even if only implicitly so, through common cultural background—and fully understood by B, the fact that once dinner is over B refuses to enter into any amorous contact, hiding himself behind a most improbable misunderstanding, then his move will count as breaking off the game, and as such will be interpreted by A as deceit. The fact that managing compatible moves is a complicated affair is demonstrated by the difficulty that B would encounter if he wanted to clear up all possible misinterpretations. If (32) is socially unacceptable, the following answer to the perfect ambiguity of (31) would hardly be less unacceptable:

A: Would you like to go to the cinema one of these evenings?
B: I'd love to, but no sex please.   (33)

A would then be in an excellent position to play the part of the person who is scandalized, giving some legitimate literal reason that she had never dreamt of anything of the sort. It is thus not possible to escape from social and linguistic ambiguity by making everything explicit, for such an approach would cause breaks and losses of face. It may be achieved, on the contrary, by improving implicit communication. B will have to be so adroit as to clarify his erotic unavailability without placing A in the position of being a rejected lover. A *soft* interaction is one in which no agent is ever placed in the situation of having to utter or to receive an explicit rejection.

The interpretation of a move occurs within each agent's mind; therefore it is nontransparent and susceptible to implicit bargaining. One of the agents may align herself with the other agent's interpretation of what is going on in the dialogue (which game has been bid?), even when her own interpretation was different, thus committing herself to playing the game the other player was proposing.

Even when the opening bid is understood correctly, the relationship between moves and games remains a complex one. The simple cases are those already described: when the partner accepts the move and the game, or when he rejects both. Slightly more complex are those situations in which the partner is willing to play the game, but not the specific move, or vice versa. Referring back to example (30), B may:

a. like the idea of going out with A, but hate the opera;
b. like the idea of going to the Metropolitan, but refuse the implications of spending an evening with A.

It is the task of the stage we are dealing with to recognize and analyze conflictual situations, providing the following reaction stage with sufficient information for the partner to be able to plan an adequate response. Furthermore, possible concordances and dissonances between the actor's proposal and the preexisting intentions of the partner must also be taken into consideration. Continuing with the same example, B might:

c. have previously decided he was going to the Metropolitan on his own and take the opportunity to go as A's guest (*concordance*);
d. have previously decided to go to the Metropolitan on his own, but refuse the interaction proposed by A. In practice, B may tell A he is going on his own, or he may decide not to go at all, despite his previous intention (*dissonance*).

4.4 Reaction

The reaction stage must produce a communicative intention. This represents the input stage in the generation of the response. From a conversational standpoint, this stage must include information for the actor regarding the effects of her attempted communication on the partner's mental state.

The importance of the conversation game emerges quite clearly when the partner has no request by A to perform an action. In this case, the conversational game itself requires the agent to generate the

communicative intention of informing his interlocutor of the communicative effect of the latter's preceding utterance. For example, this accounts
for "OK" being emitted to express agreement.

On a more general level, the communicative intentions produced at the
reaction stage are a consequence of integrating communicative effect—that
is, the output of the adjustment process—and the behavior games that
partner B is willing to play with actor A. Suppose, for instance, that in
answer to a customer's request for swordfish the waiter replies:

"I'm sorry, but we're out of swordfish."   (34)

This reply satisfies the rules of the conversation game inasmuch as the
customer will deduce that the waiter will not bring her the swordfish.
Nevertheless, the waiter's reply bears further information, for the *conversation* game would have been played correctly even if he had simply said
"No." For the *behavior* game that the waiter plays with his clients constrains
him to furnish an explanation as to why a customer's request cannot be
complied with. This example shows that the reaction is determined by
base-level rules that try to avoid a specific failure being interpreted as a
refusal to play the global game.

The conversational metalevel of the reaction stage lays down that the
reaction must be pertinent to the analysis carried out in attempting to
comprehend speaker meaning (see metarule M4 in figure 4.7). Partner B
must therefore take a stand on all actor A's intentions, no matter whether
those intentions have been successful or not. This implies that the reaction
must be relevant. But it need not be sincere.

It should be noted that exceptions exist that do not follow the metarule
expounded in figure 4.7. In these cases, the institutional context provides
specific alternatives to the usual communicative situations. This happens
in the case of the psychotherapeutic setting, where the analyst is not
obliged to respond to all the patient's utterances, or in a job interview,
where the interviewer avoids externalizing her own personal reactions to
what the interviewee is saying.

The task of the base level of the reaction stage is to plan the realization
of a communicative effect on the actor through the production of the
communicative intention to generate a response.

The reaction is planned by taking into consideration the following
elements:

a. the conversational intentions defined by the metalevel;
b. the communicative effect of the speech act produced by the actor;
and

Reaction

M4

Metarule

▶ **Subtask 1:**

If the partner takes it as shared that actor A has communicated to him that she intends to play a behavior game with him, then he will convey whether or not he intends to play that game.
"If Laura asks me to go to the opera with her, then I must give her an answer as to whether or not I will go with her."

▶ **Subtask 2:**

If the partner takes it as shared that the actor has asked him to do a certain thing, then he will communicate to her whether or not he intends to do that thing.
"If Simona asks me to kiss her, then I must answer either 'yes' or 'no.'"

▶ **Subtask 3:**

If partner B takes it as shared that actor A has communicated a certain thing to him, then he will convey to her whether or not he believes her.
"If Helen communicates to me that she loves me, then I must tell her whether or not I believe her."

The task of the reaction stage is to execute a feedback communication to actor A in which partner B informs her whether or not he agrees to the pertinent following points:
(1) the behavioral bid made by actor A;
(2) the communicative intentions of actor A that partner B carry out an action;
(3) the actor's communicative intention to share a fact with her partner.
The response generation stage is necessarily activated by the above procedure.

Figure 4.7
The reaction stage. The three subtasks are identical to those of the communicative effect stage, from which they were received and which must now be given an answer.

c. the private objectives the partner intends to achieve through producing his response.

The general objective for the partner consists in making the actor assume that actor and partner share certain mental states. It does not matter whether the partner possesses those mental states or not. Now we will examine what kind of communicative intentions the partner can generate depending on his attitude to the intentions he attributes to the actor. The simplest case is that in which the actor has managed to get her partner to carry out an action. In this case, the function of the reaction stage is to transform the private intention generated by the adjustment stage into a communicative intention: *do it communicatively.*

The type of response generated at the base level may be linguistic or nonlinguistic. If the actor tried to induce her partner to perform an action, then the reaction should provide information concerning the partner's intentions with regard to that action. In this sense, the partner may either produce a speech act, or he may openly execute the action. If the requested action is to be carried out immediately, the partner may simply execute the act. For instance, an adequate response to a request such as:

"Give me a kiss!"   (35)

consists in giving that kiss.

If, on the other hand, the action is to be deferred until later, the partner must confirm his intention to carry out that action. For example, in cases such as:

"Can you please take our child to school on Monday?"   (36)

it is not enough for the partner to plan the action. He must also make his intention to do so explicit by providing a response confirming this intention.

With regard to negative responses, the partner may render his intention not to carry out the action explicit with an utterance expressing refusal. The nonlinguistic alternative consists in openly executing an action that is clearly incompatible with the action requested. For example, one may remain seated when asked to stand up, or shout when invited to keep quiet.

If the actor has attempted to convince her partner of something, then the expected effect is that of a change in mental state. But since mental states are, by their very nature, private, the partner is required to declare whether the desired communicative effect has been achieved or not. During a conversation, if an actor affirms something, the partner cannot remain impassive. He must communicate something with regard to what has been asserted, even if this be done only by a nod of the head or a grumble.

No rule obliges the partner to be sincere about his mental states. Quite the contrary. In planning his response, the partner may decide to pursue his goals even in an insincere and deceitful manner. This is attributable to what has already been established with regard to the fact that the conversation game does not require the player to sincerely share his mental states with the actor, but only to convince the actor that they are shared.

The conversation game has provisos for other possibilities in addition to accepting or refusing the actor's proposal. Let us consider the following cases:

A: How old are you?
B: Why do you ask?   (37)

Here the partner admits he has not understood which behavior game the actor is proposing, and thus activates a clarificatory subtext before communicating whether he intends to comply with the request or not.

A: Change the channel, there's a film by Woody Allen on channel 3!
B: Do you mind if I finish watching the news first?   (38)

A: I would never live in a big city. They're far too chaotic!
B: Not even in Paris?   (39)

In the latter two cases, instead of taking up a position with regard to the actor's communicative intention, the partner begins a bargaining session with the actor in order to transform her intentions into something closer to his own mental states.

One central base-level task is ensuring that the interaction proceeds softly, as when one ensures the rules of politeness are observed. One particularly significant case is that of *excuses*, that is, justifications given for not complying with an actor's communicative intentions. For example:

A: Can you lend me the car?
B: I'm sorry, it's broken down.   (40)

The logical component of an excuse requires the partner to communicate to the actor that one of the conditions necessary to comply with the latter's request is not valid. Such a condition excludes volitional mental states: "I don't want to" is not an excuse but an overt refusal. Furthermore, as with any other conversational move, an excuse must be compatible both with social conventions and with the game being played. As regards social convention, one example of a good excuse is:

A: You remember my invitation for next Tuesday, don't you?
B: I'm sorry, but as I told you, I have got a previous engagement which I can't possibly postpone.   (41)

The following example is more amusing but unacceptable:

A: You remember my invitation for next Tuesday, don't you?
B: I'm sorry, but I hope to receive a more interesting one.   (42)

With regard to compatibility with a behavior game underway, one valid excuse for an engagement with colleagues is:

A: Are you coming to the meeting of the dissertation committee?
B: I can't. I have a meeting with the Vice Chancellor.   (43)

In an analogous situation, the following excuse would not go down well:

A: Are you coming to the meeting of the dissertation committee?
B: I can't. I have to go to the cinema with my uncle.   (44)

One typical feature of excuses is that they are, in one sense, recursive. The condition presented as an excuse may, in its turn, have to be justified:

A: Can you pick me up at eight tomorrow?
B: I'm sorry, but I'll be going to bed very late this evening, because it's my daughter's birthday. You know that my ex-wife sets great store by things like this.   (45)

The ubiquitous, almost compulsive nature of excuses when the partner manifests his intention not to comply with the actor's requests renders their absence a significant and precise message. In fact, it makes manifest to the actor that the partner does not believe he has to justify his intention not to participate in the game proposed. For example, he might believe she should not have made such a proposal in the first instance, as in the following two interchanges:

A: Can I take the day off, tomorrow?
B: The answer's no!

A: If your wife's away, we could have dinner together.
B: No, thanks.   (46)

One interesting point with regard to conversation games concerns the real nature of a dialogue. Are there any components that may be considered a necessary condition to enable an exchange of words to be defined as a dialogue? As we have seen, this is not the case with courtesy forms. A similar structure applies to taking turns while talking: in a quarrel, the turn-taking system may be altered beyond all recognition. Yet this does not mean that a dialogue no longer exists. It would appear that all the components identifiable as typical of a conversation are actually contingent rather than necessary.

My own hypothesis is that the only distinctive trait of the conversation game is communicative intent. Breaking the rule of communicative intentionality is the only way of escaping from any form of dialogue, since any deviation whatsoever from the usual norms of conversation would be interpreted as applying to a particular behavior game. Returning to the example of the quarrel, which is nevertheless one of the most discontinuous forms of a dialogue, every possible unexpected move, including silence, would be interpreted as a mode of attack, justification, exhibiting resentment or disdain, and so forth. The only way of abandoning any behavior game consists in interrupting the interaction: going away, hanging up the phone, not replying to letters.

In conclusion, the output of the base level of the reaction stage is a set of intentions directed by the partner at the actor: it is the task of the generation stage to turn these intentions into an observable response.

4.5 Response

The input of the response stage consists of the communicative intentions produced by the reaction stage. The response stage generates a representation that must be translated into an actual response. When the response is exclusively linguistic, the representation describes the form of the expression act in terms of interlocutor A, propositional content p, and literal illocutionary force f.

Just as comprehension is in two substages, comprehending the expression act and comprehending speaker meaning, so may the response stage be considered as being constituted by two processes. The first process plans the expressions of certain mental states in accordance with communicative intentions. The second process realizes such expressions of mental states through linguistic and extralinguistic behaviors. Both processes must respect the constraints imposed by the behavior game in progress: for example, some situations require a particularly high level of courteous formality.

The first task of response generation is the creation of a sort of specialized plan. I assume the existence of the capacity to transform a communicative intention directly into the expression of a mental state. For instance, one direct method of sharing a belief with someone is to express that belief. However, it is sometimes necessary to follow a more circuitous path, such as when one has to plan a specific utterance in a difficult situation, or when one has to prepare an efficacious deceitful move. In that type of case, the generation of the response may be based on a simulation of the actor's comprehension processes. That is, the partner must take into account the specific cognitive and emotive styles of the person he is interacting with.

With regard to the generation of utterances, a few observations will suffice. As was seen in the analysis of the preceding stage, not only must the partner take a stand with regard to the actor's communicative intentions, but he must also express his reactions in terms that are compatible with the rules of conversation. This, indeed, is the second major task of response generation. It consists in giving the reaction an adequate and appropriate linguistic form. Let us consider, for example, the use of pragmatic particles, as in:

A: Come 'round tomorrow evening—we're celebrating Philip's birthday.
B: Um, actually I should be leaving tomorrow afternoon.   (47)

In this case, "Um" foreshadows the fact that the partner is about to reject the proposal. In the terms of conversational analysis, B is providing a dispreferred response. The dichotomy between *preferred* and *dispreferred* does not refer to the volitional mental states of a specific interlocutor, but to the degree to which a given response is considered socially preferable. Generally, acceptance and consensus are preferred actions, in contrast with refusals and dissent, which are dispreferred. Wootton (1981) on adult–child interaction, Pomerantz (1985) on adult interaction, and Atkinson and Drew (1979) on the rigidly formal courtroom situation have demonstrated that dispreferred actions are usually marked as such. In this way, the interlocutor is made to realize that the agent is aware that he is engaging in a socially less preferable action compared to other possible actions. Conversational strategies aiming to soften the impact of dispreferred responses consist in:

Delay The execution of dispreferred actions tends to be delayed in a variety of ways: pauses, introductory presequences ("If I really must give an answer, then . . ."), or alternative sequences used to procrastinate ("Let me first explain something that will clarify my position . . .").

Indication of a Dispreferred Action The action is introduced by being marked as dispreferred by means of explicit presequences ("I was hoping I would not have to say this, but since you force me . . . "), extralinguistic signals of dispreference (facial expressions such as grimaces, gestures), paralinguistic signals and specific pragmatic particles ("ah," "um," "ehm").

Indirect Speech Acts or Their Equivalent The dispreferred action is generally carried out in an indirect or else softened form in order to avoid one of the interlocutors openly losing face ("I somehow doubt I will be able to do it," "It might be a good idea if you thought about it a bit more").

Justifications   The reasons that led to the selection of the dispreferred action are supplied to the interlocutor in the form of explanations ("Unfortunately we cannot accept: the girls are at home on their own"), motivations ("Don't believe I don't want that too, but I'm a practicing Catholic"), and excuses ("I'm afraid we can't meet next week. I'll be out of town").

In my model, the effects described would be obtained by enriching the representation of the utterance with a functional trait such as "proposal rejection," which could be processed in the reaction stage simply by comparing the communicative intentions of the actor with those of the partner.

4.6   Motivation

Motivations may be considered as a generator of intentions—a mechanism, that is, which, once activated by a series of necessary conditions, generates adequate intentions. If we examine, for instance, an elementary motivation such as feeding oneself, we may observe that when certain conditions obtain (physiological, haematic, mental, and situational), this generates a specific goal, namely, the acquisition of food.

Motivation is a threshold structure. This means that not all the preconditions need to be present. It is sufficient for those that are active to be strong enough to reach the minimum threshold activation level. The configuration of the present preconditions—and their relative intensity—will be responsible for the urgency of the intention generated: from a vague desire for food, which will be attended to only if the system has no other significant matter to attend to, to a compulsion strong enough to inhibit any other activity in progress. The type and quality of preconditions determine the particular intention generated, which may vary from a generic need for an entire class of foodstuffs to a specific desire that may be satisfied only by a single element.

The intentions that interest the student of communication are those relating to participating in a game. Considering games typical of couples, the first condition is that in one of the two actors an autonomous motivation activating the intention to play that particular game with that particular partner must be triggered. Physiological, emotional, psychological, and social needs are the antecedents of autonomous motivation. Later, the intention thus generated will have to win out over the other intentions currently active in the systems, if the resources necessary to satisfy that intention are to be mustered. For instance, I might feel like going to a concert with a friend, but this desire will be abandoned if one of my daughters suddenly feels ill just before I leave the house.

Here, I will deal neither with the structure of motivation, nor with how a motivation is activated, nor with how this then generates a specific intention among all those possible, nor with how the intention generated wins out over all the other goals concurrently active in the system. Any psychological model of motivation (e.g., Searle 2001) that explains these aspects is compatible with the theory of communication presented here.

In truth, what we do need in order to clarify the mechanisms of motivation is a theory of desire. Desires are the real engine of human action, not facts about the world or our beliefs regarding those facts. If on this splendid Saturday afternoon in October, sitting at my desk, rewriting the fourth chapter of this book for the third time, I dream, instead, I am walking on the beach of Bora Bora, this has nothing to do with the fact that Bora Bora is a much more pleasant place to live than Milan, nor has it anything to do with my own belief that I love the seaside and not the plains. The key point is my desire to go to the seaside, my desire to live happily, my desire to finish the fourth chapter. (I realize that this desire is something I probably have in common with my reader.)

All these desires are based on a set of beliefs and maintained by a flow of emotions, but they must not be confused either with those beliefs and emotions or with the motivations they trigger. Since no satisfactory theory connecting beliefs, emotions, desires, and motivations exists as yet, I will make do with a treatment of the problem that does not go into the mysterious heart of volitional states. The desires that may elicit motivations to play may relate to any aspect of the game.

Let us now analyze in detail partner B's motivation in agreeing to play the game proposed by A. Obviously, the basic motivation is identical to A's, but it is of greater interest, for the key points that we will identify are those that may prompt possible refusals. In other words, they are points that A must take into careful consideration in planning her bid. B's motivation will be set in motion if A proposes a valid game, that is, one that is relationally acceptable and that he is capable of playing, and, above all, that he wants to play. Only then will the intention to play the game proposed be generated in B (figure 4.8).

A must therefore work on these four points to maximize her chances of B accepting her proposal. In sum, the active intention of participating in the game is generated once all the necessary preconditions have been

If: (1) The validity conditions of proposed game G are verified.

(2) B is capable of playing game G.

(3) B considers A an acceptable partner in game G.

(4) B's internal state is compatible with the playing of game G.

Then: B's motivation generates the intention to play game G with A.

Figure 4.8
Conditions governing the activation of motivation in B to play game G proposed by A.

satisfied. Even the absence of one condition would impede the generation of the intention.

In the literature, all this is often solved in a rather dismissive fashion by default, assuming that B accepts any proposal made to him within a given context. This shortcut is possible, however, only because the games analyzed are extremely superficial, as are typically the games of giving and asking for information. But even in these simple cases, who would stop if the person asking for the information had a disreputable mien, or was obviously a drunk or a drug addict?

The intention generated covers both game G and proponent A. The relative importance of these two factors is not, however, constant. There are cases where B is far more interested in the game, and the specific identity of the partner is thus a secondary matter. At the Wimbledon tennis tournament, each player is placed on a list that foresees progressive direct elimination. Hence, the identity of the opponent is, in one sense, irrelevant: the participant must play against any player whom the draw of the schedule pits against him at that stage of the tournament. In other cases, what counts is the relationship with the partner, while the nature of the game is of secondary importance. The perfect courtier is willing to submit to any whim his sovereign queen might have, as long as he be at her side and please her. Any activity will be acceptable, provided it guarantees the continuation of the relationship with the object of desire.

There may also be games where the actor is interested in playing only with one specific partner. These games are, however, very rare. They are games that have a strong emotional base, and are the only ones that do not admit any substitution of the partner.

By this, I do not mean that in general one partner may be exchanged with another: a patient would never dream of changing her psychotherapist for another, nor would a child give up her mother, or a father his son.

But with the exception of these basic relationships, there are no experiential data to support the thesis of nonsubstitutability, at least over the long term.

Alexandre Dumas (1846), a clever psychologist as were all French writers of the period, recounts the story of Edmond Dantès who, when he became the Count of Montechristo, organized complicated vendettas against those who had unjustly caused his imprisonment on his very wedding day. But while Dantès takes extreme care in ensuring no one else pays in place of his enemies, he seems more willing to substitute his well-beloved Mercedes with another young, though less tragic, maiden, the beautiful Haydée, who for the sake of prudence this time is a slave instead of his fiancée.

The real way out of the simplification of default rules would be to make the fourth condition explicit, namely, the condition relating to the compatibility of a person's internal state and his willingness to take part in a given game. The minimalist reading of this stance is tantamount to asserting that bar any obstacles, the game is accepted. This is true of contracts (where B is obliged to provide a service upon receiving a well-formulated request from A) and for games that a person does not deem are fundamental. For example, a cook prepares a meal for anyone who asks for one in the required manner, without any partiality for one client or another.

For games requiring greater commitment, which involve the players' selves, the fourth condition must be interpreted in a more restrictive fashion. It is not sufficient that the players' internal states be compatible with the game proposed. There must also be the component of self-determination. This is equivalent to that something that first drove the actor to propose the game. This is not the place to develop a theory of motivation. Suffice it to observe that in this case too there is complete equality between agents, independently of the sequence of moves. Actor and partner have the same bargaining power over a game, since the game will then belong to both of them. And if the proponent necessarily had the desire, wish, or need to play that game, the partner will also have to have an analogous desire, wish, or need.

5 Nonstandard Communication

The theory outlined in the preceding chapter describes the process of comprehension and of the construction of the response in situations that may be classified as standard, that is, situations that trigger default rules. There are, however, a large number of interesting cases that go beyond the bounds of normality, which may be classified under four headings:

1. *Nonexpressive interaction*: the use of an utterance without there being any intention to express the mental state associated with that utterance.
2. *Exploitation*: the special use of a communication rule to obtain a communicative effect that is different from that normally associated with that rule (e.g., to create irony).
3. *Deception*: the attempt to convey a mental state that is not in fact possessed.
4. *Failure*: unsuccessful attempt to achieve the desired communicative effect.

The analysis of these cases is important not only in itself, but also because it provides independent evidence in favor of cognitive pragmatics, in the sense that the structural features typical of possible interactions that are nonexpressive, that exploit, that deceive, and that fail, overlap perfectly with the different representations on which the cognitive process of communication is based. An interruption in the standard inferential chain may be ascribed to one of two different reasons: either the actor wanted the interruption to come about, or else it comes about in the partner's mind without the actor's having wished it. Intentional interruption means that the actor intended to employ a form of exploitation or of nonexpressive interaction.

Alternatively, failure comes about either because the partner does not follow the inferential chain when he was meant to, or, conversely, because he follows the chain when he was not supposed to, since the actor had proposed a nonstandard mode. Finally, an attempt at deception takes place when the actor employs false shared knowledge in order to achieve her objectives.

Let us suppose that in B's presence A says:

"It's raining as usual."   (1)

The literal illocutionary force is that of an assertion, and the propositional content corresponds to the truth conditions of the utterance. In a normal situation, the actor will employ utterance (1) to express her belief in the propositional content expressed through the utterance. In those cases I have defined as nonstandard, this stricture is not true. For instance, the actor may simply be repeating in a loud voice a phrase from a book of exercises in order to learn English. When the use of an utterance is intended to be expressive, then provided he finds himself in a standard situation, the partner will attribute the belief expressed to the actor, unless there exists shared or private evidence to the contrary.

As we saw in chapter 3, it is the conversation game that governs the succession of the five stages in communication. Stated differently, the conversation game works at a metalevel—employing metarules—that ensures that at the base level all the standard inferences may follow smoothly in succession without any blocks occurring, simply by applying the base rules. The purpose of the conversation game is, on the one hand, to guarantee that each stage accomplishes its task in an adequate fashion, thereby enabling the successive stage to receive the information it requires to proceed, and, on the other hand, to intervene if a given stage fails to achieve its objectives.

Indeed, if a stage does not realize its predetermined goals, then the conversation game intervenes at the metalevel in order to specify what has to be done about the problem that has occurred at the base level. In this case, the metalevel blocks the default rules that are specific to that stage, activating an alternative inferential process that does not employ that particular type of automatic rules. Just as I have termed the communicative process utilizing default rules *standard*, so I will call *nonstandard* those processes that must have recourse to classic inferencing procedures since they cannot apply standard default rules because the latter are inappropriate to the context. Each nonstandard situation has a logical place in the framework of the comprehension process I have outlined. Nonexpressive interaction, exploitation, and deception fall naturally into the first three stages of my model. In the first stage—understanding the expression act— the only nonstandard path the actor may have followed, and which the partner must therefore identify, is that of nonexpressive interaction. In the second stage—understanding speaker meaning—all nonstandard inferences are cases of exploitation. In both types of cases, the actor tries to ensure the partner will identify the nonstandard path and follow it correctly. Should this not happen, the outcome will be failure.

The third stage—communicative effect—is where deception occurs. Deception cannot be found in the comprehension stages because deception is not realized by any special form of communication. It concerns the relationship between what the actor communicates and her private mental states.

Finally, I will analyze failures, which may occur at any stage. In order to recognize and possibly to repair a failure, one cannot use the default rules of communication: she has to fall back on classic inferential procedures.

Simplicity and complexity of a communication act   Before analyzing the four types of nonstandard communication, I would like to expand on a concept introduced in section 4.2.1 regarding indirect speech acts. There I introduced the distinction between simple and complex indirect speech acts, which I would now like to generalize to every category of communication act.

I define a *simple* communication act as that in which the passage from utterance to the behavior game of which the utterance may be considered to be a move is immediate, requiring only one single inferential step.

I define a *complex* communication act as that in which the passage from utterance to the behavior game of which the utterance may be considered to be a move requires an inferential chain of variable length.

This generalization allows us to distinguish not only between simple and complex communication acts in standard communication (as in the case of indirect speech acts), but also between simple and complex communication acts in nonstandard communication, as in the cases of irony and deception.

5.1   Nonexpressive Interaction

At the stage of comprehending the expression act, the base rules enable the partner to attribute a given meaning to the actor's utterance. The use of default rules is justified in this case by the assumption that a shared communication act will be taken as being expressive, unless there is explicit evidence to the contrary. In other words, in order to assume that an actor *is not expressing* her own mental state, the partner must be convinced that the interaction is taking place in a nonstandard context. Examples of nonstandard contexts include: a person reading from a book in a loud voice, a person who is repeating another person's words *verbatim*, a person acting on stage, and so forth.

Establishing what an actor is achieving through her utterances, instead of expressing her mental states, is not one of the tasks of a general theory of dialogue. Every different nonstandard context requires its own specific model, all of which are still to be developed. The only thing that all the specific models will have in common with each other and with the standard model will be that the interlocutors do share the awareness that the actor has emitted an utterance. In no case will it be possible to deny this fact.

5.2 Exploitation

At the stage of understanding speaker meaning, the partner's task consists in reconstructing the actor's communicative intentions starting from the recognized expression act. This is precisely the point at which the actor might have decided not to follow a standard route, proposing a form of exploitation. The term *exploitation* was originally introduced by Grice with reference to how general maxims of cooperation may be used to generate conversational implicatures. By extending the original concept, we may *exploit* the rules of the model outlined in chapter 4 to lead the dialogue along a nonstandard route.

Among the different types of exploitation, I have chosen the two cases most relevant for pragmatic purposes, because managing to explain them represents a crucial testing ground for any theory of communication: (i) irony, in which an utterance is considered as having a meaning different from, and often the opposite of, its literal content; and (ii) *as-if situations*, that is, those contexts in which a communicative exchange is enacted, generally for reasons of politeness, even though there is a shared lack of interest in the content of the exchange itself.

The two general cases cited do not exhaust all possible cases of exploitation, as a brief list of other types will show: *metaphor* ("The sea does not love vessels in chains"); *understatement* ("Attila was not overcondescending with the defeated"); *hyperbole* ("I will love you forever"). Grice interprets all these types as cases of the exploitation of the second maxim, that of quantity ("Try to make a contribution that is true"), and in particular, of the first specification ("Do not say that which you believe is false"). The reader interested in these topics should consult the extensive work of the linguist George Lakoff (1987).

These cases may be combined with irony to produce ironic metaphors, ironic understatements, and ironic hyperbole. For instance, I may say I have had a "stroke of genius" the second I have an intuition about the solution to a difficult problem. However, I might use the same metaphor ironically in a different situation to refer to an error of judgment that had serious consequences.

5.2.1 Irony

Let us suppose that B is telling A how his wife tried to use her car to knock down the woman whom he had decided to live with, and that A comments on the episode thus:

"Your wife is definitely someone who does not take things badly!"   (2)

What makes utterance (2) ironic is the fact that both interlocutors share the view that the opposite of what was asserted is literally true. This blocks the application of the rule that lays down that, within the space of shared beliefs, if the actor expresses a belief, then by default she intends to communicate that this belief will be shared by herself and her partner, unless her partner denies the fact.

In the spoken mode, the partner is sometimes aided in recognizing that an utterance is ironic also by the tone with which the actor produced it. Characteristically, we refer to an ironic tone, though it is doubtful whether a specific intonation pattern designed to express irony exists. Grice argues that a scornful, a conspiratorial, or an amused intonation pattern is sufficient to convey irony. I think that the speaker may mark the tone of her utterance to a greater or lesser extent in order to help the listener to recognize her ironic intention. It is also easy to imagine a situation in which an agent makes absolutely no alteration whatsoever to the normal intonational pattern, despite the fact that she is conveying an ironic message. If I arrive home late for supper and unwisely ask my wife what there is to eat, I might hear the following words sweetly expressed with an innocent look on the speaker's face:

"There must be some iguana in the fridge."   (3)

"Deadpan" humor, Buster Keaton–style, shows that irony may be conveyed through silence, without modifying one's facial expressions in any way, exploiting, on the contrary, one's imperturbable state to achieve even more exhilarating effects on the audience. Specularly, it may be noted that an excess of markers (grimaces, eye-winking, right up to the point of stating: "I was only joking") will completely ruin the effect. A discerning audience could even find offensive the fact that the actor does not trust their ability to recognize that a given utterance is not to be taken literally.

I will refrain from engaging in the vain attempt to define irony. The reader may consult Attardo (1997) for a deeper investigation into humor. However, one must recognize the fact that for irony to exist, the utterance must be amusing; and the humor must be benign, if the irony is of the humorous variety, or, at the very least, it must not be malicious. Irony may also drift toward stronger tints, moving toward sarcasm. In this case the tone veers toward greater aggression. The target may be the speaker herself, the main listener, or another interlocutor, who need not even be present.

Example (2) illustrates the principal feature of exploitation: it is one way of playing with sharedness. In actual fact, utterance (2) could have been interpreted as a serious confirmation by a third person who had arrived after the initial description of the events furnished by B. The point is that an ironic intention does not alter the standard sequence in which the rules are applied, but only the way in which the rules are used. I have already stated that the rules are usually exploited by taking the reverse of the literal meaning conveyed by the utterance. This, for Grice, is the essence of irony: saying p and meaning *non-p* ($\sim p$).

Grice, of course, is formalizing the traditional analysis of irony: a trope based on *antiphrasis*, which is, quite simply, an utterance to be intended as its opposite. However, two kinds of argument have been advanced against equating irony exclusively with the opposite of literal meaning. The first was propounded by Sperber and Wilson (1986, 1995), who demonstrated that ironic statements do not necessarily correspond to the opposite of literal meaning. Take the following excerpt from Voltaire's *Candide* (1759):

When all was over and the rival kings were celebrating their victory with *Te Deums* in the respective camps. . . .   (4)

According to Sperber and Wilson irony is a case of *echoic* interpretation. An echoic utterance is one that echoes the thought, and attitude toward the thought, of someone who is not the speaker herself. It echoes the thought of another person when it simply reports what that other person said. It may, however, echo traditional thoughts, as when it reports an obvious truth, a popular belief, or a proverb.

In the case of irony the speaker produces an utterance that echoes another person's thought, while concurrently manifesting a critical or disparaging attitude toward content *p*. In example (4) Voltaire is not suggesting that neither of the two kings won the battle and were celebrating victory, nor that both kings lost the battle and were bewailing their defeat. Instead, Voltaire is echoing the claims made by the two rivals. Since the two simultaneous claims of victory contradict each other, it is obvious that both parties cannot be right. The irony stems from the fact that Voltaire highlighted the attitude of the rival kings, unveiling its vacuousness.

A second objection is advanced by Morgan (1990). He points out that no one—neither Grice, nor those such as Perrault (1990) who adopt Grice's approach—ever explains why a meaning *p* should be interpreted as ~*p*, and not as a lie. Morgan considers irony to be a *transparent fiction*: the speaker says something pretending to believe it while simultaneously making it obvious through the use of paralinguistic and nonverbal features that the utterance is indeed a fiction.

The vast majority of critics of the antiphrasis position are quite vehement in their censures. Morgan defines it as a perverse obscurity, while Sperber and Wilson declare that defining irony as implicating the opposite is a bizarre practice.

Example (3) conforms that the classical account is inadequate. In grasping the irony in my wife's words, I may be reasonably certain that her utterance is false, and that the fridge does not contain any iguana. But her intent was not to reassure me that iguana was not part of our daily food. Nor can it be claimed that the meaning of utterance (3) is ~*p*, that is, that there is something in the fridge that is not iguana. However, even the echoic hypothesis does not appear to hold: there does not seem to be any thought—whether it be traditional or individual—that foreshadows the possibility that husbands arriving home late will find iguana served up for dinner. Rather, it might be said that my wife indirectly conveyed the idea that *I deserve iguana* for dinner.

As the criticisms leveled at the classical account demonstrate, Grice has solved one particular case, but not the general case: *sometimes* in uttering *p* the speaker implicates ~*p*. The same stricture applies to the echoic thesis: sometimes the speaker echoes a thought that is not hers, in order to bring out in some way those aspects she deems are negative. Case (4) is brilliantly accounted for by the echoing of the rival kings' attitudes, but case (3) does not fall within this account. Even Morgan's transparent fiction offers an excellent account of a number of standard cases. Nevertheless, his thesis cannot elucidate Voltaire's example, in which two bishops are indeed singing two *Te Deum*s to thank the Lord for having blessed each of them with victory. The weakness in Morgan's intuition, which, however, is valid in a broad sense, is that it does not enable us to distinguish between irony and *as-if* situations.

My theory is based essentially on shared knowledge, in order to explain how interlocutors understand—without the aid of the stigmatized miracles of the classical approach—that a given utterance is not to be taken literally. With regard to the meaning of irony, a more general explanation compared to those advanced so far is that the ironic utterance constructs a *possible scenario* that acts as a background against which the element of alterity introduced by the speaker without mentioning it, and which the hearer will have to infer, will be highlighted by contrast. Against this background, different meanings may emerge, including Gricean opposites, Sperber and Wilson's echoes, or Morgan's transparent fictions.

Thus, in (2), the possible scenario of a tolerant wife starkly foregrounds her attempt to kill her rival. In the case of (3), an iguana for dinner immediately lays bare the cook's attitude. In (4), the scenario, which is not merely possible but real, forcefully underscores how ridiculous the conflicting claims of the rival kings are. Even in the case of Buster Keaton's wordless irony, what the actor does is construct a possible scene that patently reveals the total incongruity between the actor's impassive behavior and the catastrophes occurring all around him.

The element that represents alterity must emerge by contrast: white if the background is black, and black if the background is white. Returning for one moment to the example in which I have no excuse for returning home late, compare (3) with the equally sarcastic alternative:

The paté de foie gras and the caviar are on the table. I'm just finishing the lobster, so you can uncork the champagne that I put on ice.   (5)

Both utterances depict unrealistic backgrounds, but the contrasts come about in opposite fashions. It may be expected that after (3), despite my unworthiness I will find something slightly more acceptable in the fridge than a reptile, whereas the sophistication of (5) makes one expect, on the contrary, something much less appetizing, namely, exactly what my indifference deserves.

Grice and those like Perrault who follow in the classical tradition focus essentially on the induction process the interlocutor must enact. However, they impose far too narrow confines, limiting it to the case, which is admittedly frequent, in which the emergent meaning is the opposite of the literal content of the utterance.

Sperber and Wilson concentrate on a particular type of scenario, one simulating a hypothetical agent, or one in which the speaker echoes thoughts of one or more agents. There is no doubt that this thesis furnishes a brilliant solution to some cases. However, not all cases of irony can be accounted for by echoic utterances. Turning to inductive processes, which Sperber and Wilson believe may be explained by the single principle of relevance, little attention is devoted to shared knowledge, which plays such a central part in the planning and comprehension of ironic utterances.

Returning to the topic of how a hearer can distinguish between a serious utterance and an ironic one, I repeat, the only means consists in assessing what knowledge the actor considers she shares with her partner. If what the actor considers as shared information is not shared at all, the irony will not be detected, even when there are paralinguistic clues that convey to the interlocutor that the utterance is not to be taken at its face value. Since the type of knowledge shared by all humans, or within a group, or exclusively by a single couple, varies enormously, what will be interpreted as ironic will vary in accordance with circumstances.

For example, if Christine says, laughing:

"Great: another beautiful day!"   (6)

while it is pouring down rain, everyone present will take her comment as ironic, independently of the knowledge they have of the speaker. Contrariwise, consider the utterance:

"It's been a wonderful evening. They prepared a buffet consisting
exclusively of French cheeses!"   (7)

which only Christine's closest friends will take as ironic, as they know she is allergic to dairy products. They are thus the only ones who know what a difficult situation she was placed in. A spectator who was not cognizant with her allergy would find nothing strange in utterance (7) and would consequently take it literally for the very reason that it is well known that French cheeses are high-quality products.

Interlocutors can recognize the incongruence of the scenario proposed only on the basis of knowledge they share with the speaker. And it is only on this basis that the speaker in her turn may employ paralinguistic clues that alert the listeners as to what is happening. The situation becomes more complicated if a particular type of knowledge, which the speaker is exploiting for her ironic ends, cannot be taken as shared by one of the hearers, who is therefore not authorized in some way to officially comprehend the irony of the message, but must take it literally.

Jones (1953) recounts a fascinating anecdote in his autobiography of Freud. In order to obtain permission to leave German-occupied Austria, the Gestapo asked him to sign a document in which he declared that he had been treated well, as befitted a scholar of his fame and stature. When the Nazi officer presented him with the declaration, Freud made no objection whatsoever. Nevertheless, he asked the officer if he could add the following phrase handwritten and signed by himself:

I strongly recommend the Gestapo to everyone.   (8)

The genial stroke of Freud's bitter addition lies in the fact that practically anyone could privately grasp the sarcasm, with the exception of the Gestapo officer who had to obtain Freud's signature on the declaration. He cannot legitimately share the knowledge Freud shares with all of us, knowledge that enables us to interpret (8) in a manner far different from its literal meaning. Even if the Nazi officer had understood the irony, he would have been compelled to ensure that Freud or anyone else did not understand that he had grasped the ironic intent behind the words.

Let us now move on to a more formal presentation of the theory. Actor A generates utterance p, which is incompatible with state of things r. She also believes she shares knowledge r with the addressee to whom the ironic utterance is directed, such knowledge having been adequately activated. Finally, her communicative intention is to contrast utterance p with background r. Any spectators present may be divided into those who share belief r with the actor and may therefore comprehend the ironic intent, and those who do not share belief r and are therefore unable to understand what A really meant.

The general formula representing this is as follows:

$BEL_A \; p \neq r$

$BEL_A \; SH_{BA} \; r$

$EXPRESS_A \; p$

$CINT_A \; SH_{BA} \; p \neq r$ (9)

Recapitulating: since actor A is convinced that p is incompatible with r, and thinks that belief r is shared with B, she utters p ironically against the background of r.

All types of irony, antiphrasis included, fall within the scope of this general framework. All that is required is to recall the concepts of simplicity and complexity introduced at the beginning of this chapter. I will speak of *simple irony* when the interlocutor can grasp speaker meaning instantly, moving directly from the utterance to the behavior game of which the utterance may be considered to be a move. (2) and (6) are prototypical examples of simplicity.

In more formal terms, if, for the sake of clarity, we concede for one moment that r is the equivalent of *non-p*, A produces utterance p that contrasts forcefully and immediately with shared belief r (*non-p*). Figure 5.1 represents the case of simple irony.

I define *complex irony* as irony in which the interlocutor must carry out a series of inferences in order to grasp speaker meaning. This consists of an utterance q that does not directly come into contrast with shared belief *non-p*. However, performing a series of inferences (from the utterance q to its implication p) will enable the hearer to arrive at the conclusion that a belief p is clearly incompatible with the activated scenario of shared beliefs. (4) and (7) are prototypical cases here.

In more formal terms, and still conceding momentarily for the sake of clarity that r is the equivalent of *non-p*, A produces utterance q from which p may be inferred, and which manifestly and instantly contrasts with shared belief r (*non-p*). Figure 5.2 represents complex irony.

Figure 5.1
Simple irony: actor A produces ironic utterance p that openly contrasts with belief *non-p* shared by herself and B.

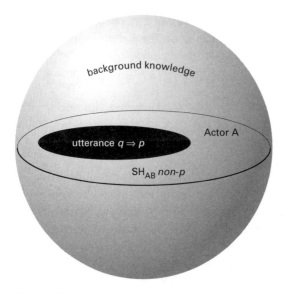

Figure 5.2
Complex irony: actor A generates ironic utterance q implicating p, which openly contrasts with belief *non-p* shared by herself and B.

We can thus use one single analytical framework to account for extremely different types of irony, without having to forgo in the analysis either the infantile prank or the most sophisticated sarcasm. I have discussed only the linguistic type of irony, but the same treatment can also be extended to extralinguistic irony, such as clapping one's hands after somebody's poor performance at a trivial task.

From a developmental standpoint, finally, the fact that irony may be grasped only through the use of shared knowledge should make it impossible for irony to be understood by children under the age of four, since this category of persons are unable to distinguish between knowledge they possess and knowledge they can assume others possess. Furthermore, it should be possible to understood simple irony earlier than complex irony because of the different length of the inferential chains the two processes require. The topic of development will be taken up in section 6.2.2.

5.2.2 As-If Situations
The second type of exploitation of an utterance takes place in what we may call *as-if situations*. These are situations in which the agents act as if their reciprocal communicative intentions were those expressed, while it

is shared knowledge that this is not so; that is, we are dealing with a social simulation of an actual interaction.

The term "as-if" has been used by other scholars to refer to a variety of phenomena. Limiting my treatment to the literature on speech acts, mention must at least be made of Robert Stalnaker's (1973) use of *acting as if* in his definition of pragmatic presupposition. Stalnaker observes that if in a normal context a speaker employs an utterance that requires a presupposition, then, whatever her real beliefs, *de facto* she *acts as if* she were taking for granted the validity of the presupposition, and *as if* she were assuming her interlocutors were also taking it for granted. The point that Stalnaker's as-if concept has in common with mine is that both agents may share the fact that they are acting in an as-if way because they have a common conversational goal. What distinguishes the two standpoints is that for Stalnaker, the as-if aspect refers to the truth of a belief, whereas for me the as-if aspect refers to communicative intentions.

In their work on politeness, Brown and Levinson (1987) examine the possibility that in order to avoid the obligation to minimize the risk of losing face, an agent *speaks as if* the crucial point were to achieve the maximum efficiency possible. This is because it is mutually agreed that when efficiency does have priority—for example, in cases of urgency or emergency—one does not need to exhibit embarrassment for having failed to respect politeness norms. For instance, a person may jump the queue if she can show she has a desperate need to do so.

From the standpoint of the theory I am expounding, a similar concept may be expressed in the following way: an actor acts as if the validity conditions of a behavior game had already been verified in order to oblige her partner to commit himself to playing the game that otherwise he could not have played or would not have wanted to play. Imagine, for instance, someone pretending she is in a great hurry in order to justify her refusal to continue an interaction that for some reason she finds extremely difficult.

We now return to my definition of as-if situations to try to clarify it through exemplification. Suppose that Laura, a colleague of Alex's, says to him:

"I heard your mother's been ill. I'm very sorry. How is she now?"   (10)

when it is shared information that Laura has never even met Alex's mother and has no reason to worry about her. The correct interpretation of Laura's utterance is not that she is inquiring about Alex's mother's health, but rather that she wants to externalize her fondness for Alex himself. And indeed Alex would not be furnishing an appropriate reply were he to launch himself into a detailed report on the condition of the patient.

Our social life is full of situations like the one just described, in which a set of utterances is produced and to which fitting replies are given even when both interlocutors share the fact that neither of the two parties is really interested in the content of the interaction. What is important in such cases is setting up or confirming behavior games of reciprocal interest to both agents. In one sense, such exchanges may be considered to be a simulation of the type of relationship the two agents intend to create in a situation that will be more interesting for them.

In other cases, an actor may establish an as-if situation for the very reason that she wishes to avoid games that call for a heavy commitment on her part. Talking about irrelevant matters is an excellent strategy when one wishes to fulfill one's social obligations without going into serious issues. Those conversations that are so frequent in our social lives and in which one pretends to be interested in the vague maladies of advancing age, in the efficiency of public services, or in the decline in moral standards allow us to preserve a semblance of interaction without incurring any costs. That is, thanks to our simulating conversation we avoid the ultimate trauma of others refusing to communicate with us.

In as-if situations, exactly as happens with irony, the rules governing dialogue do not change. It is only the use we make of them that changes. Moreover, this is the only similarity between these two modes of exploiting communication. The most significant difference between the two modes consists in the relationship between what is said and what is meant to be communicated. In irony, the fact that the literal meaning of what the actor is saying is false is shared by the interlocutors. In as-if situations, there is in principle no fixed relationship between what is said and what is shared as being true. Indeed, the relationship between what is said and what is believed is irrelevant. However, good manners lay down that we act as if the exchange were relevant and sincere.

The difference between the two types of exploitation emerges quite clearly when communication breaks down. If an ironic utterance is not recognized for what it is intended to be, then part of that knowledge that was assumed to be shared is not shared, or it has not been actively recovered. Repair on the part of the actor consists quite simply in her making her communicative intentions explicit, even though this explanation will destroy the humorous or sarcastic effects produced by irony. An as-if utterance cannot, however, be revealed for what it is. If the partner unwittingly or craftily misinterprets an as-if utterance and then replies to the as-if communicative intention interpreting it as real, the actor cannot admit the as-if nature of her preceding move(s). She is therefore obliged to continue the interaction as if her previous utterances had been true.

For example, if an unexpected visitor is given an as-if invitation to dinner, with the intention of making him understand how inconvenient his presence is when the host is about to embark on a battle to make the children eat, if that invitation is then accepted—either through perfidy or through social incompetence—the actor has no escape route to admit that her invitation was not meant to be taken seriously.

5.3 Deception

In one sense, even plants deceive, not just animals. Phenomena such as cryptic coloring in order to mask their presence in the environment and escape the detection of predatory eyes or the eyes of their prey, or camouflage to keep away a predator by exploiting the repulsiveness of the imitated species, is a widespread phenomenon in nature—from insects right up to mammals.

But it is only when the deceiver turns her attention to members of her own species that things become interesting. Deception presupposes the ability to imagine the other's behavior by creating a mental representation of the other's mental states. The fact that some of the acts of deception succeed demonstrates just how efficacious representations of the other may be. Whiten and Byrne (1988) have developed a taxonomy of acts of deception observed in primates, classifying them into five functional categories. *Tactical deception* has been defined as an act that constitutes a part of a agent A's normal behavioral repertoire and is employed so that another individual B may easily misinterpret its significance to agent A's advantage. The classification reads as follows:

1. hiding something (usually food);
2. distracting B's attention away from something and toward something else;
3. creating a false image of A so that B will misinterpret something;
4. manipulating B through another individual C: by behaving in a certain way with C, agent A modifies B's behavior to her own advantage;
5. rechanneling B's (essentially aggressive) behavior: A acts in such a way as to divert B's aggression onto another individual C and away from agent A.

The behavior pattern that has the greatest analogies with human behavior is to be found in category 3. The most famous example comes from a field observation carried out in the Ethiopian desert by Kummer (1982) in his research into baboons: a female was grooming a subordinate male, taking great care to ensure that only her head could be seen from the rock behind which they were hiding. In this way, the female was able to check the dominant male's behavior, managing to assume the latter's perspective, allowing him to see only the noncompromising part of her body.

The meaning of deception from an evolutionary standpoint is to be sought in the possibility of introducing into the struggle for survival and the reproduction of one's genes components that are not limited to brute physical force. A cogent case in point is that of the small seahorse which manages to introduce himself into the dominant male's harem by pretending to be a female while the dominant male is too busy fighting off the official challengers. Despite their suggestiveness and the interest they arouse, these deceptions are limited since animals do not possess the mental capacities required to represent shared beliefs and communicative intentions, which means that they are unable to produce any form of communicative behavior, violations included, in the strict sense of the term.

For cognitive pragmatics, deception is a *conscious violation of a shared behavior game*. Though A knows she should act in a certain way in order to respect the behavior game being played by B and herself, she carries out a communicative behavioral act that is premeditated to make B believe it is a game move even while she knows full well it is a violation of that game.

I will now present the formulas necessary to represent deception in cognitive terms. Temporal notation is obligatory. However, such notation will be suppressed in the exploration of the full example for the sake of simplicity. The deceptive utterance takes place at time t_1; the beliefs and mental states preceding the utterance are indicated at time t_0; the progressive consequences of the utterance are indicated at times t_2, t_3 . . . t_n.

t_0	BEL_A *non-p*
t_1	$\text{CINT}_A \text{ SH}_{BA} \, p$
t_2	$\text{EXPRESS}_A \, p$
t_3	$\text{BEL}_A \text{ SH}_{BA} \, p$

$$(11)$$

Summing up: A expresses utterance p, though not believing it herself, her communicative intention being that B take it as shared between them. If the deception works, A will assume that B takes p as shared. Stated differently, on the one hand, A hopes that B will believe p, and that he is convinced that A herself believes p too; on the other hand, A commits herself to behaving for the rest of the interaction in a manner consistent with this "supposedly shared belief" (whereas B thinks it is shared, A does not believe it). From the standpoint of the cognitive resources required, the difficulty of deception consists in always keeping the private belief *non-p* ($\sim p$) and the supposedly shared belief p both active in her attentional space.

This latter type of nonstandard communicative situation revolves around the relationship between the mental states that actor A communicates and the private mental states she actually holds. As we have noted previously, the conversation game is neutral with regard to the sincerity and correctness of the interlocutors' behavior. Hence the participants may carry on a conversational dialogue that is correct from an external standpoint without ever communicating their mental states. For example, a promise may be expressed in an impeccable manner without there being any real intention to keep that promise. Indeed, from Delilah to Judas the best instances of treason have always been clothed in a form that aroused no suspicions whatsoever.

Whereas the conversation game does not require there to be any agreement between private mental states and communicated mental states, things change when it comes to the behavior game. With regard to the point we are discussing, behavior games may be classified into three categories: regular games, irregular games, and façade games.

Regular games In regular games, the agents reciprocally commit themselves to being sincere and correct. These are the most frequent games to be played, if for no other reason than they are the only ones that guarantee actual behavioral cooperation.

The criterion for regular games is both clear and stringent: any insincere or incorrect communication act will cause a breakdown in the game and will be considered deceit. Insincere and incorrect example consists, for example, of A saying to B she will do something when she has already decided not to do it, or is fully aware she is in no position to do it. If, however, the breakdown was not planned, then it does not come under the category of deception. For instance, when A takes out her purse to pay the hotel bill and discovers her wallet has been stolen and she had not realized this before, then she cannot be classified as a swindler.

Irregular games   In irregular games, agents are not reciprocally committed to sincerity and correctness. Their private mental states are relevant, but local discrepancies between private mental states and expressed mental states are allowed. Any such discrepancies do not count as deceit properly speaking. Examples of this category are the bargaining that goes on between buyer and seller, or a meeting between two lawyers to discuss a divorce suit.

In irregular games an incorrect or insincere action is admissible; it does not necessarily cause a breakdown. Consequently it cannot be classified as deceit. For instance, an expert buyer of Persian carpets does not expect the seller to tell the truth about how old the carpet is, just as a person wishing to buy a horse to ride does not expect the salesman to tell her truthfully just how docile the horse really is. Both buyers will seek independent evidence, without paying much heed to the sellers' words and without being overly upset if they discover a discrepancy between what the seller declared and what he knew.

This does not mean, however, that any move is legitimate in this type of game. The agents must signal when they are embarking on an irregular game—where cooperation is suspended—and when they are abandoning it to return to the regular game. In general, the relationship constrains sincerity and correctness, *except when* the agents are reciprocally conscious that such an assumption is suspended, because an irregular game is being played at that moment. This involves a complex ballet between regular game and irregular game, if the interlocutors wish to maintain good relationships once that particular game is over.

For example, two lawyers representing different parties may be reciprocally insincere and incorrect during a specific interaction, provided that this is restricted to a specific case of an irregular game. However, certain limits must not be exceeded, otherwise the game again risks breaking down: one may withhold a vital piece of information, but one may not bug the other lawyer's telephone to gain vital information. In other words, explicit and implicit metarules exist that limit the amount of discrepancy possible.

In poker, where bluffing is an essential part of the game, the rules governing this admissible deception are formalized: A may act so as to induce her companions into believing she has a certain point in her hand, but she cannot explicitly state in words what the point she is pretending she has is. In other terms, while holding a poker hand, A may pretend she only has a pair, to bait the incautious player into bidding higher. However, if A keeps her poker hand well hidden and says:

"Don't worry, I've only got a pair." (12)

the hand would immediately be annulled and A would risk losing the esteem of the table, with penalties that will differ according to whether the game is taking place on the Mississippi or on the Thames.

Facade games In facade games, agreement between private and communicated mental states is irrelevant by mutual consensus. Games of this type cover as-if situations in which sincerity and correctness are simply beside the point: polite appreciation of the elegance of the lady of the house will be recognized as a compliment, independently of whether or not the compliment corresponds to the speaker's private mental state. Hence, deceit is not part of this type of game. When a problem arises, this is because one of the interlocutors believes a regular game is being played while the other person considers it a facade game.

A: I would give anything for the pleasure of meeting you again!
B: Well, if you were to give me a thousand bucks, it might be managed.
(13)

Even in this case, clarification will have to take place regarding the interlocutors' reciprocal communicative intentions. Such a clarification will have to take place without anyone accusing anyone else of deceit.

Analyzing deception from an evolutionary standpoint, Perner (1991) claims that this consists of an actor attempting to manipulate the mental states of her partner. That is, the actor's immediate objective is to induce the partner into false beliefs that will lead him into carrying out actions favorable to her own goals. Perner further affirms that to speak of deceit proper, we must exclude the possibility of an innate tendency to execute an act with the deliberate intention to deceive. In fact, he calls *primitive lies* communicative interactions of the following type:

A: Who drew on the wall with a crayon?
B: Not me, granny did! (14)

Primitive lies, which emerge in their simplest form ("It wasn't me!") around the age of one, are told to avoid an unpleasant consequence, and the rigidity with which they are enacted reveals that they are not acts of deception aiming to manipulate others' beliefs, but simply strategies to avoid unpleasant consequences—in the above example, being scolded. The lie thus seems to be a quick escape route out of a difficult situation. Bok (1978) defines a lie as a message deliberately aiming to deceive, couched in the form of a statement.

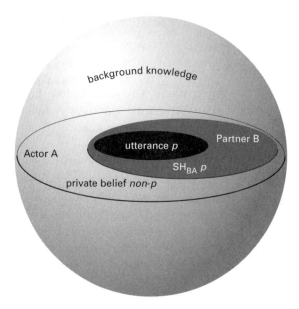

Figure 5.3
Simple deceit: actor A generates deceitful utterance p, in which she does not believe privately, with the communicative intention that her partner, B, take p as shared by them.

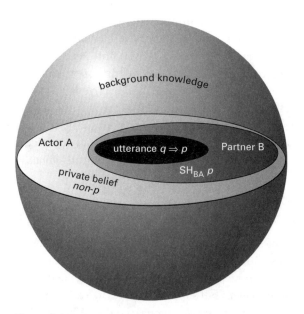

Figure 5.4
Complex deceit: actor A generates deceitful utterance q with the communicative intent that B draw inference p, in which she does not believe privately.

Analogously, Mitchell (1986) argues that not all acts whose result is deception are real cases of deceit. Only those acts that are based on the comprehension of the beliefs of others and that have been planned in order to achieve a certain goal constitute genuine cases of deceit. On this point, Leekman (1992) claims that at a first level, one can have the intent to lie without necessarily intending to manipulate others' beliefs. Returning to example (16), the child might simply wish to avoid punishment without actually intending to manipulate the hearer's beliefs. Leekman argues that it is only later that children learn more complex deceit strategies. First, they begin to manipulate the beliefs of their interlocutors. Then they manipulate the interlocutor' beliefs about their own intentions.

Not all acts of deceit have an equally complex structure. As for the other types of communication, the difficulty of an act of deception depends on the number of inferences B requires to reach the hidden game, starting from A's untruthful communication act. To carry out or discover a well-planned deceit, several aspects will have to be taken into consideration, in addition to the simple fact of whether p is true or false. In principle, there is no limit to the how complex a situation can be. Human beings are, however, incapable of dealing simultaneously with a high number of embeddings.

Employing the distinction between simple and complex speech acts once again enables us to establish a criterion by which to distinguish different levels of difficulty that a deceit may reach.

A *simple deceit* consists of the production of a communication act (p) that contrasts with something (*non-p*) which would immediately allow the partner to identify what game the actor is trying to hide from him. Simple deceit, as I have defined it, is called lying in the literature. Figure 5.3 represents a simple deceit.

A *complex deceit* consists in producing a communication act q, implying a belief (p) that leads the partner toward a move or a game which is different from that he would arrive at if he had access to A's private belief *non-p*. Figure 5.4 shows a complex deceit.

Thus, lies and deceits are not always conceptually distinct. They fall along a continuum in which the lie constitutes the simplest level. The more complex the deceit, the greater the planning it requires. But even the most intricate deceit sometimes requires the telling of a lie, by which I mean an untruth. In this latter case, the lie is only the ultimate act finalizing a planning process that is potentially extremely complex.

In order to succeed, the deceit must not be discovered by the partner. If the partner discovers an attempt to deceive him, he may declare the fact or he may pretend he has not realized, in order to plan a counterdeceit, if he so wishes. The possibility of there being a counterdeceit demonstrates that A may simulate B's mental processes only up to a certain point, and in any case the operation always involves a certain amount of risk.

Everything that has been said refers exclusively to the cognitive aspects of deceit. However, the emotional aspects are of greater importance, for they determine our reactions to deceit. For example, the same lie is acceptable when told by child to parent (that is, it is compatible with attachment), but intolerable if told by parent to child (that is, it is incompatible with care).

Finally, deceits also may be produced through extralinguistic means: from pointing to a wrong location (simple deceit) to taking off one's wedding ring before leaving for a conference out of town (complex deceit).

5.4   Failure

First of all, we must make a distinction between two types of failure: the failure to achieve an agent's internal goal and communicative failure. Figure 5.3 summarizes the relationship between these two subtypes. If we suppose that actor A has a goal M, and to achieve it she requires the help of partner B, then different things may occur. If goal M is realized, then we may safely conclude that the communication has also been successful, and that A has received help from B. If, instead, goal M has not been realized, the failure may be due to a communicative breakdown, or to other reasons that are independent of cooperation between A and B.

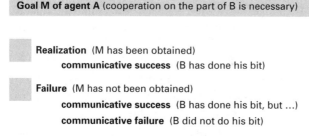

Goal M of agent A (cooperation on the part of B is necessary)

Realization (M has been obtained)
   communicative success (B has done his bit)

Failure (M has not been obtained)
   communicative success (B has done his bit, but ...)
   communicative failure (B did not do his bit)

Figure 5.5
The relationship between an agent's goal and communication.

Let us suppose, for instance, that while both are seated, A asks B to switch on the light. If B gets up and turns on the light, we are sure that A's goal was realized thanks in part to the communication having been successful. If the light does not go on, however, there are two possible explanations. Either A's request was successful: B got up and pressed the light switch, but a sudden blackout made his action ineffective, despite his goodwill; or B refused to carry out A's order, hence communication failed.

Since our subject is communication, I will ignore those cases of failure attributable to the infinite number of obstacles the world may set between ourselves and the realization of our goals. Communication may work perfectly well, but this is no guarantee that the original objectives of the agents in the interaction will be achieved. Strikes, heart attacks, earthquakes, and the like may totally modify the context. They all constitute impediments that do not fall within the category that concerns us here.

A second caveat is that only the agents can decide what is to be considered a success and what a failure. Some failures are so obvious that they cannot be questioned. Try reading a page of this book to someone who speaks no English and he won't understand a thing of what I'm saying. Other cases are less straightforward. If A asks B to give her five dollars and B gives her four, A might consider this a success in normal circumstances, but a failure if what she really needed was exactly five dollars to buy something from the vending machine. Note also that in this latter case, if B had given her a fifty dollar bill, this too would have counted as a failure.

It is again the agent who decides whether her goal corresponds to a state of the world, or to the execution of a specific action. Generally, what the agent wants is to achieve a given state of the world. However, the actions that lead to the realization of that state are not determined in detail. If A says to B:

"Switch the radio on, please."   (15)

in standard conditions, we may presume that what interests A is that the radio be switched on and not how B achieves turns it on, whether this be by turning the knob, through sheer force of mind, or even by asking the butler, C, to do so in his stead.

There are, however, cases in which the actor is interested not only in achieving the goal, but also in how the goal is achieved. If my wife says to our elder daughter:

"Simona, it's your turn to set the table."   (16)

my wife is not simply interested in ensuring the table is set. She also requires that it be Simona who sets it. She will not just want a state of the world corresponding to her request, but she will also check the procedure with which the required state is realized, thereby rendering vain Simona's efforts to make her grandmother have pity on her, corrupt the maid, or blackmail her sister.

Finally, an agent's objective may coincide perfectly with the execution itself of a given action. She may have no interest whatsoever in the consequences of that action. Julius Caesar stated, for instance, that when a battle is imminent, soldiers had better have little free time. Hence, he devised a series of irrelevant tasks (such as digging trenches) whose aim was to keep the soldiers busy, thereby distracting them from thoughts that would endanger their enthusiasm for war. It is thus important to make a distinction between a goal intended as a state of the world to be realized and a goal intended as a set of actions to be carried out and which will eventually lead to a given state of the world that is more or less relevant in itself.

All communicative failures are of interest, but from a psychological standpoint the most important is *refusal*. In this case, the difficulties occur at the level of communicative effect. If we abandon a fragmented standpoint on communication, in which only the single interaction is taken into consideration, it becomes important to consider what happens to both of the agents when B refuses to play the game or to make the move that A expected of him. A might reiterate the proposal, perhaps in a slightly modified form, thus hoping to render the proposal more acceptable to B, or she might provide some support for the proposal, or she might forgo all negotiations, recognizing her failure and abandoning her plan.

Even though it might at first seem paradoxical, from the standpoint of cooperation even a failure must be agreed on by the actors. In order to remain consistent with all the literature on the subject, I will continue to use the term *failure* in a generic sense to indicate all those cases that exhibit communicative failure at whatever level this might have taken place. I will introduce the term *shared failure* to indicate that particular case in which both the agents are aware of what has happened and accept the definition of the occurrence as constituting one of failure in the proper sense of the term. What I wish to underline is the fact that to define an occurrence as a shared failure both the agents must consciously recognize that there has been a nonnegotiable refusal, and that this refusal is to be considered as shared knowledge. If one of the two agents, either A or B, does not believe that this is what has happened, then the case cannot be classified as shared failure, despite the difficulties that have occurred.

There are people whose personality organization cognitive psychotherapists define as depressive. These people are particularly prone to immediately accepting the refusal made by another. In a certain sense, these people easily construct a shared failure by themselves. Other cognitive organizations, and in particular obsessive personalities, are much more loath to give up, hence far less prepared to consider an exchange that has not been crowned by success as a shared failure. The result is that different people construct interactions that are apparently identical in different ways: some agents incline themselves to failure while others do the opposite, with consequences to themselves and their partners that can be easily predicted. It should not be forgotten it may be as unpleasant to be the source of a refusal as it is to be the party refused. Indeed, sharing a refusal is emotionally disturbing both for the refused and for the refuser, for the latter would normally willingly do without, preferring to make do with the far less stressful situation of negotiation.

We are now in a position to define a *communicative failure* as an abortive attempt to produce a given communicative effect on one's partner. From A's standpoint, communicative failure may come about in any of the first three stages I have hypothesized: at the level of the expression act, at the level of speaker meaning, or at the level of communicative effect. An interruption at any point along the communicative chain will produce a failure to achieve the speaker's goal, that is, the speaker will fail to generate in her partner's mind the mental state she intended to generate.

There are three types of communicative failure: noncomprehension, misunderstanding, and refusal. I discuss these in turn.

Noncomprehension B fails to understand the expression act or the speaker meaning of what A is saying. An interruption in the inferential chain is detected at the level of the conversational game. Since the predefined task of the pertinent metarule has not been completed, the regular flow of the successive stages is interrupted and the reaction stage is activated. In the reaction stage the partner decides whether to render the failure explicit, for instance by asking for clarification, or whether to handle the situation in a different way. Whatever option he does adopt, failure is transparent to him, and his choice of option is a conscious one. Noncomprehension is a case of transparent failure for B, for B is aware he has not understood what A was saying.

Misunderstanding   B fails to comprehend the expression act or the speaker meaning of what A is saying in the way she intended it to be interpreted. The inferential chain takes a different route from the one A intended it to take. Misunderstanding is a case of opaque failure from B's standpoint, in the sense that B is unaware that he has failed to understand what A has said.

Refusal   B understands what A is saying, but refuses to comply with A's orientation. In this case, the private mental states of B are involved: either in the attribution process (inferring private mental states of A), or in the adjustment process (modifying B's own mental states), something followed a different route from the one A wished it to take. Refusal is a case of transparent failure for B, in the sense that it depends on a conscious decision on B's part.

The occurrence of a failure cannot be attributed to the incorrect application of a base-level rule. Such rules are meant to capture the communicative competence component of communication. At our level of abstraction the application of these rules is mandatory, and their functioning is automatically correct, under normal physiological conditions. The origin of the failure must therefore be sought in the representations that the rules are applied to. In truth, it is precisely the presence or absence of certain representations that may induce the partner to apply a rule that the actor did not want him to apply, or, vice versa, to fail to apply a rule she presumed he would apply.

One such example was presented in figure 5.6, with reference to behavior games. Two agents may have different representations of a behavior game while sharing some of the moves at a given level. Communicative failure will become evident when some event constrains the interlocutors to change the level of representation from that of making moves to a more abstract level. This will bring the disagreement out into the open.

Both misunderstandings and refusals thus come about in three main ways:

a. a default rule is applied counter to the actor's intentions;
b. a default rule is blocked counter to the actor's intentions; or
c. the actor or the partner uses a representation that is different from the one the partner or the actor respectively assumed the other interlocutor would use.

5.4.1   Failure Recovery

All the types of failures we have examined may be recognized and put right in the course of the interaction. Indeed, dialogue is an extremely flexible structure, one that is capable of repairing any sort of local malfunction. The principal objective of repair is to restore mutual knowledge when the participants are no longer certain as to what may or may not be taken as shared.

The modes available for recovering failures in grasping the expression act and speaker intentions consist basically in either repeating what was said or paraphrasing it. With regard to repetition, what is obviously required is an improvement, if possible, in the mode of producing the utterance: for example, by making it stand out better from the background, by emphasizing it, by decreasing noise. A paraphrase may expound exactly the same concept, or it may try to clarify what the actor believes is the less intelligible part of her message.

From a pragmatic standpoint, repairing the failures of communicative effect is a more interesting subject, for to do so, we must penetrate the domain of the negotiating that must go on between the actors. Figure 5.6 illustrates possible types of repair in failures of this third type.

It is worth recalling here the notion of shared failure: shared failure may only be legitimately spoken of when the actor forgoes all attempts at possible repair, including that of delaying the completion of her request, or that of proposing a move or an alternative game that might be acceptable to her partner, and when both interlocutors explicitly and consciously recognize there has indeed been a failure to all intents and purposes.

5.4.2   The Developmental Approach to Failures

The study of failure is crucial from a methodological point of view, because it allows us to observe the intermediate erroneous outcomes of the communication process. A theory able to predict errors that occur during a process is to be praised over theories that can predict only correct responses.

None of the existing pragmatic theories offers a global account of successful and failed communication. A noteworthy exception is relevance theory, which establishes a continuum between the idealizations of success and failure; Sperber and Wilson (1986) measure the efficacy of communication in terms of attempted relevance, as compared with achieved relevance. The introduction of strong and weak implicatures emphasizes the idea that each communicative instance conveys core meaning and perpetual implications. The notion of failure is spread over a wide set of implicatures, both

After a failure at the level of communicative effect, A may attempt to repair the situation, or propose that failure is shared.

a. Repair		Failure (in B)	Recovery (by A)
1	**Relationship**		
	Does the relationship between the actors provide for the game proposed?	not with you	restructuring the relationship
2	**B's motivation**		
	Does B have private motives which go counter to A's intentions?	I can't, I don't want to	modify B's internal state, pointing out his advantages
3	**Validity conditions**		
	Do the validity conditions for the game proposed exist?	it is not possible to play the game	restore preconditions
4	**A's capacity**		
	Does B think A is capable of playing the game?	you won't play your role properly	underscoring her capacity
5	**B's capacity**		
	Is B capable of playing the game?	I don't have the ability or knowledge, contingent reasons prevent me from taking part	teaching B, modifying contingency
6	**Informedness**		
	Does B consider A well-informed?	you are not reliably informed	muster independent evidence, show reliable sources
7	**Correctness**		
	Does B consider A correct?	I don't trust you	commit oneself, anticipate one's turn to demonstrate reliability
8	**Sincerity**		
	Does B consider A sincere?	I don't believe you	reiterate one's sincerity
9	**Shift in level**		
	B in no way intends to execute the move or play the game proposed	I have no intention of doing it	find a move or a game which is acceptable at a higher level
10	**Temporal shift**		
	B has no intention of keeping within the allotted time	I will not do it on time	delay

b. Shared failure

A and B both decide to recognize the fact that there has been a failure

Figure 5.6
Points at which a refusal from B may be repaired. These points are equivalent to A's failures to achieve her desired communicative effect.

those attempted and those that can be possibly achieved. Still, relevance theory has never generated systematic hypotheses for explaining communicative failures. Recently, the linguist Weigand (1999) has stressed the importance of misunderstandings in the dialogical interaction; he considers misunderstanding as an integral part of the comprehension process rather than a simple breakdown. He considers linguistic communication as an interactive process within which, in the case of *nonunderstanding*, the partner signals his problems and thus initiates the process of clarification, whereas in the case of misunderstanding the clarification is generally initiated by the speaker.

Following the assumptions of cognitive pragmatics, Bosco, Bucciarelli, and Bara (2006) investigate a taxonomy of different sorts of failure, which is grounded on the mental representations and cognitive processes involved: failure of the expression act, failure of the speaker meaning, and failure of the communicative effect. When failure of the expression act occurs, the partner fails to comprehend the literal value of the utterance; when failure of the speaker's meaning occurs, the partners fails to comprehend the speaker's communicative intention; and finally, when failure of the communicative effect occurs, the partner does not modify his mental states in the way the speaker desires, that is, he refuses to adhere to the speaker's goal. Depending on the sort of failure occurred, the speaker might enact a different kind of repair. The taxonomy allows us to generate hypotheses about the relative difficulty in recognizing and repairing different kinds of failure.

Our account follows a developmental perspective. This means studying mental processes not only as fixed states—an approach that takes into consideration exclusively the final stage—but rather concentrating on how a given function develops in the infant to the child and the adult. In particular, our subjects were eighty children aged 3 to 8 years.

Our experimental hypotheses are based on the mental representations and processes of varying complexity that we assume to be involved in the recognition and repair of different sorts of failure. We borrow two assumptions from two theories of the development of human cognition. In particular, the first assumption focuses on the emergence of communicative competence, and it assumes that the ability to deal with representations of increasing complexity increases with age (Bucciarelli, Colle, and Bara 2003). The second assumption focuses on the development of reasoning abilities, and it assumes that the ability to detect inconsistencies between representations of varying complexity increases with age and it correlates with the ability to reason (Bara, Bucciarelli, and Johnson-Laird 1995; Bara, Bucciarelli, and Lombardo 2001).

Globally considered, the results of the experiment support our taxonomy and its underlying assumptions. A first result concerns the distinction between the recognition of successful communication acts and the recognition (and subsequent repair) of the respective failures. It is simpler to recognize the success of a communication act than the respective failure. Thus, children perform better at recognizing that the speaker has succeeded in modifying the partner's mental state in the desired way, than recognizing when the speaker fails in her attempt. When we consider all the participants, the hypothesis holds for all kinds of failure and supports the assumption that inconsistencies between A's private goal and its felicitous realization are hard to detect.

As far as recognition of failures is concerned, noncomprehension is easier than misunderstanding, and failure of the expression act is easier to recognize than failure of the speaker meaning. Failure of the communicative effect is quite easy to recognize, and as predicted it posits at the same level of difficulty as failure of the expression act. Also, as we obviously

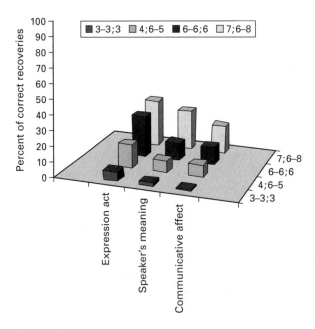

Figure 5.7
Histogram of percentages of proper repair of a failed communicative act, from the easiest to the most difficult to repair: failure of expression act, failure of speaker's meaning, and failure of communicative effect.
(*Source*: Bosco, Bucciarelli, and Bara 2006.)

could expect, it is simpler to recognize the failure of a communication act than to recover such a failure. One does not repair something if she does not think it failed.

Finally, the result concerning the trend in difficulty of repair of failures fully confirms our expectations. The repair of the expression act is simpler than the repair of the speaker meaning, which is simpler than the repair of the communicative effect (see figure 5.7). As shown in figure 5.6, the strategies for repairing failures of the communicative effect may in fact become quite complex.

6 Communicative Competence

The decision to place the chapter devoted to the evolution, development, and decay of communicative competence at the end of the book is motivated by the fact that the reader needs to become acquainted with the theoretical aspects of cognitive pragmatics before being presented with the evidence that corroborates it. The evidence in its favor is of two major types. The first type is based on Darwinian-oriented arguments regarding the evolution of communication from animals to humans (section 6.1). The second type is experimental, and concerns both the emergence of communicative competence in the child (section 6.2) and its decay. The latter may be due to physiological reasons, as in old age; to pathological causes, as in brain injuries; or to degenerative factors, such as in Alzheimer's disease.

The term *competence* refers to that abstract set of capacities which the system possesses, independently of the actual use to which those capacities are put. *Performance*, instead, refers to the capacities actually exhibited by a system in action. These may be inferred directly from the system's behavior in a specific situation. The difference is vital since it enables the distinction to be made between what the system is capable of doing in principle (competence), and what it actually does in a concrete situation (performance). For a more detailed treatment of this dichotomy, which was originally introduced into linguistics by Chomsky (1957), readers may consult my own work *Cognitive Science* (Bara 1995).

Any type of data that may be cited, whether it be experimental or from observation, it refers, by definition, to performance, since it has been generated in a given context. The fact that a subject manages to do a certain things is definite proof that that specific capacity forms part of his or her competence. For instance, if for once and once only in my life I manage to run very quickly, perhaps because I am being chased by an angry bull, this shows that running quickly is part of my potential capacities, that is,

I possess that trait at the level of competence. Taking the opposite case, the fact that a subject has never been observed doing a given thing gives rise to doubt in the observer. Perhaps the subject is capable of performing that particular action, but she has never found herself in a situation requiring the activation of that capacity. In this case, the subject might possess the competence even though performance data are not available to confirm the fact. Alternatively, she might not possess the necessary competence, which means that the pertinent performance would never be observed. If I were being chased not by one, but by three angry bulls, I would still be unable to take off the ground and fly, because I am incapable of flying. Flight not being part of my motor competence, I am unable to exhibit the performance of flying.

The more complicated case of a competence that has to mature will be dealt with in section 6.2.

In conclusion, the sole proof of the existence of a given competence is an instance of the related performance. The nondetection of a performance has no intrinsic meaning. It might indicate a deficit in competence, a deficit in performance, or a defect in the support structures. Especially at the developmental stage, the nondetection of a performance might be due to the immaturity of the support structure. The situation is complex and it warrants two comments. The first is an invitation to interpretational caution in attributing a deficit: the missing observation of an expected performance may be comprehended only when a strong theory is available that predicts the deficit and explains it in terms of competence and performance. The second is an invitation to courageously eliminate any data the collection of which is not based on a theory: these data are quite simply useless inasmuch as they are performance data not connected to competence.

For example, the inability to comprehend a communication act may depend on the fact that the person does not possess the essential tools required to do so; alternatively, the person might possess the necessary tools but might not have applied them for any reason whatsoever: she was tired, distracted, overwrought. From an experimental standpoint, it is a question of distinguishing between a systematic failure in carrying out a task, which usually indicates a problem at the level of competence, and occasional failures that may be attributed to specific causes, which may be eliminated and which are generally symptomatic of problems at the performance level.

A chimpanzee does not have the competence necessary to comprehend a deceit: it does not possess the ability to attribute mental states that are different from its own to other living beings. Even a drunken person may be incapable of understanding that he is being lied to, but such incapacity is temporary, since it is caused not by a lack of mental states, but by too high a blood-alcohol level. If the experiment is repeated a day later when his mind is clear, the subject will be capable of exhibiting the correct performance.

The objective of this chapter is to furnish as much evidence as possible in support of the theory that has been presented. The evidence I will present involves three different domains. First of all, a theory must be compatible with what is known about human evolution: the findings of communicative pragmatics tally with much of the knowledge available on human evolution, as I will show shortly (section 6.1). A second methodological point is that a theory must not only explain what happens when the system has reached stability, it must also account for its ontogenetic development: in line with developmental cognitive science, one important criterion to test the power of a theory is whether it manages to explain not only the phenomena under investigation but also how those phenomena have gradually been constructed (Bara 1995). Hence, explaining the development of communicative competence is a fundamental issue (section 6.2). Finally, starting from our awareness of the fact that our minds are biological, succeeding in correlating mental processes employed in communication with the cerebral functions that realize those processes is a further step forward in demonstrating the validity of the theory itself (section 6.3).

6.1 The Evolution of Communicative Competence

Evolutionary psychology has only recently asserted itself in the field of the cognitive sciences. The basic idea is that the human mind is a product of the evolution of the genus *Homo*, which includes modern and premodern humans: each component of the mind has been modeled by natural selection (Barkow, Cosmides, and Tooby 1992).

Evolutionary psychology holds that the architecture of the human mind is to a large extent adapted to the life our ancestors led in the Pleistocene age, a geological period that began approximately 2 million years ago and came to an end about 10,000 years ago. It has been hypothesized that it is impossible to fully comprehend the nature of any psychological mechanism whatsoever without referring to the type of life our predecessors led during the Pleistocene, the life of the hunter-gatherer in the savannah and prairies.

To comprehend the psychology of modern man, then, we cannot restrict our study to the human being in our contemporary civilized environment, in which we have been living for 4,000 years at most, that is, since we invented writing, which enabled culture to be maintained transgenerationally. Cerebral and psychological functions gained their stability over a much greater time range: the latest version of *Homo sapiens* has been around for about fifty times that long, that is, 200,000 years. It is thus not difficult to realize that the living conditions that accompanied us in the course of our phylogenesis were very different from present-day conditions. For instance, with regard to social organization we know that *Homo* spent over 99 percent of his evolution in groups that varied between 35–50 and 200–300 people (Oates 1977). These groups of individuals, organized into nomadic bands of hunter-gatherers, formed the type of organization that was prevalent until approximately 10,000 years ago.

All animals interact with members of their own species, using communicative modes of increasing complexity. A minimal degree of communication is necessary in every gendered species in order to guarantee continuity through sexual reproduction. To be more precise, those animals whose social life is more intense than that required for the elementary interaction constituted by the reciprocal declaration of one's availability to mate develop a system of communication that is correspondingly more articulated.

The complexity of social life is an excellent predictor of the richness of the communicative capacity of the species. The reason for this correlation lies in the fact that if no social structure has emerged, an advanced communication system offers no evolutionary reward compared to an elementary system. However, one should avoid positing a simple causal link, since each advance in communication leads to an advance in social interaction and vice versa.

Certain types of insects seem to constitute an exception, but bees and termites have a social structure where every type of interaction is rigidly predetermined at birth, even if the number of agents is extremely high indeed. Communication is sometimes effective, as in the dance of the bees described by Karl von Frisch (1966): a bee that has found a source of nectar is capable of indicating the location to her companions, signaling both the direction with respect to the sun and the distance from the hive.

It should, however, be noted that the entire structure of communication is preconstituted genetically, without the individual having any liberty whatsoever. A group composed of half a dozen members may have a much more complex social structure than a society made of hundreds of members.

Complexity depends on how genetically rigid interaction between members of a species is, and on how many games—courting, hunting in isolation or in a group, caring for the young—they are capable of playing freely with each other. In this sense, the language of the bee is extremely poor, even though it is marvelously efficient from the point of view of survival.

A comparative scale of communicative competence is presented in figure 6.1: at the lowest level we find the invertebrates, and on the next rung up we find the societies of insects, reptiles, and fish.

A rigid system of interaction   This kind of system may be found in all animal species, from the lowest levels on the tree of life up to the lower mammals: in a rigid system, each signal has only one meaning; composition or modification is not possible. The marmot's alarm whistle, the song the lark uses to stake out its territory, the stickleback's signals of aggression: all are particular and virtually unchangeable. Animals emit and receive a genetically determined signal that provides no scope either for the creation of a new meaning (innovation) or for the construction of a set whose meaning depends on the meanings of elementary signals (composition). Thus a duck will never be able to invent a new noise (a "word" which possesses the features of a "neologism"), no matter how useful such an invention might be in certain environments, nor can it emit a significant series of simple noises in order to compose a "phrase." Given these limitations, such a closed system is incapable of conveying more than about ten meanings.

A first qualitative leap forward, intended as a relatively elastic mode of communication compared to genetically determined communication, is to be found at the level of lone mammals (e.g., tigers, killer whales) and birds, especially those that are used to living in groups (e.g., penguins): here we already find some degree of individual freedom in interaction between peers (Thorpe 1961). The next level is that of social mammals. The latter are able to communicate elementary meanings such as reciprocal presence, or danger, among peers (e.g., horses, buffalo).

Semirigid communication systems   In a semirigid system, which is typical of higher mammals, a restricted number of base meanings may be used, showing a certain sensibility to context. A pack of wolves is able to organize a group hunt, even if most researchers do not attribute to wolves any kind of joint goals or plans (Tomasello and Call 1997). Rather, each member of the pack is attempting to maximize its own chance of reaching the prey, also through exploiting the other participant's chasing behavior.

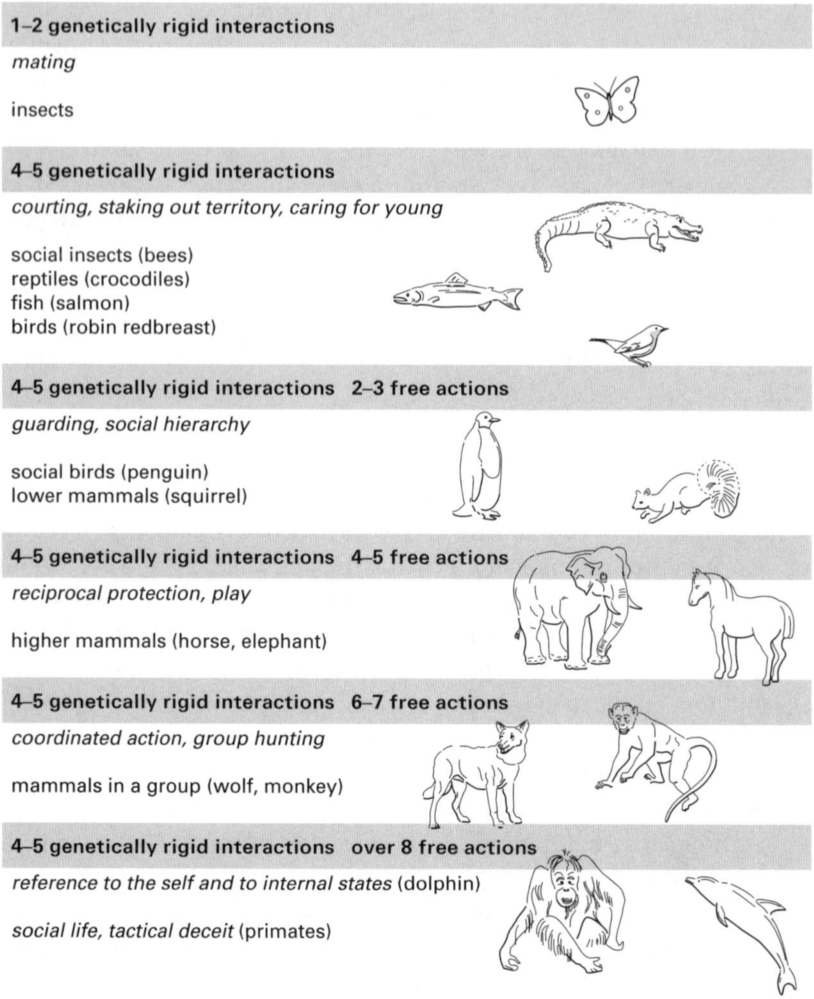

1–2 genetically rigid interactions

mating

insects

4–5 genetically rigid interactions

courting, staking out territory, caring for young

social insects (bees)
reptiles (crocodiles)
fish (salmon)
birds (robin redbreast)

4–5 genetically rigid interactions   2–3 free actions

guarding, social hierarchy

social birds (penguin)
lower mammals (squirrel)

4–5 genetically rigid interactions   4–5 free actions

reciprocal protection, play

higher mammals (horse, elephant)

4–5 genetically rigid interactions   6–7 free actions

coordinated action, group hunting

mammals in a group (wolf, monkey)

4–5 genetically rigid interactions   over 8 free actions

reference to the self and to internal states (dolphin)

social life, tactical deceit (primates)

Figure 6.1
Comparison of the capacity for social interaction, measured in terms of type and number of interactions.

Analogously, dolphins appear to communicate with each other by following elementary schemes that enable them to convey certain internal states (hunger, sexual availability, etc.). They may even use self-referential concepts, thus enabling them to express the key concept "I." Higher mammals can also use the same behavior pattern in different contexts in order to express different meanings. For example, an adult leopard may play with his cub, conveying aggressive signals to it while concurrently communicating to it that those signals of aggression are not to be taken literally, but as a game (Bateson 1956). In order to play, the leopard sends a signal of aggression that, on the one hand, has been lightened and, on the other hand, has been emitted in a context that changes its significance, so that the cub will understand that the situation is to be read as a kind of game.

The capacity of a semirigid system, that is, one that may use elementary meanings showing a certain sensibility to context, is around the twenty–thirty mark. There is also a severe limit on the number of elementary meanings that are possible, as well as on the number of relevant contexts. One stimulating study on semiclosed communication is that by Dorothy Cheney and Robert Seyfarth (1990) on vervet monkeys. I will go into a little detail on this work in order to show how easy it is for a human observer who is sympathetic to the animals she observes to credit them with capacities in excess of those they exhibit.

Vervets emit three distinct alarm calls correlated with the presence of their three most dangerous predators: leopards, snakes, and birds of prey. Each of these constrains the cercopitheci to adopt different defense strategies, which range from tree-climbing if a leopard appears, to standing on their hind legs and scrutinizing the ground if a snake comes up, and to hiding behind bushes and staring into the sky if an eagle has been spotted. The important fact is that the monkeys produce an appropriate response to the specific warning signal, even if they cannot see what type of predator has appeared. This unquestionably impressive behavior induced Cheney and Seyfarth into hypothesizing that the vervets emitted the equivalent of an assertive speech act ("There's a leopard! There's a snake! There's an eagle!").

But the results of research into other animals—cocks—which no scholar could seriously think of comparing to human beings, have had the effect of attenuating the acclaimed communicative capacity of the vervets. Hauser (1996) has shown that cocks too are capable of varying their alarm call, depending on whether the predator comes from the earth (a fox) or from the sky (a falcon). If we reflect with greater care, then we will realize that we are dealing with a rigid behavioral scheme rather than a flexible one, a scheme that is centered on a sort of simplified equivalent of directives. Stated differently, the signal emitted by cocks and vervet monkeys do not correspond to the assertive:

There is an X!

where the variable X may correspond to predators that run, slither, or fly. There are, instead, three separate signals, each emitted in a specific context, which are followed by an obligatory behavioral act:

Climb on the tree!

Stand on your hind legs and look at the ground!

Hide in the bushes!

Signals of this type reflect much more the cognitive capacities of vervets and cocks. Do they resemble directives? Only in a metaphorical sense, certainly not in the proper sense of the term. In any case, a directive is much simpler to understand than an assertive: the hearer has no inference to draw (*Now that I know a leopard is around, what should I do?*). It has just to execute the action ordered (*Climb the tree!*).

Finally, an impressive leap forward is made by great apes (orangutan, gorilla, chimpanzee, bonobo). The communicative competence of these animals compared to any other animal species is extraordinary. All field studies show that the social behavior of these primates is rich and articulate when they are living in the wild. And the resemblances with analogous human social behavior has also been underscored, for instance, by Goodall (1986) with regard to chimpanzees. Even *Homo* belong to the class of primates, but in order to avoid making the treatment overly dense I will exclude human beings from my use of the term "primates."

Savage-Rumbaugh et al. (1993) point out that we still possess insufficient information on the communicative capacities developed by these primates living in their natural habitat. Savage-Rumbaugh et al.'s preoccupation with this fact leads them to exaggerate the possibility that there may well be languages that have not yet been discovered. There remains the unacceptable fact that in a few years time such data will be forever lost, given the threat of extinction hanging over all primates because of the incessant homicidal violence of their more developed cousins. And studying gorillas in a laboratory cannot yield the same results as studying this creature in the wild.

The point is that neither cocks nor vervets have mastery over directives, and even less so does a bonobo have mastery over any type of language. All these animals have adapted magnificently to the environment they inhabit, exhibiting behaviors that humans cannot even dream of possessing. However, such capacities do not include language, nor anything that remotely resembles language. Relocating animal communication to its real level does not mean devaluing or undervaluing it, but simply ordering it in a sensible evolutionary scale.

Open systems of communication   Open systems, employed exclusively by humans, are those in which elementary meanings are potentially infinite, just as the number of phrases that may be generated through the mechanism of syntax is potentially infinite. The result is that the number of meaningful messages possible is infinite. Human language composes words on the basis of elementary units, such as the letters of the alphabet or the signs of ideograms. The number of words that may be composed is infinite, since the number of times a letter or a sign in the same word may be repeated is infinite. The number of words employed in an ordinary conversation is around the thousand mark: Basic English, from which every other term in English may be defined, is composed of approximately 900 words. Reading a newspaper requires a knowledge of approximately 1,500 words, while a highly educated person has a vocabulary of 40,000 to 50,000 words. The major edition of Webster's dictionary, one of the most authoritative and comprehensive for the English language, has 320,000 different entries.

Starting from this basis, meaningful phrases that are always different may be generated, without even needing to invent new elementary meanings or to coin neologisms. Open systems may thus use over 300,000 words, with which it is possible to compose, thanks to syntax, a number of meaningful utterances that would cover the needs of many lives.

6.1.1 Comparative Communication

As we have seen, communication is not only linguistic. I am, however, now obliged to refer principally to language, for practically all the arguments advanced by scholars of the subject concentrate on this domain. I will therefore abide by the convention, while waiting for concepts such as communicative intention and shared knowledge to be developed from an evolutionary standpoint, concepts that are potentially capable of indicating the emergence of human extralinguistic communication.

When, then, did human language emerge?

I am forced to supply a purely inductive answer, based on considerations pertaining to anatomy, neuropsychology, archaeology, and

Years ago

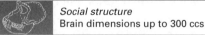

200 million | **Mammals**

Auditory apparatus

65 million | **Apes**

Social structure
Brain dimensions up to 300 ccs

5–8 million | **Separation between primates and hominids**

Anatomy: *separation of primates* (chimpanzee [385 ccs],
orangutang [405 ccs], gorilla [495 ccs]) *from hominids*
Paleoneurology: *brain increase* (400 ccs)

4 million | **Australopithecus**

Anatomy: *distinction between Africanus, Robustus, and Afarensis*
Paleoneurology: *Lucy, Australopithecus Afarensis* (450 ccs)

2,200,000 | **Homo habilis**

Anatomy: *phonic apparatus, manual capacity*
Paleoneurology: *brain increase* (700 ccs)
Archaeology: *first stone tools*
Extralinguistic communication: already developed
Archaeolanguage: vowels connected to consonants

1,700,000 | **Homo erectus** Common progenitor of Neanderthal and of Homo sapiens

Anatomy: *erect, free use of hands*
Paleoneurology: *development of the frontal and parietal areas* (900 ccs)
Archaeology: *rudimentary tools; discovery and conservation of fire;
group hunting*
Protolanguage: useful for organizing information and social exchanges

500,000 | **Archaic Homo sapiens**

Anatomy: *practically equivalent to present-day anatomy*
Paleoneurology: *further development of the neural cortex* (1,200 ccs)
Archaeology: *tools built in series; first artistic products*
Language: symbolic

200,000 | **Anatomically modern Homo sapiens**

Anatomy: *contemporary man*
Paleoneurology: *present-day brain development* (1,400 ccs)
Archaeology: *burial* (40,000 B.C.); *rock paintings, sculpture* (30,000 B.C.)
Language: different languages
Writing: succession of stages in Mesopotamia: *calendar* (10,000 B.C.);
pictograms (3,500 B.C.); *phonograms* (3,000 B.C.); *alphabet* (1,700 B.C.)

Figure 6.2
Genesis of language.

anthropology. Figure 6.2 schematizes my reconstruction of the evolutionary steps that brought language into being. I have tried to integrate different sources in order to present a single, unified framework expounding the essential data of an evolutionary type. The most important references come from the neuropsychologist John Bradshaw (1997) and the evolutionary psychologists Morten Christiansen and Simon Kirby (2003).

It should always be borne in mind that the temporal distinction between the various species of *Homo* are by no means clear cut: there are long periods of overlap, in the order of hundreds of thousands of years, during which *Homo* belonging to different levels of evolution cohabit. The most enthralling description of what was not overly peaceful interaction has been provided by the writer Jack London (1907) in his stories of Big Tooth, *Homo habilis*, the intermediate stage between Tree Men (the primates) and Men of Fire (*Homo erectus*), who fell in love with the charming Erect Woman (*Femina erecta*), whose superior intelligence allowed their common offspring to make the qualitative leap necessary to proceed toward *Homo sapiens*. A more up-to-date and ironic work is that by Roy Lewis (1960), who writes the autobiography of the son of the greatest ape-man of the Pleistocene age, namely the one who discovered fire, to the indignant horror of conservative Uncle Vanya, an ape-man of solid principles tied to the arboricultural tradition.

In order to speak, not only must one possess an adequate phonic apparatus, but also a corresponding auditory system capable of discriminating the sounds emitted with the same degree of efficiency (Kuhl 1987). In the wake of Crelin's (1987) accurate reconstruction, we may state that *Homo habilis* already possessed a phonic structure that enabled them to generate consonants associated with vowels, that is, a very wide range of precisely definable sounds creating clear borders between words. At the same time, the auditory apparatus, whose development had begun back with higher mammals, exhibited the indispensable corollary capacity of sound recognition.

Philip Lieberman (1991, 2000) has best clarified the relationship between language and neuroanatomy. The human vocal tract guarantees a selective advantage over all other possible structures because it is capable of producing nonnasalized sounds. Nasalization produces sounds that are less recognizable, whereas our vocal tract produces sounds that are quite distinct, thereby diminishing the probability of perceptual errors. *Homo habilis* may therefore connect vowels up to consonants, producing sounds such as *to* and *ba*. This is more than sufficient to allow premodern *Homo* to take a communicative pathway that other primates are denied access to. De Waal

(1988) points out that phonic communication in nonhuman primates is based essentially on vowels, because their oropharinx does not allow consonants to be produced. This means that the sounds emitted by primates merge into one another, thereby limiting the number of fully recognizable sounds to the twenty–thirty mark.

Thanks to the natural borders furnished by consonants, the human natural lexicon is enormously greater. If we take into consideration only five vowels and ten consonants, we already have fifty basic phonemes at our disposal. This means that *Homo habilis* can already build words, generating them from about fifty elementary constituents. In passing, it may be noted that Neanderthal did not have this type of oropharinx, and this undoubtedly limited his capacity for spoken language.

An exception to the inability of the monkey to produce complex verbalizations is represented by the gelada monkey: Richman (1976) has documented the fact that the gelada can produce sounds equivalent to consonants interspersed with vowels. In a later study, Richman (1987) also showed that synchronized exchanges of *contact calls* among geladas exhibit melodic and rhythmic features analogous to those of human language. Such exchanges increase in relation to the need to solve emotional conflicts inherent in many social situations. Furthermore, the frequency of such exchanges increases proportionally in relation to the intensity of the social bond between the monkeys.

To account for the anomaly of this conversational ability in monkeys with a neocortex that is relatively small compared to that of their cousins, the baboons, Robin Dunbar (1993) looks to the needs created by their social life. Geladas live in groups that are the most numerous among nonhuman primates: on an average their bands count approximately 120 members. Such an intense social life constitutes a selective driving force toward a more evolved oral system of communication capable of diminishing the risks of continual interaction, especially on an emotional plane.

An analogous function of maintaining group cohesion is realized in other monkeys by *social grooming*, that is, a series of physical interactions based on reciprocal scratching, looking for fleas, and combing hair (Dunbar 1991). Social grooming serves to establish and maintain friendship and coalition, characteristics that render the social structure of primates unique in the animal world. It bears a linear correlation with the number of individuals constituting the group, a number that varies, in primates, between 30 (gorillas) and 50 (chimpanzees). If we estimate the number of humans living in a Neolithic village at about 150–200 individuals, then if social grooming were the only means available for maintaining cohesion the investment in time would be intolerable: approximately 50 percent of each day. Language is a unique tool enabling the achievement of social cohesion necessary for the development and maintenance of groups of over 150 people, since it guarantees that interpersonal ties will not be overlooked under the pressure of survival.

In this sense, one essential function of language is that of enabling the establishment of social relations through talking about oneself and about others. Language allows the exchange not only of information concerning the world, but also of information concerning individuals and the relationships among individuals. This applies as much to prehistoric humankind as it does to contemporary humankind. However, possessing the required anatomical structure is not sufficient a condition to move from vocalizations to language: it is the brain that counts. This is demonstrated by those people who have undergone a laryngectomy. These individuals learn to emit by means of modulators placed in other parts of the body sounds that other people recognize as words.

We now move on to neuropsychological evidence. Speech capacity requires both highly developed brain capacity as well as a specific cerebral region. In humans, this has been realized in Broca's area and Wernicke's area. In this sphere too, *Homo habilis* was the first species of *Homo* to exhibit the brain capacity crucial to sustain language: 700 ccs against the 450 ccs of the Australopitheci who preceded him, and significantly greater development in the parietal and frontal areas, which are respectively responsible for the control over language and over the hands. With *Homo erectus* the volume of the brain reaches 1,200 ccs; with the entry on the stage of modern *Homo sapiens*, 200,000 years ago, the brain reaches its present capacity of 1,400 ccs (Stephan, Frahm, and Baron 1981; Falk 1987; Aiello and Dunbar 1993).

Human protolanguage may be traced as far back as over 1.5 million years ago, with *Homo erectus*. But to identify language proper we have to reach late *Homo erectus*, and perhaps even further forward, to the appearance of an archaic type of *Homo sapiens*. Approximately 1.7 million years ago, our ancestors discovered fire and began to organize hunting in groups. This made the use of language an indispensable tool for the exchange of information. We have already seen that human groups totaled over a hundred members, a phenomenon that never occurs in other primates. Life in such a numerous group makes language a crucial instrument of oral communication in order to ensure successful social interaction, that is, interaction that will guarantee the emotional flexibility required for frequent, intense, and demanding social exchanges.

After the elementary exchange of information on the world (e.g., for hunting) and on social life, the next step in the evolution of language is the emergence of the symbolic function. This symbolic capacity may be reasonably attributed to *Homo sapiens*. One of the reasons that has been hypothesized to account for the extinction of Neanderthal is that his inferior communicative capacity would have placed him at a severe disadvantage in what was most probably a competition for survival with *Homo sapiens*.

Language as we know it today is a prerogative of modern *Homo sapiens*. It is therefore biologically extremely recent. It appeared less than 200,000 years ago. Merlin Donald (1991) argues that all known languages may be traced back to a common ancestor, which developed about 100,000 years ago. In recent years, technological progress has been enormous, yet language has presumably remained unchanged. Anthropological observation offers indirect evidence in support of this contention, showing that even human groups who never went beyond the Stone Age possess languages exhibiting characteristics equivalent to those groups that made significant technological progress. Lexicon apart, the language of the Bushmen is not inferior to modern English at the level of competence. No language in use today can be considered primitive, in the sense that it has a simpler, more elementary structure. The counterevidence is the fact that children brought up in a culture that is equivalent to that of the Stone Age can fully adapt to modern industrial society, as is shown by the fact that they obtain degrees in modern universities.

The archaeological evidence takes the same argumentative line. It is based on the production of handmade goods that demonstrate the existence of a social life sufficiently complex as to warrant the stabilization of a developed language system capable of satisfying the interactive needs of *Homo*. The most ancient stone tools found in Kenya once again date back to the appearance of *Homo habilis*, 2 million years ago. But it is only 400,000 years ago that the construction of tools witnessed a boom that gave rise to systematic production. The earliest evidence of artistic production, which is interesting not only as a form of external representation but also as an expression of aesthetic pleasure that only humans possess, may be traced back to a period that comes shortly after the one we have been discussing: rock paintings and the first prehistoric sculptures are both 30,000 years old. Archaeologists such as Iain Davidson (1991) contend that the genesis of language coincides with these sophisticated levels of figurative expression. Davidson (2003) points out that *burial* of human cadavers (at least as far back as 40,000 years ago) can be taken as a solid indicator of the sorts of displacement and reflectivity made possible by the use of symbols. Both in Europe and Australia, prehistoric burials are accompanied by clear signs of ritual, particularly through the use of ochre. In Europe, the burials are also accompanied by personal decorations such as beads and bracelets.

However, the cognitive capacities required to construct objects are not less complex than those required to speak. Children up to the age of three can learn to *use* an instrument such as a spoon or a pencil, but the ability to construct one is another matter altogether. On the basis of all these findings and considerations, I would shift the appearance of some form of language to at least 2 million years ago, that is, to when the first manufactured products appeared. Taking manufactured products as an indicator implies that the evolution of language is linked up with the evolution of cognitive capacities.

In sum, if one accepts the idea that the capacity to communicate evolved progressively, then *Homo habilis* may be said to have already been capable of communicating in the proper sense of the term 2 million years ago. On the basis of an extensively developed communicative capacity, language evolved still further in the course of the following 1.5 million years. In the last 200,000 years linguistic communication came to full maturity. The consequence of assuming that a communicative capacity existed that was common to both the linguistic and extralinguistic modes is that the appearance of an antecedent primitive of language must be traced back to a much earlier period in humankind's history.

6.1.2 Writing: The Dream of Permanence

No animal uses instruments in order to leave a mark. Some species of molluscs and insects leave a secretion that enables them to return to their departure point, and many animals leave a recognizable trace of their presence—for instance to stake out their territory—but this is never realized by means of a tool outside their own bodies (Gallistel 1992). Even animals such as anthropomorphous apes that possess the capacity to handle external tools never use such tools to leave behind a significant trace for themselves or for members of their own species. Humans, by contrast, seem to be innately endowed with notational competence, both for drawing and for writing.

Humanity's most brilliant invention consists in using our capacity to draw symbols to ensure the preservation of knowledge at the group level, that is, beyond the life of the single individual. The invention of writing enables external cognition to become permanent, thus making transgenerational evolution possible. Stated differently, the conditions necessary for the existence of culture, intended as the possibility to transmit knowledge acquired individually to other members of the group, are external cognition and its consolidation, that is, its relative permanence (see section 1.1.2).

External cognition allows a system to use environmental indicators as a support of its own cognitive activities: it thus facilitates mental processing by lightening the cognitive processing load. The idea of cognition as being a concurrently internal and external process is close to what Lucy Suchman (1987) suggested with her concept of situated action: building an action plan does not take place wholly in the mind; rather the plan is constructed gradually as the actor interacts with the world. The *situated* paradigm has permeated cognitive science, opening up an ecological perspective that concentrates greater attention on the interaction between human beings and their environment. It is above all the expert of ergonomics Donald Norman (1988) who underlines the importance of external support to human intelligence, from the simplest type of support to the most technologically sophisticated.

But the most important realization of all, as Varela, Thompson, and Rosch (1991) argue, is that cognition is embodied, that is, it is realized in a specific body equipped with special features. In this sense our intellectual capacities are also connected to our manual capacities. The latter had already grown noticeably with the development of the opposable thumb. The development of the frontal areas in *Homo habilis* increases this growth even further. All primates have opposed thumbs, but they have not developed any form of culture, despite the fact that they have the capacity to modify the surrounding environment even in quite a sophisticated manner. Exclusively bodily potential is in itself insufficient. What is needed is a brain to exploit that physical potential. The biological mind is essentially a structure dedicated to the control of the biological body (Clark 1997).

Other animals that are endowed with a large brain but do not possess an opposed thumb—such as dolphins—do not have the possibility of developing a transgenerational culture. What is missing this time is precisely the necessary physical support. *Homo*, on the contrary, possess all the necessary conditions: a brain (internal cognition), environmental conditions (external cognition), and the necessary corporeal characteristics (embodied cognition) that enable communicative capacities to be developed to the fullest.

From the standpoint of the reconstruction of cognitive evolution, external memory is a technological support that aids the full expansion of the symbolic function as represented by language. It is only when memory—or in a wider sense, cognition—achieves concrete realization in writing and subsequently in all those resources built from the alphabet that modern culture is born. Succeeding generations master the conquests of their predecessors, building on knowledge that has been consolidated and physically embodied, without having to start each time from scratch. Manufactured products are generalized in the group. Once the first *Homo* has made a knife, this remains, for good or evil, as the legacy of the following generations over and beyond the physical existence of the first ingenious craftsperson. It is external cognition that allows progressive accumulation of knowledge, without there being any limits.

A full reconstruction of the evolution of writing is in Bara 2003, which I here summarize. The first step toward writing is the moment when the first human artists begin to paint and sculpt cave walls. In a continuous evolution lasting at least 40,000 years, aesthetic, magic, and sacred functions are complemented by those conveying cognitive content. We may state that the earliest traces of graphological symbols go back 35,000 years, and consist of small, equidistant engravings whose significance is still incomprehensible, but whose function may be stated as being that of acting as an external support for an individual's memory, or perhaps for that of a group.

Around 30,000 B.C., we find highly stylized representations, whose origins are uncertain, of animal heads and sexual organs. Around 20,000 B.C. the organization of the pictures improves: special features of the species are represented, such as the horns of the bison and the trunk of the mammoth. Once we reach 15,000 B.C. painting and engraving techniques are practically the same as those that exist today: the horses of the Pyrenees caves, like the black bulls of Lascaux (see fig. 1.4), are accomplishments well beyond the capacity of anyone who is not a real artist, whether he be Neolithic or modern.

Returning to the distinction between linguistic and extralinguistic communication, and given the fact that the feature of permanence may be attributed to both modes, we should be able to recognize an extralinguistic mode of writing as well as the linguistic mode that we are used to. Alexander Marshack (1991) has documented what is still today the first instantiation of protowriting. This goes back to the Paleolithic age, around 10,000 B.C. A bone fragment was discovered in Tai, France, bearing mathematical notation as well as writing. Presumably this was allotted to marking the passage of time—a sort of elementary calendar.

We may distinguish between the various forms of writing by using the number of signs employed as our classificatory criterion: thus *pictograms* employ over a 1,000 signs, *logograms* employ between 1,000 and 40 signs, and an *alphabet* uses fewer than 40 signs.

The most ancient example of pictogram is the calcareous slab found in the Sumerian city of Kish in Mesopotamia. The drawing of a foot, a hand, and a sleigh, beside which are symbols that are presumably numbers, appears for the first time around 3,500 B.C. The clay tablets found inside the temple in the city of Uruk in Mesopotamia exhibit 1,500 different symbols. Each of these pictograms refers to an object: the head of a bull represents a bull, the outline of a mountain a mountain.

The efficacy of the pictogram simultaneously constitutes its limit: everyone can immediately grasp the meaning of the signs drawn on the tablet, seen as a sequence of images. It constitutes a kind of representation by association: its true meaning can only be comprehended by those who are already familiar with facts represented before their eyes. Pictography leaves aside the times, modes, and logical links that connect subjects and events. This is why I classify pictography as a permanent version of extralinguistic communication: a set of symbols having associative, noncompositional structure. I will now examine the transition stage to the permanent representation of linguistic communication.

To increase the effectiveness of pictographic writing, signs must be stylized, which reduces the number of signs that may be used. This is what happens to logograms. The Egyptians, who needed an efficient system of writing in order to rule their large empire, solved the problem around 3000 B.C. What the eye is about to perceive becomes schematized. Thus a pubic triangle is used to represent a woman, an eye to represent seeing, and so forth. But the crucial step consists in introducing a rudimentary form of syntax, which allows the communicators to move from the property of association, which characterizes extralinguistic communication, to that of compositionality, the feature that defines linguistic communication.

Two of the most important indicators of the inception of the principle of compositionality are the plural form and the combination of logograms. Two signs of the same type indicate the plural: the sign for a bird indicates a bird, two signs of a bird indicate birds in the plural. It is also possible to create new ideograms by combining two or more different signs: for instance, mouth + bread = eat; woman + mountain = serve; woman + dress = mistress of the house. It should be noted that ideograms are a direct reflection of the meaning of the sign—there is no link with the way the word is pronounced.

The final crucial step toward writing as we know it today is the substitution of ideograms by phonograms, which comes about in Mesopotamia around 2,500 B.C. This reduces the signs employed to fewer than 100. The main mechanism that realizes this operation is a crossword-puzzle-type principle, a principle related to the idea of *rebus*. For instance, in order to represent the concept of a date, the writer does not use a symbolic representation of the calendar (a sun followed by a moon). Instead he draws a date (the fruit). What creates the form–meaning link is not the sign in itself, but the uttering of the sign. We have thus reached the stage of syllabic writing, such as the systems in Mesopotamia and Egypt, which are no longer simply looked at as were pictograms, and are not yet read as are alphabet systems: these are *deciphered*.

To achieve the transition from symbol to sound, the Egyptians used ideographic signs to represent concepts with analogous sounds. Since, for instance, in the language spoken by the Egyptians "chair" was pronounced *pe*, the drawing of a chair was used to indicate not only the concept "chair" but also the sound <*pe*>. One of the earliest examples of the application of this method is to be found in Narmer's tile (2,900 B.C.) depicting the victorious King Narmer: the sovereign's name is inscribed employing the rebus principle, by means of the hieroglyph of the fish (N'R) coupled with that of the scalpel (MR). It should be noted that the phonic substance associated with hieroglyphs is purely consonantal: the vowels had to be inserted by the reader. Figure 6.3 illustrates the name "Narmer" in the phonetic version of hieroglyphics. The price of its greater effectiveness is the interpretational ambiguity it produces: in order to decipher a text one must not only know the language, one must also possess ample knowledge of the context the document refers to.

The final step consists in the invention of the alphabet by the Phoenicians, around 1,700 B.C. This time the pressure for change came from trade,

Figure 6.3
Narmer's tile: fish (N'R) and scalpel (MR).
Source: Ifrah 1981.

not from conquest, as was the case with the Egyptians. The Phoenician alphabet had 22 signs; it used only consonants, leaving the reader with the task of adding the vowels. Vowels were introduced into the alphabet by the Greeks around 1,000 B.C., thereby achieving total correspondence between spoken and written linguistic communication.

The possibility of rendering a compositional symbolic system permanent consolidates every intellectual success and greatly facilitates cultural transmission not only from one individual to another, but also from one generation to another. For of course, culture must be taught and learned. Indeed, since human children are incapable of autonomous survival in the first seven to eight years of their lives, beyond their familiar duties (such as babysitting, thus allowing for bigger family sizes) society destines them to undergo direct education (Del Giudice, Angeleri, and Manera 2009). One reason this process is possible is that the child's brain has plasticity, a characteristic that is lost at puberty. In other words, the small child is a prodigious machine for learning, a fact that also indicates that the parent is symmetrically predisposed to become his teacher. If the key to human adaptation is the intergenerational resource flow from the old to the young, then skill learning (both social and technical) becomes the primary function of our long juvenility: it represents a fruitful investment in "embodied capital."

Other primates too may act as teachers to their young ones through direct demonstration: from their observations of chimpanzees in their natural habitat of the rain forests of the Ivory Coast, Boesch and Boesch-Ackermann (1991) report that mothers teach their little ones to break nuts using a sort of hammer. In actual practice, not only does the mother furnish her offspring with a hammer, but she also shows him how to hold it and what position to place the nut in. However, these adults teach their young in a nonsystematic and occasional manner that is vastly different from the effort and commitment human parents and teachers put into the task.

It is enlightening to compare teaching-learning styles in humans with those of primates (Tomasello 1990). Whereas humans show a natural inclination to teach, and reciprocally a great willingness to learn, primates limit themselves to occasionally showing their young how something is done, and the young learners match this by exhibiting a lack of spontaneous interest in learning to master the ability in question. The lack in primates of any real imitative capacities means that cultural learning, in the sense of learning that can be extended to a group of individuals, is not an option open to them (Tomasello, Kruger, and Ratner 1993). One important consequence of this highly circumscribed imitative capacity in chimpanzees is that they cannot generate any interpersonal gesture conveying a stable meaning that is identical for all members of the group: every chimpanzee is capable of inventing a new communicative signal which it can add to its own repertoire, but no other member of the species will reproduce a signal it has seen another member make, preferring to create a new one. Such a mode of communication makes cultural transmission within a group difficult, and any transgenerational transmission that does not occur between parent and child impossible. What transmission does take place is of the most elementary type, such as is found in any mammal.

Summing up: communication is a function that evolves autonomously, starting with *Homo*. Naturally, this protolanguage already constitutes a tremendous advantage for both cognition and communication. There would not appear to be unchallengeable proof that one of these functions predominated over the other. Hence, I will consider them both foundational. Communication leads to protolanguage, and the latter in turn gives rise to language. In addition to the fundamental genetic determinants, the structure of present-day language is also due to its complex relationship with thought, social activities, communicative needs, manual skills, and cultural transmission.

If with regard to the emergence and initial development of language we may concede that language had an extremely high degree of autonomy compared to other mental processes, when it comes to the consolidation of language, then the communicative function becomes the preeminent factor, especially rewarding from the point of view of survival. We will delve further into this matter in section 6.1.4.

6.1.3 The Micro–Macro Cortical Ratio

A first elementary biological observation is that the larger an animal, the larger its brain is. This consideration is, however, unsatisfactory, for each animal must devote the same percentage of its brain to bodily control functions. For instance, an elephant has a brain that is four times as large as that of a human being, but it is certainly not more intelligent than a human being. It simply has a body to manage that weighs about a ton.

A more accurate analysis will lead us to consider the proportional variation in the weight of the brain in different beings, and in particular the extraordinary increase in the neocortex in human beings compared with the dimensions of the body. On the basis of a rich collection of data on comparative neuroanatomy, the biologist Harry Jerison (1973) has proposed an *encephalization quotient* (EQ). The EQ is based on the relationship between the brain and the body. It represents the measure of how much the real dimensions of the brain exceed the dimensions that would be predicted for an animal of that size. For instance, apes, dolphins, and parrots have brains that are significantly larger than would be expected for animals of their size.

Primates tend to have brains twice the size one would expect when compared with other mammals. In their turn, humans have brains three times the predicted size compared with other primates, and, therefore, six times the size of mammals. Jerison argues that primates achieved a critical brain mass that would support their cognitive capacities. Further development of the critical mass led to the development of language. Jerison also proposes a threshold of 600 ccs as necessary to support the language capacity. The simple equation that is adopted is that the higher the EQ, the more intelligent is the being possessing that brain (Jerison and Jerison 1988). However, the issue is more complex than that.

Another biologist, Richard Passingham (1982), has highlighted the fact that even if brain dimensions increase principally in absolute terms, it is the cerebral cortex, which in primates accounts for 70 percent of the total volume of the brain, that has the greatest increase. Monkeys have from 50 percent to 70 percent more cortex than Prosimians, once the parts they have in common are subtracted, and primates have about 300 percent more. Once Passingham has assigned monkeys an EQ of 1, he calculates an EQ of 2.5 for apes and Australopithecines, an EQ of 4 for *Homo habilis*, with *Homo sapiens* reaching an EQ of approximately 7.

Using a more sophisticated measurement technique for calculating the subtraction of common brain areas, the anthropologist Terry Deacon (1997) claims that the increase in brain volume in apes compared with other species has been systematically undervalued, and in particular humans diverge radically from the predicted developmental trend. The encephalization quotient is a valid approximation for lower species, not for the comparison between primates and other species, and even less so for comparison between different species of primates.

The measurements made by Jerison and Passingham do not therefore do justice to the difference between humans and apes. However, the issue is not simply a quantitative one: not only do humans have larger brains, but they have a brain that is very special, for it enables them to think and speak. According to Jerison in the first instance, and Passingham after him, what counts is the amount of cortex available to the human compared with the other primates. It is again Deacon who criticizes this position, for achieving symbolic referential capabilities cannot be a result simply of reaching a given threshold in computational power. It is not just the size of the brain that renders language possible, but rather the brain's macro-architecture that reorganizes its structure in such a way as to enable the human brain to achieve the qualitative leaps that other animals fail to make. In practice, each time brain volume increases, the new parts are not simply added on to the preexisting sectors; instead, the brain reorganizes the entire structure so as to render it more functional.

Deacon does not go as far as assigning numerical values to the effects of brain reorganization, which is, instead, what I will try to do now. What concerns me is not so much an exact quantification of the differences, but establishing the degree of magnitude of the comparison. If the thesis of functional reorganization is correct, then the criterion to be employed is not addition, but multiplication. Naturally, the key lies initially in micro-architecture, but it is macroarchitecture that renders human capacities incommensurable with those of other primates. I will now try to justify why I hypothesize a relationship of multiplication instead of one of addition.

Great apes reach a brain capacity of 400 ccs. In actual fact, the gorilla goes well over that mark. Nevertheless, given its body size, we may consider this animal as comparable with the other apes. However, Australopithe-cines, our real ancestors, already possessed a brain capacity of 450 ccs. The 50 cc difference may seem a modest quantity, but they acquire great impor-tance if they are devoted to cognition and communication. Let us return to the data from Jerison which I quoted earlier and which demonstrate that primates have twice the predicted brain size in relation to their bodies.

If we assume that half of a primate's brain (200 ccs) is allotted to bodily control and that the other half (200 ccs) to cognition, then we see that the brain of Australopithecines, who have to manage a body roughly equiva-lent in size to that of the larger apes, has a potential capacity that may be assigned to cognition of 250 ccs, which is a good 25 percent more com-pared to their tree-bound cousins. It is that extra 25 percent, which becomes an exceptional 150 percent extra in *Homo habilis*, that makes the differ-ence: *Homo* have the same body dimensions and equivalent physical abili-ties, and assign the entire increase in brain volume to cognition and to the reorganization of the way the brain works.

Homo sapiens finds himself today with the usual 200 ccs with which to manage his bodily functions, and something like 1,250 ccs available for higher psychological functions. The numerical factor alone is significant in itself, because we possess a brain three times the size of other primates. The EQ, which only takes microarchitecture into consideration—it calculates only the number of neurons—increases the ratio even more, reaching a figure of 6/7 times that of primates (1200:200 = 6). But even this ratio is not sufficient to explain the intellectual distance that separates us from primates.

Let us therefore now consider macroarchitecture, that is, the special organization of the human nervous system, whose peculiarity has been highlighted by all the studies on neuropsychology. Let us suppose that 3 percent of every increase in brain volume is assigned to organization, that is, is given the responsibility for macroarchitecture. What I am interested in is establishing the principle that part of the brain is dedicated to the management of the brain itself, to optimizing its functioning. I do not have hard data to support my approximate assessment of 3 percent, which is based more on architectural considerations than on anatomical considerations. The equations I will work out, however, do not vary very much in relation to the variation of the percentage of the brain's macroarchitecture.

If we start off again from Australopithecines, this means that 3 percent of 50 ccs (1.5 ccs) is allotted to handling the brain's macroarchitecture. The part that handles the organization of the brain cannot simply be added on: since it makes the brain work in a different fashion, it must be treated as a multiplication factor and not an addition factor. It is as if in a team of 33 workers, one were to stop working directly and were to devote himself to optimizing the work of the other 32 men.

It is this figure (1.5) that becomes the multiplication factor for the rest of the brain (i.e., 48.5 ccs, obtained by subtracting 1.5 from 50). The result (48.5 × 1.5 = 72.7) must first be added to the brain that both humans and primates have in common (72.7 + 200), and must then be divided by the brain volume of primates (200 ccs). The result of this calculation, (272.7/200), is the figure 1.6: Australopithecines have a cognitive capacity of approximately one and a half times that of other primates, and not the same capacity as Passingham has argued. As far back as Australopithecines there is no comparison possible between humans and primates.

The *micro–macro cortical ratio*, which takes into account the growth of micro- and macrocognition, in relation to that part of the cortex common to both species being compared, may be represented by the following equation:

Species A

microcognition (cognitive cortex)   ×

macrocognition (cortex allotted to the handling of the architecture)   +

common cortex

Species B

microcognition (cognitive cortex)   ×

macrocognition (cortex allotted to the handling of the architecture)   +

common cortex

The volume of brain assignable to body functions is 200 ccs. The volume of common cortex is therefore 200 ccs (400 − 200 = 200). When comparing *Homo* and primates, the only common denominator will be common cortex.

With regard to modern *Homo sapiens*, the figures to be considered are those relating to the brain, which measures 1,400 ccs. Of these, 200 ccs are assigned to bodily function control, and another 200 ccs constitute the cortex they have in common with other primates. Of the remaining 1,000 ccs, microcognition is carried out by 97 percent of the volume, that is, 970 ccs. Macrocognition management functions occupy the remaining 3 percent, that is, 30 ccs. With regard to primates, of their total brain volume of 400 ccs, and subtracting the 200 ccs allotted to bodily control functions, only the 200 ccs of common cortex are taken into consideration.

We may now calculate the cortex's micro–macro ratio between contemporary *Homo sapiens* and primates: (970 × 30 + 200): 200 = 146. This figure indicates that the modern human has an intellectual capacity over 100 times superior to that of an ape. Although the figure might seem to be decidedly high, it nevertheless comes much nearer to assessing the differences between humans and primates in realistic terms than do the figures of previous studies. Even the most primitive of *Homo* possesses an intellectual capacity that is far, far higher than that of the most ingenious primate ever described by a fascinated observer. I am not talking about fitness, because if we consider swallows, foxes, or whales in relation to their environment, then we find they are capable of mastering the challenges that environment sets them. Comparisons become vacuous if we forget that the topic we are focusing on is the ability to communicate.

The micro–macro cortical ratio may also be used to quantify differences between different types of *Homo*. The basic idea remains that of separating

	Primates	Australopithecus	Homo habilis	Homo erectus	Archaic homo sapiens	Modern homo sapiens
Total brain	400	450	700	900	1200	1400
Bodily control	200	200	200	200	200	200
Common cortex	200	200	200	200	200	200
Microcognition 97%	0	48.5	291	485	776	970
Macrocognition 3%	0	1.5	9	15	24	30
Primates	1	1.4	14	37	94	146
Australopithecus		1	10	27	69	107
Homo habilis			1	2.6	6.6	10
Homo erectus				1	2.5	3.9
Archaic homo sapiens					1	1.5

Figure 6.4

The micro–macro cortical ratio, with macrocognition estimated at 3 percent. The upper half of the figure furnishes brain capacity in absolute terms, expressed in ccs, which then constitutes the basis for the comparison outlined in the lower half of the figure.

the cortex assigned to microcognition from that assigned to macrocognition, and subtracting the common parts. For example, the difference between *Homo erectus* and *Homo habilis* is the following:

Homo erectus
encephalous 700 ccs (900–200)
common cortex 200 ccs
microcognition: 485 ccs, that is, 97 percent of 500 ccs
macrocognition: 15 ccs, that is to say 3 percent

$$\frac{485 \times 15 + 200}{291 \times 9 + 200} = \frac{7,475}{2,819} = 2.6$$

Homo habilis
encephalous 500 ccs (700–200)
common cortex 200 ccs
microcognition: 291 ccs, that is, 97 percent of 300 ccs
macrocognition: 9 ccs, that is, 3 percent

A ratio of 2.6 means that *Homo erectus* is approximately two and a half times more intelligent than *Homo habilis*.

Performing the calculation in the same way yields a ratio of 2.5 to describe the relationship between *Homo sapiens* and *Homo erectus*. It is clear that these differences are extremely significant. They are achieved in small incremental steps, generation after generation. After all, to progress from one species of *Homo* to another takes at least a million years, during which many thousands of generations follow each other. Figure 6.4 shows the micro–macro cortical ratio for the various types of *Homo*.

If we also take macroarchitecture into consideration, then the reason we should expect a qualitative jump between animal communication and human communication is quite clear. Corticalization explains a maximum ratio of 7:1 between humans and primates, while brain reorganization brings about relationships of multiplication in *Homo*. Without allowing figures to overly fascinate us, it must nevertheless be admitted that the relationship between humans and primates is better described by tens instead of numbers under ten.

The human species has not simply added a large number of neurons. Rather, a significant number of those neurons has been assigned to handling the function of the other neurons, modulating human cognitive capacities with a degree of efficacy that was previously impossible. From a computational standpoint, not only do we possess the most oversized machine extant in nature, but we have also developed the ability to exploit it to the full.

Brain development I will end this section with a few observations on the development of the brain, from childhood to adulthood. My treatment will follow the accurate picture offered by the developmental neuropsychologists Bates, Thal, and Janowsky (1992), integrating it with data provided by Elman et al. (1996). At birth, the human brain is much more immature than it is in other primates, and it remains extraordinarily plastic for many years. The main postnatal developmental processes are hemispheric specialization, synaptogenesis, the growth of the dendrites, and myelination. By the age of 8 to 9 months, most of the brain connections between the major cortical areas have been established. In addition, the metabolic activity in the brain reaches the level of adults.

The feature that is most closely connected to cognitive and linguistic development between 16 and 24 months is the spectacular increase in the number of synapses within and between the cortical regions. Between 9 and 24 months the density of synaptic connections reaches a level of 150 percent that of an adult. Metabolic activity at all levels of the brain reaches its peak at the age of 4. The extremely high ability to learn in our early years is based on this increase in brain activity that substantiate it.

But perhaps the most interesting point about the development of the brain is that this rapidly achieved peak of neurons, connections, synapses, and metabolic activity in the brain is followed by a slow decline, from the age of 4 on. In this second stage of development, with the exception of myelination, for each of the additive events described we find a complementary event that is subtractive. Cell formation and migration are followed by the death of many cells; the projection of axons is followed by a phase of retraction of axons; synaptogenesis by a phase of synaptic degeneration; the explosion of metabolic activity by a slow decrease of all levels of cerebral metabolism.

Brain development consists of a first stage of rapid superproduction, followed by a stage of relatively slow selective elimination. For instance, neural density in the frontal cortex at 2 is over 55 percent more than that of an adult (even if the so-called *pruning* process is active from birth), decreasing to over 10 percent above typical adult levels around the age of 7. Analogously, synaptic degeneration and metabolic activity diminish gradually until the age of adolescence when they become stable.

Deacon (1997) offers an interesting explanation for this rapid growth and slow decline of all the brain's microfunctions. He hypothesizes that selectively eliminating neurons solves the problem of the specificity of the objective, which is underdetermined from a genetic standpoint, essentially to guarantee that plasticity of the brain which characterizes our species.

Neurons tend to superimpose axons, and the latter connect up to a large number of potential objectives during the initial stages of growth; only a small fraction of these connections are maintained in adulthood—those that have shown their efficacy. The remaining connections are eliminated by competition between axons coming from different neurons and converging on the same synaptic objectives. This Darwinian-like process is responsible for a large part of the sophisticated control and adjustment of the patterns of neural connections that account for and explain the precise adaptation of the brain's functions.

As an alternative to the pruning metaphor, it seems to me that the brain is *sculpted* in the passage from childhood to adulthood, both in terms of the number of neurons and of the dendritic connections between them, and in terms of active synapses. The idea of a sculpture underlines not only the aspect of the global growth of the brain's activity observable from birth to the age of 4, but also the subtractive activity that offers a more accurate picture of the transition from the age of 4 to the age of 16.

The sculpture that emerges is equipped with an overall efficiency coefficient that is greatly superior to the coefficient that would be obtained if the number of neurons, dendrites, and synapses remained unchanged from birth to adulthood. We obtain an accurate picture of what happens to the human brain only when we consider both the micro and macro aspects of the brain, that is, the elements and their organization.

6.1.4   The Evolution of Language

Before I can complete my argument, I must outline the main different hypotheses that have been advanced with regard to the evolution of communication.

The linguistic continuity hypothesis   The linguistic continuity hypothesis was first formulated by Jean Piaget, even though the Swiss scholar limited himself to ontogeny, making only a small number of observations on phylogenesis. This hypothesis asserts that language derives directly from extralinguistic communicative capacities, as shown in figure 6.5. Piaget (1923) believed that the motor system was the precursor of language. But strictly speaking, language has no precursor, as Chomsky and Fodor point out to Piaget and his collaborators in the debate faithfully reproduced by Piattelli-Palmarini (1980). On that occasion Piaget attempted to reconcile Chomsky's vision with his own theories. However, in a series of conversations whose harshness the old and influential Swiss psychologist was totally unaccustomed to, Chomsky reiterated the fact that the two

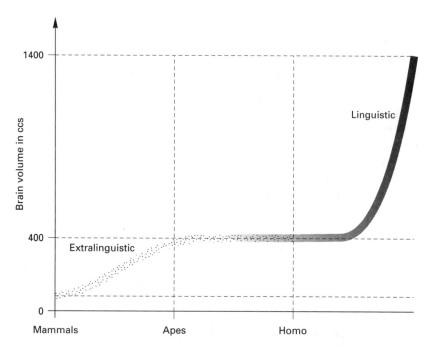

Figure 6.5
The linguistic continuity hypothesis.

viewpoints were irremediably opposed. In particular, Chomsky pointed out that if the theory of the motor system as a precursor was true, then tetraplegic children should exhibit serious language deficits. On the contrary, a block in the motor system is not accompanied by any difficulty in acquiring complete mastery over language.

The continuity hypothesis has been implicitly adopted by the first scholars who tried to teach primates some type of language. All of them encountered insurmountable obstacles. For a review of the various attempts made, I refer readers to Joel Wallman's (1992) accurate critical analysis. His reconstruction of the different projects devoted to educating chimpanzees to language use leaves no room for doubt: there is no likeness whatsoever between human communication and animal communication. Notwithstanding the efforts of human teachers, everything—from lexicon to syntax to semantics—remained different, both from a qualitative and quantitative point of view.

With regard to pragmatics, two scholars of primates, Patricia Greenfield and Sue Savage-Rumbaugh (1993) claim that chimpanzees are able to employ the pragmatics of repetition. Once four chimpanzees (two *Pan troglodytes* and two *Pan paniscus*) had mastered a symbolic system developed for human beings, they managed to repeat a part of or an entire set of symbols used by the research workers in the same way as the symbols had been used by children who formed the control group.

It is by no means proved that the sequence of actions carried out by the chimpanzees has the same meaning for the chimpanzees as it has for the children with whom the animals were compared. Other animals may also be taught to respect the turn-taking rule: parrots brought up in captivity even give the impression of carrying out a conversation with the humans they live with. What this demonstrates is that parrots and chimpanzees have sufficient brain capacities to be able to learn to do something that, *when it is spontaneously executed by a young human*, witnesses his innate capacities.

Similarly, a 6-year-old child may be taught to swim under water. It would, however, be peculiar to claim that swimming under water demonstrates that humans exhibit the same ability as fish to remain under water, even if an ingenuous observer with a limited temporal viewpoint might believe that such swimming abilities show startling analogies between the innate abilities of fish and the acquired abilities of humans.

The linguistic discontinuity hypothesis   For decades, Chomsky has been the most radical advocate of the linguistic discontinuity hypothesis, to the point of contending that the principles of Darwinian selection cannot be applied to language. Starting from the assumption of linguistic modularity, Chomsky hypothesized that the language capacity that typifies human beings arose from a sudden, complex genetic mutation with no history of gradual selection. In Chomsky's opinion, language did not evolve at all, since it is meaningless to speak of one-tenth of a language, then of two-tenths of a language, and so on.

Massimo Piattelli-Palmarini (1989) subsequently toned down Chomsky's claims, conceding that language might have evolved, although not with the evolutionary function of improving communication. In his opinion, the primary advantage linguistic mutants had was that language increased the human potential for thought. Only as a secondary benefit was language used for communication; that is, it parasitized on the selective pressure that thinking necessities exerted over the human brain. On this view, language grafts itself onto the human system as a fortunate "side effect," enriching the capacities of cognition and communication already present in humans by equipping them with an enormous potential they did not previously possess (see figure 6.6).

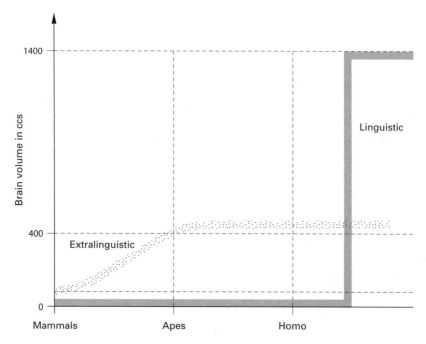

Figure 6.6
The linguistic discontinuity hypothesis.

Hauser, Chomsky, and Fitch (2002) dealt with the theme of language evolution in a more technical manner, distinguishing a uniquely human "narrow" faculty of language from the "broad" faculty of language which consists of adaptations for communication that have analogies or homologies in other animal species. They further claimed that *recursion* is the core (and perhaps the only) component of the narrow faculty of language so defined. In these authors' view, the recursion mechanism is probably not an adaptation for communication, but might have been shaped by the demands of other cognitive tasks (e.g., spatial navigation) and later made available to communication. In this perspective, the inclusion of recursion in the language faculty is a discontinuous event in the evolution of human communication, even if the recursion mechanism might have evolved gradually for other reasons. Pinker and Jackendoff (2005; Jackendoff and Pinker 2005) argued against this thesis, maintaining that the evidence points at language as a complex adaptation for the communication of knowledge and intentions, and criticizing the broad–narrow distinction as overly restrictive and too coarse from an evolutionary point of view.

The most serious criticisms leveled at linguistic discontinuity have been formulated by the linguist Steven Pinker (1994, 1997). Pinker demonstrates that Chomsky's original claim was based on a misinterpretation of the principles of Darwinian evolution. Even small increments help improve the possibility of individual reproduction: natural selection does not require great leaps. Small advantages available through hundreds of thousands of years may have been sufficient. If we reject the hypothesis of grammatical competence all of a sudden being instantly available to *Homo* and distinguishing them from other animals, then any intermediate linguistic structure can suffice to guarantee an evolutionary advantage to those who possessed it.

According to the linguist Derek Bickerton (1990), *Homo erectus* possessed a protolanguage similar to the child's two-word stage of development or to contemporary pidgin languages spoken by adults. *Pidgin* is an elementary language with an elementary grammar. It is associative rather than compositional, and humans develop such a form when they have to communicate without any interlocutor knowing the language spoken by any of the other participants. Sometimes, pidgin becomes a sort of *lingua franca*, as is the pidgin English presently used in the South Pacific. Bickerton (1981) has produced a masterly reconstruction of the creation of a case of pidgin when at the beginning of the century the Hawaiian sugar plantations underwent explosive growth, and were obliged to have recourse to labor from China, Korea, Japan, the Philippines, Portugal, and Puerto Rico. In these conditions, pidgin developed rapidly. Protolanguage constitutes the intermediate step between full syntactic competence and the complete lack of a computational structure devoted to it.

Pinker (1994, 1997) also clarifies another delicate point: since language needs, by definition, at least two interlocutors, whom could the first grammatical mutant talk to? The answer is that even if her companions lacked specialized brain circuits, they could at least have understood in part what the mutant was saying by using their general intelligence. To this argument I would add another, that of shared context. It should not be forgotten that we are speaking of special primates who possess a neocortex that is 300 percent larger than that of other apes, who have already become skilled communicators without language, and are now capable of connecting vowels to consonants. Selection may have rewarded small increments in linguistic abilities, favoring in each generation those speakers that hearers could best comprehend and those hearers who could best understand what speakers said.

The hypothesis of extralinguistic continuity and linguistic discontinuity I beg the reader's pardon for the title, but a pedantic label is better than an obscure one. The aim of this third hypothesis is to be compatible with the strong Chomskyan assumptions of an evolutionary discontinuity of the language module, while at the same time saving part of the communicative heritage of primates, to be precise extralinguistic communication.

I will employ as my basic reference Robbins Burling (1993), who best synthesizes the key idea. After a careful investigation of all the evidence on how primates communicate both in natural and in artificial conditions, he reaches the conclusion that communication among primates possesses a remarkable set of features similar to nonverbal human communication. These characteristics are:

1. The gradualism of the signal From a smile one may pass on to a grimace without any break. Gradualism must be compared with the nature of language, which is discrete and based on continuous contrasts.

2. Little need for learning One learns when to smile, but how to smile is almost completely genetically determined.

3. Capacity to inform Primates display excellence at conveying information concerning emotion and volition, and a parallel poverty in conveying information concerning the external world; by contrast, language is not especially suitable for transmitting information regarding emotional states, but it is highly effective when talking about the world.

4. Incomplete voluntary control One can make an effort to smile, but managing to do so in a credible fashion is hard. A convincing demonstration of how difficult it is to exert voluntary control over one's nonverbal communicative abilities is the gallery of horrors of photographs taken of people posing and trying to smile.

5. Lack of productivity Meanings never produced previously cannot be constructed in the way new words and phrases are generated. Although it is possible to state that something—for example, a poem or an original idea—has never been expressed before, asking whether a smile or a tear is the repetition of previous smiles or tears is meaningless.

6. The nonexistence of displacement Displacement in space or time, namely the exchange of information concerning something that is not happening "here and now," is not possible. Language, on the contrary, allows one to speak of events that are distant in time and space.

The final two features are taken up by Charles Hockett (1960) in his pioneering work on the differences between animal languages and human language. Burling is highly skeptical about the continuity between animal communication and language, while he underlines the similarities between animal communication and nonverbal human communication. Burling's conclusion is that *Homo* possess a nonverbal communicative competence that is essentially analogous to that exhibited by higher mammals. What distinguishes man is not communicative ability in general, but that aspect of communicative competence which is specifically linguistic. Language constitutes an element of *discontinuity* in the evolution of communication, and not its smooth continuation, as figure 6.7 illustrates.

The main criticism that may be leveled at Burling is that, apart from points 5 and 6 as developed by Hockett, the remaining four points do not allow us to discriminate between language and extralinguistic communication. Instead, these points allow us to distinguish intentionally communicative behavior (be it linguistic or extralinguistic) from noncommunicative behavior. Furthermore, in remaining faithful to the Chomskyan position, Burling neglects the important points of convergence between extralinguistic communication and linguistic communication in humans.

A similar position has been assumed by the evolutionary neuroscientist Michael Corballis (2002), who depicts a scenario like the following. With

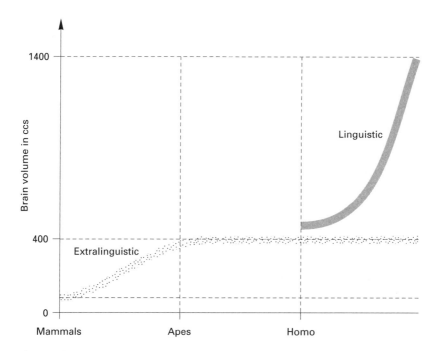

Figure 6.7
The hypothesis of extralinguistic continuity and linguistic discontinuity.

the emergence of bipedalism, the early *Homo* evolved more sophisticated ways to gesture to one another than their primate ancestors. These gestures consisted of relatively isolated signs until around 2 million years ago, when brain size increased. This led to the combining of gestures to form new meanings: thus, eventually, was syntax born. The face became increasingly involved in gesturing, especially when the use of tools increasingly occupied the hand. Corballis's gestural theory implies that the switch from visual gestures to vocal ones was gradual, and that for much of our evolutionary history gestures were both visual and vocal. At first, manual and facial gestures were accompanied by grunts, as later vocal language is embellished by manual gestures.

Giacomo Rizzolatti and Michael Arbib (1998) try to ground the gestural theory of language on the *mirror neurons system*, that is, the premotor neurons that discharge not only when the monkey (or the human) executes an action but also when the monkey (or the human) observes a similar meaningful hand movement made by the experimenter. In an audacious move, they claim that the mirror system's capacity to generate and recognize a set of actions provides the evolutionary basis for *language parity*, in which an utterance means the same for both speaker and hearer. Mirror neurons offer the first brick for the development of communication, especially of the extralinguistic type. Thanks to them, each gesture we perceive resounds within us, allowing an immediate and intuitive comprehension of its basic function. However, to extend their role from grasping recognition to dialogue generation, from motor simulation to mental sharedness, is a stretching exercise that risks lowering the acknowledgment of their importance for the motor system and its correlates. Communicative gestures are perceived for their "gestural" component by the mirror system, and for their "communicative" component by the intentional network I shall present in section 6.3.1. Thus, the activation of the mirror network when a communicative gestures is perceived does not mean that mirror neurons are responding to communication.

A brilliant side development of this framework has been produced by Jean-Louis Dessalles (2007), who considers language a game in which the "prize" is to join a network of relationships, to be accepted, and to win a valued place in it. He criticizes a simplistic application of the cooperation principle (intended as a symmetrical exchange of information, as in Dunbar 1996) in order to explain the actual language use. Even when the speaker is freely spreading useful information, she is not driven by simple altruistic motives. In fact, in a conversation it is the speaker who plays the role of the supplicant, seeking to gain a social favor from her interlocutors, while the hearers play the role of the judge, assessing the salience of what they hear. Dessalles's idea is that information is exchanged for status: hearers are willing to grant status to relevant speakers. Humans try to earn social prestige through communication; hence we need a more complex notion of cooperation to explain language use.

The cognitive discontinuity hypothesis   What differentiates *Homo* from other primates is their respective quantity of neocortex, which is put to both communicative and globally cognitive use. My hypothesis, therefore, is that the neocortex increases general intelligence enormously, rendering human communicative capacities no longer comparable with those of other great apes, as shown in figure 6.8.

The increase in brain volume that comes about in *Homo habilis* is due to mutually reinforcing factors of a cognitive, communicative, and manual nature, which trigger off a virtuous circle that continues to reward further investment in neocortex. What escapes Burling and the supporters of extralinguistic continuity is that human beings' extended cognitive capacities also modify previous abilities, such as that of using gestures for

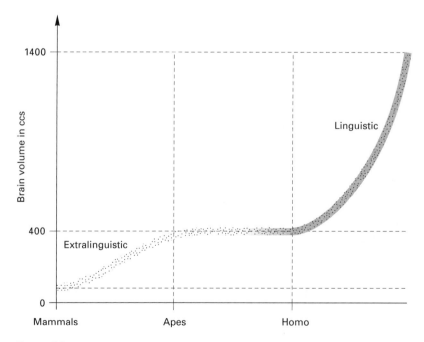

Figure 6.8
The cognitive discontinuity hypothesis.

communicating. With regard to communication, I do not believe we share much in common, not even with those highly intelligent animals, the apes. True, they are the ones most like us and our nearest evolutionary relatives. But this does not mean that the differences between primate and human communication are themselves continuous and gradual. Even the oft-cited datum, according to which 95 percent of the DNA sequence is shared between humans and chimpanzees (e.g., Britten 2002), should, I feel, be interpreted in relative and not in absolute terms. In the first place, as Pinker has underscored, 5 percent of the genome, appearing in the right place, makes a world of difference—especially if differences concern regulatory genes. Second, I am aware that I have more things in common with a gorilla than with a giraffe, and more in common with a bear than with a lizard, and much more in common with a ladybird than with a fig, and infinitely more with a cyclamen than with the Riace bronzes. The scales of likeness are suggestive, but only on condition that the differences be kept well in mind.

The cognitive discontinuity hypothesis posits that a first, fundamental leap comes about thanks to the increase in the size of the brain, which modifies *Homo*'s overall cognitive capacities, and hence their communicative capacities, in a spectacular fashion. At this point, extralinguistic communicative capacity abandons the developmental pattern of other animals. With regard to language, we may hypothesize one or more genetic mutations thanks to which a first *Homo* exhibited some form of linguistic capacity. The difference with Chomsky is that he hypothesizes this mutational event to be (at least initially) unrelated to communication. From an evolutionary standpoint, instead, the initial mutation brings a protolanguage into being, and this protolanguage is maintained and developed for the purposes of communication (though other, subsidiary goals are also achieved through the use of protolanguage). Of the other uses to which language is put, and which contribute to its consolidation, the most important are those that are connected to the support it may lend to cognitive activity, in particular to thought and memory. A virtuous circle is established between thought and language, as a result of which any increment in the former facilitates the latter and vice versa.

In other terms, on my hypothesis it is those (already existing) enhanced cognitive structures that ensure that language can be *immediately* available for use. On the one hand, the increase in the neocortex makes it possible for a large amount of cerebral matter to be dedicated exclusively to language. On the other hand, brain plasticity allows central cognitive processes to develop a new equilibrium in communicative competence by balancing out the emergence of a functional language module with the preexisting extralinguistic modality, which already includes the system's capacity for interaction, stratified in various degrees of complexity in animals, mammals, and primates. This first qualitative leap realizes the inception of extralinguistic communication and creates the conditions for the following step.

This second step corresponds to the onset of protolanguage in *Homo erectus*, which may be accounted for by an initial genetic mutation. Subsequently, communicative efficacy which had never been realized before in nature turns out to confer an evolutionary advantage that is sufficient to consolidate the new trait in the population's genetic pool. This sparks off a synergy in which communication (which, previously, had only been extralinguistic) improves along with protolanguage, and protolanguage develops further thanks to the pressures exerted by communicative needs. In enriching itself with the linguistic component, communication forges the protolanguage, gradually transforming it into something very like the language we know now. Once human beings have developed linguistic capacity, their global communicative competence gains an explosive potential.

We now reach the third step, which brings us to modern humans. We must recall that in approximately the same time span both the brain areas allotted to language and those assigned to manual activity developed. A virtuous circle similar to that described above between cognition and language is now triggered off between communicative capacity and embodied cognitive capacity. Indeed, the combined resources of language and manual dexterity launch *Homo habilis* in the direction of the brain development of early *Homo sapiens*, and the latter in the direction of modern *Homo sapiens*.

An innovative path of investigation into language evolution has been traced by the mathematicians Martin Nowak and Natalia Komarova (2001). Through an ingenious use of evolutionary game theory, they formulate the *paradox of language acquisition*. They define grammatical coherence and find a coherence threshold that gives conditions for a population of speakers to evolve and maintain a stable language. They explore the conditions under which natural selection favors the emergence of a recursive, *rule-based grammatical system*, responsible of language. In contrast to such rule-based grammars, one might consider *list-based grammars* that consist only of a finite number of sentences. Such list-based grammars can be seen as a primitive evolutionary alternative to rule-based grammars. Individuals would acquire their mental grammar not by searching for underlying rules, but simply by memorizing words or sentences and their meanings: list-based grammars do not allow for creativity at the level of syntax (Komarova and Nowak 2003).

A possible extension of their work is to see linguistic communication as a rule-based grammar, whereas extralinguistic communication is a list-based grammar. The respective properties of the grammars would be similar to those specified by Nowak and Komarova.

The phase we are living in now began only 35,000 years ago, when the union of the potential for language and for external cognition gave rise to permanent linguistic structures, generating writing. Human beings have invented history: a third qualitative leap has come about. Figure 6.9 highlights the relationship of the evolution of the species to the increase in communicative capacity.

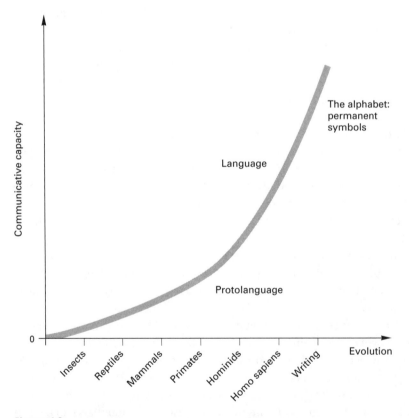

Figure 6.9
The relationship between evolution and communicative capacity.

The key point in my reconstruction is that the brain areas assigned to cognition are significantly enlarged in *Homo,* with respect to the same areas in other primates. Obviously, all animals—and mammals in particular—know how to interact with one another, but the brain resources allotted to communication are in no way comparable with those of *Homo.* It can, of course, be affirmed that we share with other mammals, and above all with primates, a basis of social interaction; but thanks to superior cognitive capacities, *Homo* have been able to develop an extralinguistic competence that can in no way be compared to that of other living beings. To this must be added linguistic competence, a capacity that only arose in our own lineage. Finally, a third level is guaranteed by external cognition that supports language, enabling communication to acquire permanence, thereby allowing transgenerational cultural transmission. Figure 6.10 illustrates the three qualitative leaps that distinguish humans from other animals from the standpoint of communication: cognitive, linguistic, and cultural.

Let us return to what primatologists say in their field and laboratory studies: primates are excellent communicators, with a complex social life.

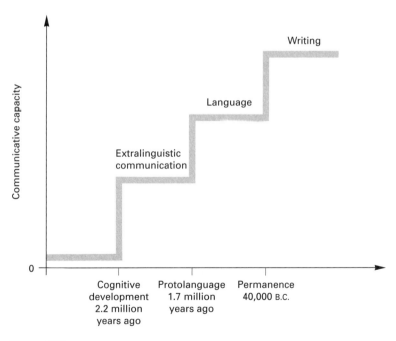

Figure 6.10

The three qualitative leaps made by communication from animals to contemporary human beings. The temporal axis is not to scale.

The same scholars concurrently illustrate the limits that nonhuman apes are unable to overcome in acquiring any type of language whatsoever—linguistic or extralinguistic. The most well-known study (Premack 1988) demonstrates that chimpanzees never, under any circumstance, achieve the communicative competence of a 2.5-year-old child. Couched in my terms, nonhuman apes are animals that have adapted perfectly to their own natural habitat, but there is an enormous gulf between their cognitive resources and those of a child, even a newborn child. In this sense, the 2.5-year rule is extraordinarily optimistic: I believe no comparison can be made between an adult chimpanzee and a child even of 12 months. A 1-year-old child who exhibited the cognitive capacities of an adult chimp would be instantly recognized as being seriously mentally disabled. If we then take brain structure into consideration, the differences at birth are absolute.

Tomasello (2008) offers evidence that the evolutionary foundations of human language lie in the attempts of primates to influence the behavior of conspecifics, not their mental states. Attempting to influence the attention and mental states of others is a uniquely human activity, and so must have arisen only after the human and chimpanzee lineages split from one another some 6 million years ago.

A nonhuman ape is not a human being with a smaller number of capacities, but an animal that is different from us. We do not "descend from apes," as the imaginative vulgarizations of Darwinian theory would have us believe. Instead, we share common ancestors from fairly recent times, which may be traced back to about 15 million years ago. However, 15 million years is a gigantic amount of time for creatures with our life span: approximately 1 million generations. It would be the same as establishing relationships with other mammals (primates excluded), with which we have many points in common (first and foremost, breast feeding) and with which we again share common ancestors, if we go back some 200 million years. All these numbers are as colossal from a human standpoint as they are ridiculously minute on a planetary scale. For this reason the likeness metaphor must be taken with great caution: as I have already stated, human beings share almost every feature with any other living creature, if we compare any living organism on Earth with any system on Earth that does not possess life. We do not resemble only chimpanzees, but also rhinoceroses, ostriches, and butterflies; even orchids and oak trees are our cousins, to a certain extent, relative to comparing ourselves with a stone or with the north star.

Games in evolution   Where can we pinpoint the origin of our behavior games, as I have defined them so far? The basic structure of a behavior game is based essentially on those speech acts classified as *commissives*, where agents commit themselves to carrying out a given action, or at least to try to carry it out in good faith. For an actor to be able to carry out a commissive, and for her partner to be able to validate that act, they must possess a communicative competence capable of handling time: past, present, and future.

In fact, A can commit herself to some future action, provided B commits himself to carrying out some other action in an even more distant future. For instance, A may promise to make a spear for B, provided B promises to give A part of the prey that he will kill with the spear. Something of this nature must really have happened; otherwise we would have found no trace of the systematic production of hunting tools and household tools, which started approximately 500,000 years ago. No toolmaker would have the time and the opportunity to organize this sort of protoindustry, if he had not been able to exchange his products with other goods.

True, many exchanges take place in the present, here and now. A gives B a spear, and B gives A some meat. But any barter system requires its agents to be able to conceive of and handle temporal dislocation. In the first chapter I pointed out that only linguistic communication can enable a speaker to refer to a time and a place which are different from the ones in which the interaction is taking place. Hence, to be able to speak of behavior games we must wait until the symbolic language is developed; and only *Homo sapiens* have mastered this instrument.

Furthermore, in order to construct a game of any complexity, a social pact must exist that the actors can refer to as a guarantee that their promises will be fulfilled. The oldest social pacts that tied together groups of humans concern a limited number of areas: sexual behavior, food acquisition, and the protection of the young.

Broadly speaking, humankind organizes sexuality on the basis of a relatively stable couple. Within this relationship procreation is carried out and the father guarantees he will provide for the mother and the child. In exchange, the mother, who depends with her children on the father's ability to procure food, guarantees faithfulness; that is to say, the father does not run the risk of committing his life to bringing up children who are not his. It is vital that the female's faithfulness and the male's reliability extend over a long period, possibly 6–7 years, until the young become relatively independent. Unfaithful females and unreliable males are unattractive partners for *Homo* who wish to perpetuate their genetic inheritance.

Even hunting in groups, as practiced by *Homo erectus*, requires tight organization. This activity, however, seems to depend less on long-standing social pacts. A commitment of even a few days is sufficient to organize a cohesive group. Finally, if the protection of the village and of the young is to be effective, it must be handled communally. Nevertheless this activity too would seem to require a commitment that lasts several days. Subsequently, by laying solid foundations of trust through successful mutual interaction, the possibility of long-term reciprocal trust is built up, thereby giving the group stability.

In addition to the three types we have already seen, the social precursors of behavior games should also include those stipulated individually by pairs, in which the group is less involved, though the latter remains in the background as the model or guarantor.

6.2 The Emergence of Communicative Competence

As I mentioned at the beginning of this chapter, the distinction between competence and performance becomes somewhat problematic when we are dealing with a system undergoing development. In fact, it is not clear what is meant by abstract capacities (competence) when those capacities have not yet had the opportunity to manifest themselves because the supporting cognitive structures have not yet reached maturity. A normal child does not speak at six months, but everyone would grant that he possesses linguistic competence, even if this will become evident only some months later. In this case, a systematic deficit in performance is not an indication of incapacity, but of maturity that has not yet been achieved.

Competence must therefore include not only abstract capacities, but also the system's *potential* for those capacities. Even if an ability does not manifest itself, it need only be potentially available, for it to constitute part of the system's competence. A healthy child has the necessary competence to swim, even though he might never learn to do so: all that is required is that he be potentially capable of swimming. Whatever performance the system might produce does not affect its competence.

A further complication is that certain communicative abilities require the support of other structures that must be fully functional. For example, for a child to be able to understand the dynamics of deceit, he must have a theory of mind available, that is, he must be capable of attributing mental states to other people that differ from his own (e.g., I know that the pen is in the drawer, and I believe that Helen does not know this), and he must possess a working memory capable of handling embedded mental states (e.g., I believe that Helen is convinced that I know where the pen is). Both of these abilities, that of possessing a theory of the mind and that of having a sufficiently powerful working memory, mature over time. Thus, an eighteen-month-old child is incapable of comprehending even the simplest of deceits.

Nevertheless, a child's communicative competence with regard to deceits is not at issue: performance is defective because the cognitive support structures are as yet incapable of supporting competence. Strictly speaking, therefore, the "development" of communicative competence is an improper term; either the system possesses communicative competence or it does not. I will therefore speak of the *emergence* of competence, not of its development. If it exists, then it manifests itself gradually, as this is rendered possible by the structures related to it.

Whereas the distinction between competence and performance may be validly subjected to a synchronous test in an adult, in a child experimentation must be diachronic. In other words, at a general level, for an adult it is sufficient to understand what he can do and what he cannot in principle at the moment the experiment is carried out, whereas for a child competence must include not only what he can do today, but also what he will be capable of doing tomorrow.

We are now in a position to make a prediction regarding the child's acquisition of language: approximately up to the age of 3, he should be able to communicate efficiently in the extralinguistic mode. The limit of 3 years indicates the point at which language has been fully mastered, thus influencing every aspect of the child's life, definitively modifying the picture. However, at birth, children already possess a device that is ready to be activated and will select the specific characteristics of the language spoken in the environment the child is born into. This demonstrates that there is a fundamental genetic component in language acquisition.

Bruner (1990) erroneously hypothesizes continuity between prelinguistic communication and language. His idea is that the pragmatics of communication is the determining factor in language acquisition, as well as its direct precursor. Following this line of thought, some scholars have attempted to find direct evidence of the greater importance of pragmatics compared to syntax, thereby confusing temporal antecedence with a cause–effect link, and hence falling into the same type of fallacious logic that entrapped Piaget.

The crucial point turns on the independent origin of the two structures, despite the fact that the function of both structures is that of achieving communication. Communication as a goal places exactly the same constraints on language use as it does on extralinguistic communication: such constraints are personal, social, and cultural. Since the constraints are identical, it is a natural consequence that the two communicative modes should both exhibit many of the same structures, even though one does not originate from the other. It is the environment in which communication takes place that gives them shape.

In contrast to the hypothesized continuity between prelinguistic communication and language, I claim that the two systems are separate. Since both constitute situated cognitions that take place in the same context, they share certain characteristics. These common characteristics are proof not, however, of continuity, but of the fact that both language and gestures realize the same communicative function: it is the world that imposes constraints.

The Darwinian theory posits a similar case, which has been termed *convergent evolution*. This term indicates the fact that the environment may influence the evolution of the species living in that environment, so that those different species will exhibit similar morphological features, even though they did not inherit them from a common ancestor. For instance, dolphins and swordfish have many features in common: elongated bodies, fins, and so forth. Such similarities do not, however, constitute proof that the dolphin descend from the swordfish or vice versa. It is simply evidence that both species live in water, and that interaction with the environment in which they evolved has conditioned their forms, modeling in a similar fashion the morphology of animals belonging to such diverse species as fish and mammals.

Both extralinguistic and linguistic abilities necessarily require the involvement of central processes. Using the two modes of expression to communicate obliges them to interact continually, bringing about reciprocal modifications. The communicative use of language retreads pathways already laid down by the extralinguistic mode of communication. Hence, the latter will inevitably influence the former. The paralinguistic features of linguistic communication are an evident form of contact between the two modes of communication, for paralinguistic features are in actual fact a partially nonlinguistic means of conveying emotional tones and the like transmitted through the linguistic mode. We have already noted that expressing emotions is the most difficult task to achieve in linguistic forms, whereas extralinguistic forms provide an ideal vehicle for conveying emotions. If we examine the issue from the other standpoint, linguistic communication exerts enormous influence over extralinguistic communication: nothing can ever be the same once it has been expressed in words.

I will now attempt to outline those constraints common to both communicative modalities of communicative competence, and to pinpoint their inescapable differences.

6.2.1 The Primitives of Communication

The basic idea underlying my analysis of language acquisition is that the child is born with innate pragmatic competence that precedes any form of structured communication by a few weeks. This competence is realized first by extralinguistic means, and then by linguistic means. Since both modalities have the same functional goal, there will be many similarities, despite their structural separateness.

In chapter 2, I introduced the concept of the *primitives* of communication, that is, those basic structures that are essential if the process of communication is to work. I will now illustrate the role they play in ontogenetic development. The idea of something's being a primitive is that this entity precedes development and is therefore inborn in the system. It is only through the unconditional activation of these structures that a phenomenon as complex as communication can be realized in the briefest of periods by a newborn child.

Common attention   The first step in communication consists in tuning into the same wavelength as one's partner, by replying to his attempts to enter into contact or by trying to actively capture his attention. Robson (1967) has shown how 1-month-old babies establish eye contact with other people. Within 2 months they are able to keep up prolonged contact, for the length of time necessary to communicate successfully.

Bruner situates the common attention stage at 3 months. This stage is indispensable if both actors are to share each individual communicative move. It is at 3 months that Jonathan's mother—Jonathan being the first subject studied longitudinally by Bruner from 3 to 18 months—begins to introduce objects in the space between herself and the child as objects requiring common action. If the child was not making eye contact when the object was presented, the mother would employ a vocative to draw his attention. Initially, the vocative was *"Jonathan."* At five months this was integrated with *"Oh, look,"* *"See what I've done,"* and the like, all uttered with a rising tone. It is the rising tone and not the specific utterance itself that is particularly effective in catching the child's attention.

At 7 months children can comprehend signals indicating that the mother is paying attention to something that the child should also look at, thereby demonstrating acquisition of what Bruner has termed a feeling for undifferentiated deictics. The corresponding ability is that of discovering what is occupying another person's attention. Scaife and Bruner (1975) filmed children aged 3–12 months to study how a child manages to follow the direction of another person's glance toward an object placed at a certain distance from them both. Two-thirds of children between 8 and 10 months follow a change in the direction the experimenter's look, and at 12 months of age all children do so. In addition, at 12 months of age, children look along the direction of the other person's glance, seeking an object, and if they fail to find one they return to the person's gaze for a second look, after which they turn to seek the object anew.

What I wish to stress here is that if, on the one hand, the child is autonomous in focusing on diverse aspects of the world that surrounds him, he is also extraordinarily precocious in establishing the precursors to common attention (at 1 month of age), and then in using common attention (at 3 months of age). These abilities, as the psychiatrist Daniel Siegel (1999) has shown, are the basis not only of the intellectual tuning in the mother–child couple, but also of their affective tuning.

Communicative intentionality   As was seen in chapter 2, communicative intentionality is a complex concept to grasp and to formalize because of its circularity. A intends to communicate something to B when she intends not only that that something be understood by B, but also that her intention to communicate be recognized as such. How do children manage to use a mental state corresponding to the intention to communicate so quickly and so efficiently?

Let us begin by observing a fact that anyone who has ever interacted with a newborn child, or has at least observed an adult interacting with one, will agree on. Whatever the behavior of the child, and even if there is no observable behavior, the mother attributes to the child the intention to communicate with her, interpreting each action in terms of as-if intentionality. The child finds himself in a situation in which intentionality is attributed to him. I know of no other method better suited to activating an innate competence.

The *holophrase*, that is to say a word standing for a complete utterance, is a unit integrating the linguistic and extralinguistic modes handled by a single communicative competence, and is highly effective in exploiting the resources available. These resources become richer in the linguistic mode around the 1-year mark, thereby integrating looks and gestures that the child already knows how to put to communicative ends. In my terms, we may consider the holophrase as a word that refers to an entire behavior game. On this point, John Dore (1975) speaks of *primitive speech acts*. These consist of a one-word utterance, they emerge around the age of 1, and are to be considered the direct precursors of a proper speech act. In fact, the examples considered above constitute precursors of directives and assertives. For the utterance to be well formed, the child must master lexicon and syntax. Nevertheless, a primitive speech act is readily understood by those who interact with the child regularly.

Tomasello (2008) sums up infantile development by systematically comparing it to that of primates: he points out that the basic difference is to be found in our cooperative mode of interaction, while primates possess only the competitive mode. By around 9–12 months of age infants encounter what Tomasello terms the *nine-month revolution* which suddenly renders them much better at comprehending the social world surrounding them. In particular, they become better at and acquire greater flexibility in following an adult's gaze, in exploiting the adult for social referencing, and in using an object in the way it has just been used by an adult (*imitative learning*).

These joint attentional engagements are triadic (and no longer simply dyadic, as in the first nine months of life). They involve the child coordinating his interactions with adults and objects in the external world, thereby creating the "referential triangle" between child, adult, and the object/event which lies at the center of shared attention. Colle, Becchio, and Bara (2006) offer an explanation of the neural mechanisms involved in the transition from dyadic (mirror neurons) to triadic (mirror neurons and Who system: see sec. 6.3.1) interaction.

Around their first birthday, infants:

a. begin to monitor others' intentional states directed at objects willingly trying to engage in and continue joint attentional activities; and
b. begin to monitor others' intentional states even with respect to their own states, thus creating the prerequisites for the handling of communication proper.

Shared belief Even the mental state of shared belief should be considered innate. Any other hypothesis comes up against the difficulties outlined in section 2.2.2: essentially, if a child did not possess shared belief as a primitive, but had to deduce it through a logical chain, he would be unable to interact communicatively until the age of 12–13, when his cognitive resources, and in the first place working memory, were sufficiently powerful to handle a long series of embeddings.

Theory of mind   All developmental psychologists today agree that the ability to distinguish between living beings and nonliving objects, and the ability to attribute to others mental states such as beliefs, desires, and intentions, is innate. I refer readers to Josef Perner's (1991) excellent book for the details. Here I will recall the most important experimental results that support the different theories, avoiding going into sophisticated interpretative issues.

The first experimental paradigm is that which Wimmer and Perner (1983) have termed the *false belief task*. The objective of this task is to establish at what age children can discriminate between what they themselves know and what others know about a specific state of the world. The child is shown a scene in which a small boy called Maxi places a piece of chocolate in a cup and then leaves. While he is gone another child arrives and moves the chocolate into another cup. The child is asked where Maxi will look for the chocolate when he returns. Children up to the age of 3 commit the error of realism, having Maxi look for the chocolate where it really is. Only around the age of 4 do children reply that Maxi will look for the chocolate where he believes it is, even if they as observers know that it is no longer there.

The second experimental paradigm is that denominated the *representational change task*. The child is shown a box of Smarties, that unmistakeable small tube which contains chocolates of various colors, and asked what the box contains. After he has replied that the box contains Smarties, the box is opened and the child is shown that the box contains a pencil instead. The experimenter now asks the child to say what he believes another child who were to arrive now would think the box contained, and what he himself believed the box contained before he opened it. Once again children up to 3 reply that both they themselves initially believed and the new child will believe that the box contained a pencil. Around 4 children manage to separate the two representations, replying correctly that both the new child and they themselves at the outset believed that it contained Smarties.

Numerous variants have been added to the basic pattern, but all the results show that something important happens in the child's mind between the ages of 3 and 5, as a result of which children are able to attribute to others mental states, and especially beliefs, that differ from their own. If a child has not mastered the theory of mind, he can in no way understand nonstandard speech acts such as irony and deceit. Indeed, this theory is crucial for the very existence of human communication, since this is an intentional activity aiming at modifying mental states in others.

If no experimental evidence exists testifying to the presence of a theory of mind in children under 3, then it becomes difficult to explain how they can communicate before this age. Tirassa, Bosco, and Colle (2006) advance the hypothesis of the existence of a stage, starting from earliest infancy, where children act as if all their mental states were shared with others, realizing only later that their own mental states are not necessarily transparent to others. The infant might therefore communicate not by using a fully developed theory of mind, but simply as a result of his innate ability to share his mental states with others. The theory of mind, inasmuch as it constitutes the ability to differentiate one's own mental states from those one attributes to others, is a later acquisition in the child's development.

Cooperation Probably the most significant paradigm shift with respect to what are assumed to be innate features possessed by human beings has been triggered by the strong and hotly challenged claim made by Tomasello (2009) with regard to cooperation. His empirical research on cooperation in children and chimpanzees focuses on two basic phenomena:

Altruism one individual sacrificing himself in some way for another; and
Collaboration multiple individuals working together for mutual benefit.

Our unique disposition for cooperation is rooted in our phylogeny, and has no need to be taught and learned in our ontogeny. We are simply biologically equipped to cooperate with our conspecifics, and we are intrinsically motivated to do so. No further reason for such a type of disposition to act is therefore required.

Context-dependency The specific cultural and social norms of the particular environment the child lives in are taught, either directly or indirectly, from the very first day of the child's life. From the very start the child learns to interact with those people—parents, grandparents—who look after him.

Behavior games constitute an indirect manner of transmitting the culture in which the infant is immersed. Subsequently, socialization within first the family, and later in wider society, will ensure the child is capable of interacting within his own environment. Around the age of 5–6 children are entrusted to public education, which is formally assigned the task of transmitting the group's culture. Educational structures operate in all the cultures known today, and they take upon themselves the task of handling the future member of society's apprenticeship until adolescence.

Adopting my standard developmental perspective, Bosco, Bucciarelli, and Bara (2004) have proposed a taxonomy of the different categories of context that contribute to reconstructing the speaker's communicative intentions. A number of domains enter into the definition of context, with different levels of importance, varying in accordance with the specific situation. The context is a dynamic, interpersonal construct, in continuous progress, potentially oscillating among its dimensions and their changing relevance.

The context is determined by the features of the physical environment, by the features of the social world, and by those of the psychological world. Because cognitive pragmatics already takes into account the psychological dimension of the agents (beliefs, emotions, and motivations), in our study we focused on the physical and social worlds. In the physical dimension, we posit the categories: *access*, *space*, and *time*. In the social dimension, we posit: *discourse*, *move*, and *status*. The empirical validation of the proposed taxonomy is based on the idea that different contexts pertaining to the same category induce the partner to assign different communicative meanings to the same expression act proffered by the actor. The results from 72 subjects aged 3–7 years reveal that different context categories play different roles in the reconstruction of the speaker's communicative intentions in children belonging to the different age groups.

6.2.2 How Children Comprehend Communication Acts

At the Center for Cognitive Science at the University of Turin, I and the research team of Monica Bucciarelli, Francesca Bosco, and Livia Colle investigate linguistic and extralinguistic communication within a coherent developmental perspective. Our work has two ambitions:

1. To study in parallel the emergence of linguistic and extralinguistic communication, reunified under a single theoretical paradigm.
2. To offer a baseline against which to compare abnormal performances in relation to linguistic and extralinguistic conditions.

Abnormal children show different deficits in the comprehension and production of communication acts, depending on the type of cerebral pathology. The same is true for decay due to traumatic impairments: children with head injuries, hydrocephalus, focal brain damage, and autism (Bara, Bosco, and Bucciarelli 1999). But the point is that it is hard to understand the deficits when one does not know how normal development takes place.

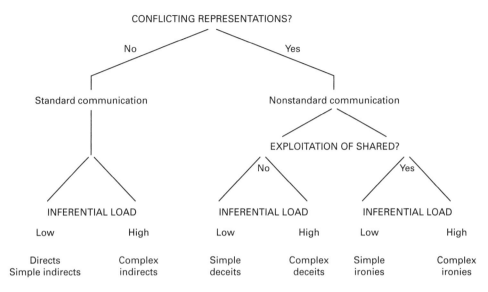

Figure 6.11
Factors that determine the difficulty of comprehension of pragmatic phenomena.
Source: Bucciarelli, Colle, and Bara 2003.

I will now report a single comprehensive work, which is paradigmatic of the approach we follow. Bucciarelli, Colle, and Bara (2003) claim that three factors determine the complexity of the mental representation involved in the comprehension of a pragmatic phenomenon (see figure 6.11).

1. *Conflicting representations*

Here representations involve a difference between what is communicated and what is privately entertained by the actor. In the case of no conflict, we are dealing with standard communication; in the case of conflict, we are dealing with nonstandard communication.

Direct communication acts, conventional indirect communication acts, and nonconventional indirect communication acts are all examples of standard communication, namely, those involving an actor whose beliefs and communicative purposes are in line with what she said. In terms of mental representations, the partner has merely to refer her utterance to a valid behavior game. This is not the case for nonstandard communication acts, such as deceits and ironies, where the mental representations involved are more complex (see below). It may consequently be predicted that standard phenomena are easier to deal with than nonstandard phenomena.

2. *Representations where shared beliefs are exploited*

Representations involving a belief expressed by an actor that is in contrast with a belief shared with the partner are more difficult to handle than representations that do not involve such a contrast.

When comprehending deceit, the observer recognizes the difference between the mental states that are expressed, and those that are privately entertained by the actor. An uttered statement becomes ironic when, along with this difference, the observer also has to recognize the contrast between the expressed mental states and the scenario provided by the knowledge the actor shares with the partner. The contemporary activation of the representation of actor's utterance (*p*) and of the contrasting shared belief (*non-p*) makes ironic statements difficult for a child to manage. It follows that, as long as we are concerned with simple pragmatic phenomena, deceits should be easier to deal with than ironies.

3. *Inferential load*

The necessity of building a long chain of inferences is what discriminates between simple and complex communicative acts.

In standard communication, this is what makes for the difference in difficulty between direct and simple indirects versus complex indirects. In nonstandard communication this, too, is what explains the difference in difficulty between simple and complex deceits, and between simple and complex ironies. In our experiment, we investigated only simple pragmatic phenomena of different sorts, with the exception of complex indirects, which involve actors whose beliefs and communicative purposes are not immediately in line with what has been said. Thus, the partner has to construct a chain of inferences in order to refer the move of the actor to the behavior game in question. In other words, complex indirects should be harder to comprehend than simple indirects. The same prediction holds for all other types of communication acts (deceit, irony, etc.): a simple act is always easier to understand than a complex act.

A group of 160 children participated in the experiment. They were divided into four age groups, equally balanced by gender: 2.6, 3.6, 4.6, 6. Half of them were randomly assigned to the linguistic protocol, and half to the extralinguistic one. The global results are summarized in figure 6.12.

The results of the experiment globally confirm our predictions. As regards predictions *within modalities*, standard communication is easier to comprehend than nonstandard communication, both in the linguistic protocol and in the gestural protocol. Also, in both protocols, directs and

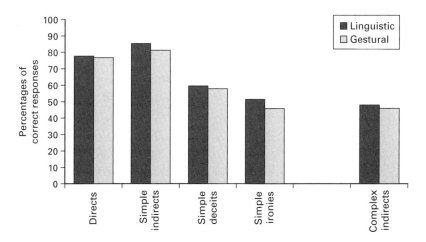

Figure 6.12
Histogram of the global percentages of correct responses given by children aged 2.6 to 6 in the linguistic or extralinguistic condition.
Source: Bucciarelli, Colle, and Bara 2003.

simple indirects are equally easy to comprehend, and they are easier than simple deceits, which are easier than simple ironies. Finally, direct and simple indirect communicative acts are easier to comprehend than complex indirect communicative acts in both protocols.

Globally, the results also reveal that a pragmatic phenomenon has the same difficulty of comprehension, whether it is realized through linguistic or extralinguistic means. In particular, results *between modalities* reveal no difference in children's performance in the two protocols, neither for the phenomena across the board, nor for standard and nonstandard phenomena, nor for the single phenomena considered separately. Irony is an exception, but only for the 6 year olds, who find it easier to comprehend simple irony within the linguistic protocol than within the gestural one.

6.2.3 From Protoconversation to Conversation
In line with my approach to the development of conversation, I will assume that to be able to speak of communication proper the child must have all the primitives specified above at his disposal. But what happens *before* all those necessary capacities are in place, a state that will come about much later in the child's development?

The child and his parents create from the very first weeks of the child's life a number of patterns of interaction that are extremely significant for all the participants. Such protoconversations employ reciprocal glances, gestures, and vocalizations, in a situation that is heavily charged with emotion. Classic examples experienced by everyone include:

The child looks at the mother and vocalizes; the mother responds.
The child smiles, the mother speaks to him, smiles, or laughs.
The father caresses the child, the child smiles or vocalizes.

The ethologist Colwyn Trevarthen (1977) has pointed out that these first interactions are *objectless*, a sort of implementation of intersubjectivity that is an end in itself. What the child offers is his own innate willingness to interact, which teams up functionally with the mother's willingness to treat him *as if* he were conveying to her something meaningful for him. Any directed vocalization brings the mother's vigilant and intense reply: "*What lovely words! What's up, my darling? What do you want to tell me? Is that so, my duckling?*," a response that is pedagogically extremely effective.

After the very first few weeks of life, protoconversations turn into what has been called *baby talk*, that is, an infantile manner of speaking. When adults talk to a child, they tend to use a language that has special features, which they intuitively believe will help make interaction between themselves and the child easier. The variants that have been subjected to more intensive study are, on the one hand, the interaction between mother and child, which has been termed *motherese*, and, on the other hand, the language spoken by father and child, called *fatherese*. For an important investigation into parent–child language, see Wells and Robinson 1982.

The differences identified by scholars between motherese and fatherese are not constant. They depend, among other things, on the sex of the child. Whether one is talking to a boy or a girl is different, both for the father as well as for the mother. But the global situation is the most important factor. Father and mother reciprocally adapt their behavior depending on the role the other person has taken, balancing each other out. The social role the two parents must play is different, and both tend to play it as soon as the situation allows them to do so. Differentiation will reach its utmost when the three interact together. When the mother is alone with the child, her motherese will be a little less maternal; and vice versa, when the father finds himself alone with the child, he will tone down his fatherese.

The most interesting aspect of baby talk in relation to our topic does not concern the language variety used by the parents, but the language variety used by the child when talking to other children, for he too adapts his language to context, producing a kind of motherese (a *childese*, we could say [Feldmann, pers. comm.]) in his own turn. Indeed, in such contexts, children suddenly become much more pragmatically competent than their parents would ever have believed possible. In more general terms, the child exhibits the ability to "switch code," to adapt his language to context, selecting the appropriate variety, in Hymsian terms (Hymes 1971).

When the child interacts with an adult, he rapidly tunes in to the adult's wavelength in order to adapt to the attitude that the adult implicitly has toward him: teacher, guardian, or other. At 5–6, the child masters appropriacy to context—he can adjust perfectly to the role in which the interlocutor casts him. The ability to pretend, which underlies an infinite number of games played by children, develops at an extremely early age (Nelson 1996). A 2-year-old child gives his stuffed animal food, treats his wooden horse which hurt itself while out on a gallop, scolds the doll who wet herself, and later, between the ages of 3 and 5, begins role-playing with his playmates of the same age, all of whom take turns to act as if they were someone else, reproducing the behavior and mental states of real or imaginary characters: children play at being doctors, teachers, mommy, the vet, and animals. Just like an actor, the child enters the part he has chosen to play, learning to impersonate other people, and experimenting with the various roles that each game allows one to play.

When my younger daughter Helen was 5, she very much liked playing "the tedious mother" with me, not only repeating in the appropriate context what my wife and I usually told her to do (*"Tidy your room," "Have you washed your hands?"*), but also what my wife said to me (*"Don't forget to lock the door!"*), and, finally, creating novel as well as appropriate utterances (*"What an oaf you are: you haven't buttoned up your jacket correctly!"*). The game, which had been invented by my daughter Simona when she was 7 and was promptly taken up by her sister who was 30 months younger, was a source of constant pleasure to my daughters, creating in me a violent need to disobey all the sensible rules I was taught. This experience allows me to confirm from a phenomenological standpoint what thorough observers have demonstrated experimentally: children are not only children; they often play the role of children.

The adult who treats a normal 4-year-old child as an irresponsible fool forces the child to disobey her in order not to lose his self-respect. If the child does not receive orders, then he will act in a manner appropriate to the situation. We should not forget the difference between *being* a child and *acting like* a child: an intelligent child knows the difference perfectly well, right from the first year of his life.

6.3   Neuropragmatics

The aim of using a neologism in the title to this section is to draw attention to an area that has not yet been consolidated, but which is of great methodological importance: that dominion which investigates the correlations between the mental processes involved in communication and those areas of the brain that are responsible for those processes. In particular, in view of the fact that research in this sector is still in its initial stages, the data that will be examined are those that link up different types of cerebral lesions, both diffuse and focal, with particular impairments in communication (Bara and Tirassa 2000).

Taking up one of my initial methodological assumptions, namely that the mind is a biological structure, I will take it for granted that a valid theory of communication should be able to identify which areas of the brain underlie the physical realization of communication. This means specifying which areas of the brain are activated when a person is engaged in communicative activity, and, to look at the issue from the opposite viewpoint, what types of deficits may be predicted as a result of lesions occurring to any of these areas.

Although the new techniques of exploring brain activity *in vivo* have diminished the absolute certainty with which the pioneers of neuropsychology localized language in Broca's and Wernicke's areas, nevertheless the basic fact cannot be denied. Language is normally situated in the counterlateral hemisphere to the dominant hand, hence in the left hemisphere for dextrals. However, both hemispheres have areas devoted to language, a fact that should not surprise us, after having shifted the focus of attention from language to communication.

In contrast to what Chomsky strongly argues for syntax, and a little less strongly for semantics, no specific module dedicated to pragmatics is invoked. The very definition of pragmatics as the study of language used in context introduces so many elements (connected to language, and to using language for a specific purpose, and to the different contexts in which all this occurs) as to make the hypothesis that one specific cerebral area is unambiguously connected bidirectionally to the complex management of pragmatic competence highly improbable.

The philosopher Asa Kasher (1991) has analyzed the relationship between modularity and pragmatics, taking as his starting point the assumption that language use is supported by two different types of pragmatic competence. One type of pragmatic competence is purely linguistic and is devoted to the production and comprehension of speech acts. The other type is nonlinguistic and is devoted to handling general cognitive structures, such as intentional action. Linguistic pragmatic competence is characteristically analytical and represents our basic pragmatic knowledge. It is therefore used in handling basic categories of speech acts, such as assertions, questions, and orders. This is realized by a set of modules whose definition, however, excludes some of the properties postulated by Fodor such as the opaqueness of consciousness.

By contrast, central pragmatic competence, which is synthetic, is composed of knowledge that is not exclusively linguistic, and is used to master rule systems concerning "what we do with words," as Austin would put it. Central pragmatic competence, founded on cognition in a wide sense, is vital to the handling of nonbasic speech acts, such as indirect speech acts, metaphor, and sarcasm. In Kasher's view, the set of modules that constitutes linguistic pragmatic competence is located in the left hemisphere, while the right hemisphere looks after nonlinguistic pragmatic competence.

Kasher's stance places language in a dominant position. In the rest of this section I will express the point of view of cognitive pragmatics, namely, that pragmatic competence is equally distributed over language and gestures.

Given the definitions I have provided so far, communicative processes may be divided into two main parts: a *central part,* where the inferential processes required either to attribute a communication act to a behavior game, or to generate a communicative move in a game, take place, and a *peripheral part,* where input and output processes take place, as mediated by the afferent perceptual cells and by the efferent motor nerve cells. Pragmatic competence (the set of abstract capacities) is handled by central pragmatic competence, while pragmatic performance (together with the system's capacities exhibited in action) comes under the control of both central (e.g., inference) and peripheral processes (e.g., gesture perception and speech production).

Central pragmatic processes are spread presumably over a large part of the cortex, since they involve a series of capacities that I will now list in detail. The actor must be able to pass from one internal physiological, emotional, and cognitive state to the motivation to play an interpersonal game, and, consequently, to plan an adequate communicative action; subsequently, she must be able to attune to the communicative behavior exhibited by her partner. The partner must be able to draw inferences in order to comprehend what the other person wants; he must be able to balance out the proposal made by his partner with his own physiological, emotional, and cognitive state, in order to activate a motivation that will drive him to participate in the game or to renegotiate the initial offer; and finally, he too must be able to tune into his partner's communicative behavior.

It should be noted that if one wishes to study language use in context, all the above-mentioned processes are indispensable. Hence, the hypothesis that each of these functions may be located in one specific area of the brain becomes untenable, given the fact that all mental activity is affected by these processes: it is obvious that thought, memory, desires, and motivation cannot be located in one specific area. Nor can a selective lesion of the central pragmatic processes be hypothesized. If this were so, then the lesion would be so serious that the person would no longer be conscious of his existence—he would be incapable of thinking, remembering, desiring, and feeling emotions.

Peripheral pragmatic processes are connected to the perceptual and motor channels that are devoted either to linguistic or to extralinguistic communication. In contrast to central pragmatic processes, peripheral pragmatic processes could be located in specific brain circuits, respectively linked to language cortical areas and to motor cortical areas. Inasmuch as they are dependent on precise input and output paths, peripheral processes might suffer selective damage. In the case of peripheral damage, pragmatic competence would not be diminished, while communicative performance might undergo specific impairments limited to the comprehension or the production of language or of gestures.

Theories in pragmatics are typically analytical and developed on autonomous grounds. The neurosciences, and in particular the neuropsychology of mind–brain impairments, provide them with a natural empirical testing ground. Clearly, whereas the pathology of a cognitive function may always shed significant light on its physiology, in the case of communication the research strategy based on pathology becomes virtually obligatory because of the intricacies of carrying out experiments in pragmatics in the normal, healthy adult.

Different neuropsychopathological diseases will affect communicative performance in different ways, depending on what relevant cognitive subsystems are damaged and how. Competing theories of communication make different claims as to the nature of these subsystems and of the their interconnections and therefore yield different predictions as to the patterns of their decay. It therefore becomes possible to compare them, and possibly even to falsify them. The same line of reasoning, applied to development, also suggests that the acquisition of communicative abilities in the child with genetic or traumatic disorders should be studied.

Neuroscience and pragmatics have quite distinct roles in this enterprise, the former being somewhat ancillary to the latter: given a powerful theory of communication, all that the experimenters need is a reliable description of the particular neurosyndrome they wish to investigate in order to be able to predict its consequences on patients' performances. The payoff for neuropsychology, however, would be a more precise, theoretically driven picture of what happens to the communicative skills of these patients and why. This would, in turn, add to our understanding of several diseases whose symptoms include deficient communicative performance. Quite interesting results have been already reached by *clinical pragmatics* in the area of pragmatic disorders (Cummings, 2008).

With different collaborators, I have carried out some research in this direction. Most of the work, however, remains to be done: we have only been able to test a few classes of subjects, such as individuals suffering from traumatic head injuries (Bara, Tirassa, and Zettin 1997; Bara, Cutica, and Tirassa 2001; Cutica, Bucciarelli, and Bara 2006), patients suffering from Alzheimer's disease (Bara, Bucciarelli, and Geminiani 1999), neuropsychologically abnormal children (Bara, Bosco, and Bucciarelli 1999), and autistic children (Bucciarelli, Colle, and Bara 2003). The aim of our protocols was both to establish a basic trend of difficulty for each class of subjects along which to order a few simple pragmatic phenomena, and to explore in detail how each type of neuropsychological damage actually affects communication. Basically, in these studies we have found a trend analogous to that reported above in figure 6.12. Characteristic differences may in principle be attributed to the specific kind of deficit linked to each neurological damage.

The assessment of pragmatic abilities in patients affected by acquired cerebral lesions is relevant, since a deeper understanding of their specific communicative deficits will be crucial for both theoretical advances and clinical suggestions. Traditionally, communicative deficits have been interpreted as linguistic disabilities, but in more recent years clinical researchers have highlighted the need for a more comprehensive assessment that will offer a complete picture of patients' communicative effectiveness in their everyday life (e.g., Holland 1991; Penn 1999).

Our research group has recently created a new assessment battery, ABaCo (Assessment Battery for Communication), that can be profitably used to evaluate the various abilities involved in communication, comprising a wide range of pragmatic phenomena and communicative modalities (Sacco et al. 2008). ABaCo comprises five evaluation scales—linguistic, extralinguistic, paralinguistic, context, and conversational—which include several kinds of pragmatic phenomena—for example, deceit, irony, social appropriateness, Grice's maxims—for a total of 190 items. The idea was to create a new clinical tool, which could also represent a valuable starting point for a complete understanding of pragmatic deficits involved in different types of cerebral lesions.

In fact, we used ABaCo in a study aimed at investigating the pragmatic performances of traumatic brain injury (TBI) patients (Angeleri et al. 2008), which represent an interesting typology of subjects since TBI results in a range of communicative impairments that cannot be adequately explained in terms of linguistic deficit only. In this study we have outlined a precise profile of impairments for these patients, and the resulting picture has gone beyond the well-known assumption of a generic pragmatic deficit in TBI. In more detail, we have found that although patients' comprehension is damaged, it is nevertheless linguistically valid; on the other hand, they perform worse than control subjects in extralinguistic comprehension of deceit and irony; production, unlike comprehension, is worse than in normal subjects in both linguistic and extralinguistic modalities. Moreover, we found that the difficulty in manipulating mental representations has a great impact on patients' performance, since there is an increasing trend of difficulty in managing different kinds of pragmatic phenomena that involves dealing with embedded mental representations: both comprehension and production of standard communication acts are easier than deceits, followed by ironies, which represent the most difficult task.

TBI patients also show a pronounced impairment in managing paralinguistic aspects, neglecting the emotional meaning expressed through modalities other than language, such as, for example, facial expression or prosody. Finally, we found that TBI patients have difficulty in grasping subtler conversational violations, such as in the case of sensitivity to violations of Grice's maxims, and that they can achieve good conversational performance when the conversation focuses on simple or superficial topics, although they are inclined to persevere on the same topic during the dialogue.

Even if our results cannot be generalized to the entire clinical population because of the extreme variety of the clinical outcomes following TBI, our study represents the first attempt to detail pragmatic performance in these patients, in the attempt to delineate a specific profile of impairment, well justified by a priori theoretical assumptions.

Within the aim of strengthening our comprehension of the mind/brain relationship, I will now concentrate in some detail on a single topic, which is crucial for cognitive pragmatics: the empirical investigation of communicative intentions.

Recognition	Agent attribution	Aim representation
What?	Who?	Why?
Enables identification of the intention from the observation of action, distinguishing among different types of motor intention	Enables attribution of the intention to its author, distinguishing between self and others	Enables identification of the aims of an intended action

Figure 6.13
Processes contributing to the understanding of intention.
Source: Becchio, Adenzato, and Bara 2006.

6.3.1 How the Brain Understands Intention

At the Center for Cognitive Science, Mauro Adenzato, Cristina Becchio, and I are jointly investigating the different neural circuits that identify the componential features of intention. Becchio, Adenzato, and Bara (2006) assume that three basic aspects are involved in the understanding of intention: intention recognition, agent attribution, and aim representation (figure 6.13).

Recognizing intention Accumulative empirical evidence suggests that recognizing the intentions of others is based, at least in part, on the same mechanisms underlying the formation of one's own motor intentions (Frith 2002). The idea is that the same cortical areas that are activated when we execute an action are also activated when we observe other people performing a similar action.

The discovery, made in the mid-1990s, of a particular class of motor neurons in a sector of the ventral premotor cortex of monkeys, called F5, provided the first convincing physiological evidence for a direct match between action execution and action perception (Rizzolatti et al. 1996). In fact, quite unexpectedly, the study of motor functions showed that not only does the F5 area accommodate purely motor neurons, but it also houses neurons that fire when a recorded monkey observes another monkey, or even an experimenter, performing a similar action. These neurons were designated as *mirror neurons*.

As Jackson and Decety (2004) noted, the existence of a system matching executed and perceived actions offers a parsimonious explanation of how we recognize other people's intended actions—that is, by a direct mapping of the visual representation of the observed action onto our own motor representation of the same action. Hence, the same motor representation is used for one's internal intentions for actions to be executed, as well as for recognizing other people's intentions to perform actions.

Attributing intention The fact that agents in normal conditions are indeed able to correctly attribute actions to their authors implies the need for a specific causal process that disambiguates representations by articulating who the agent is—that is, a *"Who" system* (Georgieff and Jeannerod 1998) specifically dedicated to action attribution.

Various neural mechanisms have been proposed to explain how such a system might operate. One hypothesized mechanism is the monitoring of signals arising from body movements, that is, a comparison between the control signals that contribute to generating a movement and signals arising out of its execution. There is firm evidence that the inferior parietal cortex and the insula are crucial components of this mechanism, which is specifically involved in perceiving the *spatial* features of movements (Jackson and Decety 2004).

Aim-representation: Distinguishing between individual and social aims
The processes described thus far concern the recognition and attribution of intention. Both of these aspects contribute to what Searle (1983) calls intention-in-action, that is, the mental and causal component of an action. An intention-in-action is the cause of an agent's movement. Yet, it should be noted that the causal domain of the intention-in-action extends only as far as the bodily movement of an action. To cover the effects that an action should cause we need to analyze the stable (prior) intention that orients the action as a whole.

In contrast to intention-in-action, which represents conditions of satisfaction of an act in progress, the prior intention is formed in advance, representing goal states that are in some way very distal to the chain of events that lead to their fulfillment. If action is a "causal and intentional transaction between the mind and the world" (Searle 1983), *prior* intention can be said to initiate a transaction by representing the end or *aim* of the action before the action is undertaken.

The same behavior performed by the same agent can be initiated to bring about different *aims*: enlarging the temporal horizon, by shifting from intention-in-action to prior intention, allows us to focus on what the agent aims at by his or her action. This aspect of intention—aim-intention, in Raimo Tuomela's (2002) terminology—determines the *mode* of the intention. Consider the case of an agent, John, lighting a candle. John may light a candle because the electricity has failed and he wants to read a

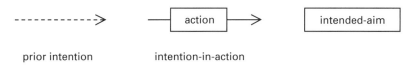

prior intention   intention-in-action

Figure 6.14
The relationship between action, intention-in-action, prior intention, and intended
aim. Arrows represent time and causation.
Source: Becchio, Adenzato, and Bara 2006.

book, or because he is planning a romantic evening with Mary, or to celebrate Independence Day. In the first case, John is acting in the pursuit of
a merely individual goal, driven by an *I-mode* intention; in the latter case,
lighting a candle satisfies a shared *we-attitude* (Tuomela 2002). The action
is the same, and so is the author. What changes is the "mode" of intention:
the "I-mode" involves acting and having an attitude privately, as an individual subject, whereas the "we-mode" involves having it as a group
member. The instance of John planning a romantic evening with Mary
may represent a sort of intermediate case: although John is not acting for
a shared social reason, he is oriented toward future social interaction.

Henrik Walter, Mauro Adenzato, Angela Ciaramidaro, Ivan Enrici, and
I have launched a new series of brain mapping experiments, with the
objective of distinguishing between merely individual aim-intentions and
social aim-intentions. In a first fMRI experiment, participants were asked
to read short comic strips that depicted an unfolding story (Walter et al
2004). The participants' task was to choose the most logical story ending
from three answer pictures. Story content was either physical, that is,
nonintentional (a ball blown by the wind breaking several bottles) or
intentional. In turn, intentional strips pertained to three conceptual categories, depicting either the intentional action of a single agent (changing
a broken bulb in order to read a book) or of two agents acting independently (an agent building a doghouse while another agent sets up a tent),
or social interaction between two people communicating through gestures
(requesting that another person pass a bottle, by pointing to it).

The most interesting result was a significant increase in neural activation associated with the social interaction condition. Seeing two agents
communicating resulted in significant activation in the medial prefrontal
cortex, especially in the anterior paracingulate cortex. The finding is coherent with the prevalent view that medial prefrontal cortex (MPFC) is the
key area subserving the ability to explain and predict the behavior of conspecifics, based on the observation of their intentional actions (Amodio

and Frith 2006; Frith and Frith 2006). However, Rebecca Saxe (2006) has argued that the right temporo-parietal junction (TPJ) plays a more specific role in the attribution of mental states. The fact that Walter et al. (2004) found no neural activation during the reading of comic strips depicting either one agent acting or two agents acting independently of each other suggested that the activation observed was not due simply to the intentional content or to the number of agents represented in stories. Indeed, the activation of the anterior paracingulate cortex required two socially interacting agents.

In this first experiment, social interaction always involved two communicating agents. Communicative intention is necessarily social, for it involves taking other people into account, as part of one's reasons for acting. In contrast to individual intention, which can be realized by an isolated person, a communicative intention can occur only during social interaction. According to the cognitive pragmatics approach, however, communicative intentions represent a "special" sort of social intention, consisting not only of the intention to communicate meaning, but also of the intention that this first intention should be recognized by the addressee. Thus, one question raised by the results of our first experiment was as follows: to what extent can the paracingulate cortex activation be attributed to the specificity of the communicative interaction? Would a social interaction not involving communicative intention have resulted in the same activation?

In our second fMRI experiment (Walter et al. 2004) we introduced a new conceptual category: *prospective social intentionality*, which we referred to as the intention of a single agent whose individual action is oriented toward subsequent social interaction (e.g., John preparing a romantic evening with Mary). The reasoning underlying the experiment was that if anterior paracingulate cortex activation was due to the presence of two agents actually interacting—or, more specifically, communicating—no activation should be observed in the prospective social intentionality condition. Conversely, if the activation depended on the social nature of the aim an agent pursued, anterior paracingulate cortex activation should still be observed.

The experimental results allowed us to propose a model of a dynamic intentionality network consisting of four regions (precuneus, left and right TPJ, MPFC). The model accounts for some crucial distinctions among varieties of intentions: first, they differ with regard to the nature of the intended aim (individual or social). Second, they differ with regard to the temporal dimension of the social interaction: present in the case of communicative intention, and future in the case of prospective social intention. Even if these two dimensions are not exhaustive, they cover the most interesting ecological cases of human interaction (Pacherie 2006). Our results confirm the crucial role of both the MPFC and the right TPJ, but show that these areas are differentially engaged depending on the nature of the intention involved. Whereas the right TPJ and the precuneus are necessary for processing all types of prior intentions, the left TPJ and the anterior paracingulate cortex are specifically involved in the understanding of social intention. More specifically, the left TPJ is activated only when a subset of social intentions are involved: communicative intentions which are both recursive and in the present (Ciaramidaro et al. 2007; see figure 6.15).

An activation of the anterior paracingulate cortex similar to our cooperative social interaction was found by Gallagher et al. (2002) in a PET experiment involving competitive interaction.

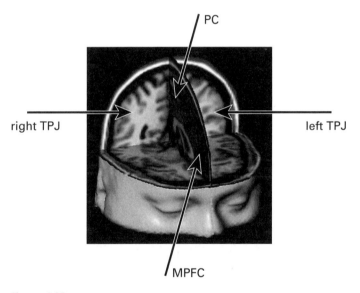

Figure 6.15
The intentionality network including the right and left temporo-parietal junctions (TPJ), the precuneus (PC), and the anterior paracingulate cortex (aPCC), located in the medial prefrontal cortex (MPFC). This network shows different activation patterns in relation to the nature of the intentions: the comprehension of an individual intention involves only the precuneus and the right TPJ. By contrast, the comprehension of a potentially shared-in-the-future social intention (prospective social intention) recruits the right TPJ, the precuneus, and the aPCC. Finally, the comprehension of a recursive, shared-in-the-present social intention (communicative intention) recruits all four areas, including left TPJ.

Type of interaction	Number of agents	Modality of interaction	Time of interaction
Cooperative	One agent (prospective)	Participated	Present
or	or	or	or
competitive	more (actual)	observed	future

Figure 6.16
Anterior paracingulate cortex: conditions for activation. It is located in the prefrontal cortex.
Source: Becchio, Adenzato, and Bara 2006.

Clinical extensions of this line of research showed a hyper intentionality style of intentional attribution in paranoid schizophrenics, and a hypo intentionality style in autistic subjects (Walter et al. 2009). Taken together, these results demonstrate the progressive recruitment of the intentionality network along the theoretical dimensions introduced by cognitive pragmatics.

With respect to previous evidence, the interesting aspect of our findings such as those by Walter et al. (2004) consists in the fact that they open the way to experimental investigation of aim-intention and social intention, showing that the anterior paracingulate cortex is activated in representing social aims, independently of interaction type (cooperative vs. competitive), time (present vs. future), and modality (participated vs. observed): see figure 6.16.

An unexplored question was whether the imposition of a communicative meaning on an action affected action kinematics, that is, how the action itself is implemented at the motor level. In a series of studies we investigated the effects of communicative intention on action (Sartori et al. 2009). In a first experiment participants were requested to reach towards an object, grasp it, and either simply lift it (individual condition) or lift it with the intent to communicate a meaning to a partner (communicative condition). Movement kinematics were recorded using a three-dimensional motion analysis system. The results indicate that kinematics is sensitive to communicative intention. Although the to-be-grasped object remained the same, movements performed for the "communicative" condition were characterized by a kinematic pattern which differed from those obtained for the "individual" condition.

What our results reveal is that the imposition of a communicative intent is not neutral with respect to action kinematics: the intention to communicate alters the parameterization of the movement. Therefore, the very same action—for example, reaching toward and grasping a sphere—is executed differently depending on whether it carries a communicative or a purely individual intent. Along these lines, a higher speed of finger opening for the "communication" condition may signify that when the task was to use the object so as to communicate to another person, participants needed more time during the "closing" phase to compute a careful approach to the object.

As I explained above, communicative intentions:

a. always occur in the context of a social interaction with a partner;
b. are overt, in the sense that they are intended to be recognized as such by the partner; and
c. their satisfaction consists precisely in the fact that they are recognized by the partner.

Implementing these three requirements, our experiment provided the first measure of the influence that communicative intentions exert at the level of action kinematics. In particular, the modification observed in key kinematic parameters fits well with the idea that communication actions are planned as a function of the partner's recognition. Further strength to this hypothesis comes from the results obtained in a second experiment in which a control condition implying the presence of a blindfolded partner was used. This manipulation proved to be sufficient to eliminate the "communicative" effect.

The ideal continuation of this experiment consists in the analysis of the possibility to distinguish between communication acts and individual actions on the basis of motor information. When we observe people performing actions, do we use kinematic information to learn about their intentions? Are motor cues sufficient to discriminate between actions carrying communicative and individual intents? By providing information about movement kinematics without added information about the actor's shape or structure, *point-light* stimuli offer a critical opportunity to explore this issue. The point-light technique is a method for representing human movement through limited visual information. With this method, the movements of a body are represented by a small number of point lights indicating the major joints of a moving person. Despite this drastic degradation of the stimulus, information available has proven to be sufficient for recognizing actions as well as different variations of a particular action, and for determining the identity of a figure, his or her gender, his or her age, and his or her emotional state.

In order to study the perception of communicative intentions of conspecifics on the basis of visual motion information, we created the first set of point-light communicative interactions (*Communicative Interaction Database*, by Manera, Schouten, Becchio, Bara, and Verfaillie 2010). The Communicative Interaction Database contains 20 communicative interactions performed by a male and by a female couple. In order to reproduce action kinematics realistically, stimuli were constructed combining motion capture technique and animation software. For each action, we provide movie files from four different viewpoints as well as text files with the three-dimensional spatial coordinates of the point lights, allowing researchers to construct customized versions. Including various types of actions performed with different social motives, the database contains a diverse sample of nonconventional communicative gestures. Normative data collected to assess the recognizability of the stimuli suggest that, for most action stimuli, information in point-light displays is sufficient to clearly recognize the action as communicative as well as to identify the specific communicative gesture performed by the actor. The full set of stimuli may be downloaded from www.psychonomic.org/archive/ and from http://ppw.kuleuven.be/labexppsy/lepSite/resources/CID.rar.

Normative data collected by Manera et al. (2010) to assess the recognizability of the present stimuli add to the findings by Sartori et al. (2009), suggesting that—for most action stimuli—visual information about body movements is indeed sufficient to clearly recognize an action as communicative, as well as to identify the specific communicative gesture performed by the actor. In line with motor theories of social cognition, these results together provide preliminary evidence in favor of the hypothesis that the motor system participates in understanding communicative intention (Decety and Sommerville 2003; Jacob and Jeannerod 2005).

The cognitive sciences are currently undergoing an evolution that, whatever its outcome will be, will change both the types of scientific questions that are being asked and the very framework in which they are being asked. The conception of the mind as the software of a digital computer is progressively losing ground in favor of its conception as an emergent property of the functioning of the brain. Correspondingly, as the classic stances of computational philosophy and methodology decline, the links between psychology and biology gain greater strength—in particular, with evolution theory, with dynamic systems theory in the wake of the work carried out by Maturana and Varela (1980), and with the neurosciences. Furthermore, viewing the mind as an evolved control system that governs an organism's interactions with the world, instead of considering it as a rational mechanism devoted to the manipulation of abstract symbols, brings previously neglected issues (e.g., developmental, social, and clinical questions) into focus. Areas like neuropsychology and pragmatics may play a pivotal role in this evolution, provided that they are prepared and equipped to do so.

A final remark is that a more ecological framework for the study of mind–brain in terms of situated (that is, interaction-centered and context-sensitive) macroprocesses ought to substitute the classic approach that, instead, typically builds on artificially isolated microprocesses. I believe that the time has come to abandon the parceling approaches that were typical of information-processing psychology, and the consequent construction of theoretical and empirical microworlds. The neurosciences will undoubtedly provide inestimable results once the psychological problems that real human beings have to cope with are made the object of study.

The picture I envisage should be clear by now. Communication is interesting both in itself and as a crucial part of what human beings do in their physical and social world. Furthermore, the questions posed by the study of communication require that stances be taken with respect to several problems worrying the cognitive sciences. Neuroscience may furnish a crucial contribution to the shaping and the framing of these questions and problems. The payoffs of a better study of the mind–brain will be the knowledge acquired and, even more importantly, a richer perspective on the nature of human beings.

6.4 Silence

There is one final aspect which tends to go unnoticed and whose importance is, on the contrary, absolute: silence. We may first distinguish between three types of silence:

Noncommunicative silence This is the silence of a person who has not even realized she has begun interacting, hence she has no intention of communicating anything to anyone.

One example of this type of silence is that of the traveling companion abstractedly looking out of the window, lost in thought, or immersed in meditation, and indifferent to the surrounding social world.

Nondeliberate and aware silence This is the silence of the person who cannot find the words with which to express her thoughts in a given situation. The interlocutor may undoubtedly infer something from the other person's silence, but it is not a meaning that may be judged as being openly communicative.

This type of silence conveys difficulty or embarrassment, when a person can do little else, as if temporarily incapable from a psychological standpoint, as has happened to many people who are timid, or who are overawed by another person, or who are suddenly love-struck.

Intentionally communicative silence   This silence is employed by an actor to convey a message to her interlocutor in an open and clear manner, given the background in which the interaction takes place and the shared knowledge.

One example of this type of explicit silence is when it conveys a confession, as is the case with many literary and cinematographic sinners. Silence indicating a refusal to answer or, more generally, a refusal to continue a conversation, also falls within this category.

But there also exists a more interesting and more specific sense of silence. This type of silence is neither equivalent to nor antithetical to communication. Rather, it represents a means by which communication is realized. It is has the same relationship to a speech act as a canvas has to the picture that is painted on it: it is a necessary complement.

Western culture is highly suspicious of silence in conversation, and tends to fill out any gap quite obsessively, even to the point of creating a redundancy of useless information that becomes difficult to stave off. Suffice it to think of the slight embarrassment that takes hold of anyone momentarily finding herself in the presence of strangers, as in an elevator. Such slight embarrassment may really and truly become collective difficulty if one of those present is so totally incapable of withstanding silence as to require an artificial and uninterrupted conversation at any cost.

That such behavior is culturally determined is borne out by the fact that different cultures treat silence in more respectful ways. Indeed, in those cultures that handle the relationship between speech and silence differently from ours, understanding when and for how long one may speak is as important as knowing what may and what may not be said.

For instance, Native Americans have a totally opposite philosophy with regard to silence compared to Western culture. For them, the norm is to remain silent unless one has something important to say. The anthropologist Keith Basso (1970) lists a set of situations in which for an Apache— though it is virtually the same for a Navajo or a Sioux—*it is right to give up words*. These are:

meeting strangers, whether they be Apache or not: as a general rule, if the stranger speaks, then you infer he is not a real Native American;
courting a person: an engaged couple begin speaking freely to each other only after months of intimacy;
meeting relatives after a long absence;
being angry: if someone shouts, then Apache norms lay down that the correct response is silence;
moral pain, especially in connection with mourning;
medical ceremonies: only the medicine man speaks, patient and onlookers remain silent.

In such situations, silence is not simply permissible, it is mandatory. The reaction to those situations in our culture is quite the opposite to silence. Thus, a Westerner finds conversation with a Native American difficult. The Westerner speaks and then waits for an interval that her culture defines as the correct time to wait for a response; however, the Native American norm establishes a much longer gap in order to avoid interrupting the person speaking; hence the Westerner starts speaking again in order to avoid the embarrassment of a conversation with an uncooperative partner; in this kind of sequence, the Native American finds it difficult to find the time to say something. The conclusion is that a Native American thinks that a Westerner intrudes on his privacy and that she is unbearably prolix, while the Westerner believes that the Native American is silently hostile and never has anything to say.

While I in no way wish to belittle our cultural tradition, it seems to me that the suspicion with which silence is greeted is bringing about the disappearance of one of the most powerful modes of interaction: that by means of which words acquire power and meaning, by virtue of their use being exceptional. Maximum communicative efficiency is linked to a communication act's managing to detach and distinguish itself from the background. Constructing silence creates the best contrast possible.

We have become accustomed to permanent background noise, so much so that we are surprised when we no longer perceive it, as in the case of finding oneself away from traffic or as when a power failure shuts down our television and stereo. But silence is our natural background, not words. Against a background of silence, words acquire value without needing to be shouted or repeated. There is no communication without silence—noble silence.

References

Aiello, L. C., and R. I. M. Dunbar. 1993. Neocortex size, group size, and the evolution of language. *Current Anthropology* 34:184–193.

Airenti, G., B. G. Bara, and M. Colombetti. 1984. Planning and understanding speech acts by interpersonal games. In *Computational Models of Natural Language Processing*, ed. B. G. Bara and G. Guida. Amsterdam: Elsevier, 9–31.

Airenti, G., B. G. Bara, and M. Colombetti. 1993a. Conversation and behavior games in the pragmatics of dialogue. *Cognitive Science* 17(2):197–256.

Airenti, G., B. G. Bara, and M. Colombetti. 1993b. Failures, exploitations and deceits in communication. *Journal of Pragmatics* 20:303–326.

Alighieri, D. 1309–1321. *Divina Commedia. Inferno canto XXXIII.* Translated as *The Divine Comedy.* Cambridge, MA: The Harvard Classics, Harvard, 1909–1914.

Angeleri, R., F. M. Bosco, M. Zettin, K. Sacco, L. Colle, and B. G. Bara. 2008. Communicative impairment in traumatic brain injury: A complete pragmatic assessment. *Brain and Language* 107:229–245.

Amodio, D. M., and C. D. Frith. 2006. Meeting of minds: The medial frontal cortex and social cognition. *Nature Reviews. Neuroscience* 7:268–277.

Atkinson, J. M., and P. Drew. 1979. *Order in Court.* Atlantic Highlands, NJ: Oxford Socio-Legal Studies.

Attardo, S. 1997. The semantic foundations of cognitive theories of humor. *Humor: International Journal of Humor Research* 10(4):399–420.

Austin, J. L. 1962. *How to Do Things with Words.* Oxford: Oxford University Press.

Bara, B. G. 1995. *Cognitive Science: A Developmental Approach to the Simulation of the Mind.* Hove: Psychology Press.

Bara, B. G. 2003. *Il sogno della permanenza: L'evoluzione della scrittura e del numero.* Turin: Bollati Boringhieri.

Bara, B. G., F. M. Bosco, and M. Bucciarelli. 1999. Developmental pragmatics in normal and abnormal children. *Brain and Language* 68:507–528.

Bara, B. G., M. Bucciarelli, and G. C. Geminiani. 1999. Development and decay of extra-linguistic communication. *Brain and Cognition* 43:1–3.

Bara, B. G., M. Bucciarelli, and P. N. Johnson-Laird. 1995. The development of syllogistic reasoning. *American Journal of Experimental Psychology* 108(2): 157–193.

Bara, B. G., M. Bucciarelli, and V. Lombardo. 2001. Model theory of deduction: A unified computational approach. *Cognitive Science* 25:839–901.

Bara, B. G., I. Cutica, and M. Tirassa. 2001. Neuropragmatics: Extralinguistic communication after closed head injury. *Brain and Language* 77:72–94.

Bara, B. G., and M. Tirassa. 1999. A mentalist framework for linguistic and extra-linguistic communication. In *Proceedings of the 3rd European Conference on Cognitive Science*, ed. S. Bagnara. Rome: Istituto di Psicologia del Consiglio Nazionale delle Ricerche, 185–190.

Bara, B. G., and M. Tirassa. 2000. Neuropragmatics: Brain and communication. *Brain and Language* 71:10–14.

Bara, B. G., M. Tirassa, and M. Zettin. 1997. Neuropragmatics: Neuropsychological constraints on formal theories of dialogue. *Brain and Language* 59:7–49.

Barkow, J. H., L. Cosmides, and J. Tooby, eds. 1992. *The Adapted Mind: Evolutionary Psychology and the Generation of Culture*. Oxford: Oxford University Press.

Basso, K. 1970. To give up words: Silence in a Western Apache culture. *Southwestern Journal of Anthropology* 26:213–230.

Bates, E., A. Thal, and J. S. Janowsky. 1992. Early language development and its neural correlates. In *Handbook of Neuropsychology*, ed. I. Rapin and S. Segalowitz. Volume 7: *Child Neuropsychology*. Amsterdam: Elsevier, 69–110.

Bateson, G. 1956. The message "This is play." In *Group Processes: Transactions of the Second Conference*, ed. B. Schaffner. New York: Josiah Macy Jr. Foundation.

Bateson, G. 1972. *Steps to an Ecology of Mind*. New York: Chandler.

Bateson, G. 1979. *Mind and Nature: A Necessary Unity*. New York: Ballantine.

Becchio, C., M. Adenzato, and B. G. Bara. 2006. How the brain understands intention. Different neural circuits identify the componential features of motor and prior intentions. *Consciousness and Cognition* 15:64–74.

Berne, E. 1964. *Games People Play*. New York: Grove Press.

Berne, E. 1970. *Sex in Human Loving*. New York: Simon & Schuster.

Berry, J. W., Y. H. Poortinga, and J. Pandey. 1997. *Handbook of Cross-Cultural Psychology*. Boston: Allyn & Bacon.

Bickerton, D. 1981. *Roots of Language*. Ann Arbor, MI: Karoma.

Bickerton, D. 1990. *Language and Species*. Chicago: University of Chicago Press.

Boesch, C., and H. Boesch-Ackermann. 1991. Dim forest, bright chimps. *Natural History* 9:50–57.

Bok, S. 1978. *Lying: Moral Choices in Public and Private Life*. New York: Pantheon.

Bosco, F. M., M. Bucciarelli, and B. G. Bara. 2004. The fundamental context categories in understanding communicative intention. *Journal of Pragmatics* 36:467–488.

Bosco, F. M., M. Bucciarelli, and B. G. Bara. 2006. Recognition and repair of communicative failures: A developmental perspective. *Journal of Pragmatics* 38(9): 1398–1429.

Bosco, F. M., R. Angeleri, L. Colle, K. Sacco, and B. G. Bara. Forthcoming. Communicative abilities in children: An assessment through different phenomena and expressive means.

Bowlby, J. 1973. *Attachment and Loss, II: Separation: Anxiety and Anger*. London: Hogarth Press.

Bowlby, J. 1988. *A Secure Base*. London: Routledge.

Bradshaw, J. L. 1997. *Human Evolution: A Neuropsychological Perspective*. Hove: Psychology Press.

Bratman, M. E. 1990. What is intention? In *Intentions in Communication*, ed. P. R. Cohen, J. Morgan, and M. E. Pollack. Cambridge, MA: MIT Press, 15–31.

Bridgman, P. W. 1927. *The Logic of Modern Physics*. New York: Macmillan.

Britten, R. J. 2002. Divergence between samples of chimpanzee and human DNA sequences is 5%, counting indels. *Proceedings of the National Academy of Sciences* 99: 13633–13635.

Brown, P., and S. C. Levinson. 1987. *Politeness: Some Universals in Language Use*. Cambridge: Cambridge University Press.

Bruner, J. S. 1983. *Child's Talk: Learning to Use Language*. New York: Norton.

Bruner, J. S. 1990. *Acts of Meaning*. Cambridge, MA: Harvard University Press.

Bucciarelli, M., L. Colle, and G. B. Bara. 2003. How children comprehend speech acts and communicative gestures. *Journal of Pragmatics* 35(2):207–241.

Burling, R. 1993. Primate calls, human language, and nonverbal communication. *Current Anthropology* 34(1):25–53.

Caesar, G. J. 58–52 B.C. *De bello Gallico*. Translated as *The Gallic War*. Cambridge, MA: Harvard University Press, 1917.

Carassa, A., and M. Colombetti. 2009. Joint meaning. *Journal of Pragmatics* 41: 1837–1854.

Carlson, L. 1962. *Dialogue Games*. Dordrecht: Reidel.

Cheney, D. L., and R. M. Seyfarth. 1990. *How Monkeys See the World: Inside the Mind of Another Species*. Chicago: Chicago University Press.

Chomsky, N. 1957. *Syntactic Structure*. The Hague: Mouton.

Christiansen, M. H., and S. Kirby. 2003. *Language Evolution*. Oxford: Oxford University Press.

Ciaramidaro, A., M. Adenzato, I. Enrici, S. Erk, L. Pia, B. G. Bara, and H. Walter. 2007. The intentional network: How the brain reads varieties of intentions. *Neuropsychologia* 45:3105–3133.

Clark, A. 1997. *Being There: Putting Brain, Body, and World Together Again*. Cambridge, MA: MIT Press.

Clark, H. H. 1992. *Arenas of Language Use*. Chicago: University of Chicago Press and Center for the Study of Language and Information.

Clark, H. H. 1996. *Using Language*. Cambridge: Cambridge University Press.

Clavell, J. 1975. *Shogun: A Novel of Japan*. New York: Dell.

Cohen, P. R., and H. Levesque. 1990a. Persistence, intention, and commitment. In *Intentions in Communication*, ed. P. R. Cohen, J. Morgan, and M. E. Pollack. Cambridge, MA: MIT Press, 33–69.

Cohen, P. R., and H. Levesque. 1990b. Rational interactions as the basis for communication. In *Intentions in Communication*, ed. P. R. Cohen, J. Morgan, and M. E. Pollack. Cambridge, MA: MIT Press, 221–255.

Colle, L., C. Becchio, and B. G. Bara. 2008. The non-problem of other minds: A neuro-developmental perspective on shared intentionality. *Human Development* 51: 336–348.

Colombetti, M. 1993. Formal semantics for mutual belief. *Artificial Intelligence* 62(2):341–353.

Colombetti, M. 1999. A modal logic of intentional communication. *Mathematical Social Sciences* 38:171–196.

Conan Doyle, A. 1887. A study in scarlet. *Beeton's Christmas Annual*.

Corballis, M. C. 2002. *From Hand to Mouth: The Origins of Language*. Princeton, NJ: Princeton University Press.

Crelin, E. S. 1987. *The Human Vocal Tract: Anatomy, Function, Development, and Evolution*. New York: Vantage.

Cummings, L. 2008. *Clinical Linguistics*. Edinburgh: Edinburgh University Press.

Cutica, I., M. Bucciarelli, and B. G. Bara. 2006. Neuropragmatics: Extralinguistic pragmatic ability is better preserved in left-hemisphere-damaged patients than in right-hemisphere-damaged patients. *Brain and Language* 98:12–25.

Davidson, I. 1991. The archaelogy of language origins: A review. *Antiquity* 65:39–48.

Davidson, I. 2003. The archaeological evidence of language origins: States of the art. In *Language Evolution*, ed. M. H. Christiansen and S. Kirby. Oxford: Oxford University Press, 140–157.

Deacon, T. W. 1997. *The Symbolic Species: The Co-evolution of Language and the Brain*. New York: Norton.

Decety, J., and J. A. Sommerville. 2003. Shared representations between self and other: A social cognitive neuroscience view. *Trends in Cognitive Science* 7: 527–533.

Defoe, D. 1719. *Robinson Crusoe*. London: Taylor.

Del Giudice, M., R. Angeleri, and V. Manera. 2009. The juvenile transition: A developmental switch point in human life history. *Developmental Review* 29: 1–31.

Deshimaru, Taisen, ed. 1977. *Textes sacrés du Zen*. Paris: Editions Seghers.

Dessalles, J.-L. 2007. *Why We Talk: The Evolutionary Origins of Language*. Oxford: Oxford University Press.

de Waal, F. B. M. 1988. The communicative repertoire of captive bonobos (Pan paniscus), compared to that of chimpanzees. *Behavior* 106:183–251.

Donald, M. 1991. *Origins of the Modern Mind: Three Stages in the Evolution of Culture and Cognition*. Cambridge, MA: Harvard University Press.

Dore, J. 1975. Holophrases, speech acts, and language universals. *Journal of Child Language* 2:21–40.

Dostoyevsky, F. M. 1866 [1964]. *The Gambler*. New York: Bantam Books. (Originally published in Russian.)

Dumas, A. 1844. *Les Trois Mousquetaires*. Translated as *The Three Musketeers*. London: Routledge, 1853.

Dumas, A. 1846. *Le Comte de Monte-Cristo*. Translated as *The Count of Monte Cristo*. London: Chapman and Hall, 1946.

Dunbar, R. I. M. 1991. Functional significance of social grooming in primates. *Folia Primatologica* 57:121–131.

Dunbar, R. I. M. 1993. Coevolution of neocortical size, group size and language in humans. *Behavioral and Brain Sciences* 16:681–735.

Dunbar, R. I. M. 1996. *Grooming, Gossip, and the Evolution of Language*. London: Faber & Faber.

Duranti, A. 1997. *Linguistic Anthropology*. Cambridge: Cambridge University Press.

Elman, J. L., E. A. Bates, M. H. Johnson, A. Karmiloff-Smith, D. Parisi, and K. Plunkett. 1996. *Rethinking Innateness: A Connectionist Perspective on Development*. Cambridge, MA: MIT Press.

Erickson, M. E. 1982. *My Voice Will Go with You*. Ed. S. Rosen. New York: Norton.

Falk, D. 1987. Hominid paleoneurology. *Annual Review of Anthropology* 16: 13–30.

Fagin, R., and J. Y. Halpern. 1987. Belief, awareness, and limited reasoning. *Artificial Intelligence* 34:39–76.

Flaubert, G. 1856 [1950]. *Madame Bovary*. London: Penguin. (Originally published in French.)

Flaubert, G. 1863 [1977]. *Salammbò*. London: Penguin. (Originally published in French.)

Fodor, J. 1983. *The Modularity of the Mind: An Essay on Faculty Psychology*. Cambridge, MA: MIT Press.

Francik, E. P., and H. H. Clark. 1985. How to make requests that overcome obstacles to compliance. *Journal of Memory and Language* 24:560–568.

Freud, S. 1899. *Die Traumdeutung*. Translated as *The interpretation of dreams*. In *Standard Edition of the Complete Psychological Works*, vols. 4–5. London: Hogarth Press, 1953/1974.

Freud, S. 1901. *Zur Psychopathologie des Alltagslebens*. Translated as *The Psychopathology of Everyday Life*. In *Standard Edition of the Complete Psychological Works*, vol. 6. London: Hogarth Press, 1953–1974.

Frith, C. D. 2002. Attention to action and awareness of other minds. *Consciousness and Cognition* 11(4):481–487.

Frith, C. D., and U. Frith. 2006. The neural basis of mentalizing. *Neuron* 50:531–534.

Gallagher, H. L., A. I. Jack, A. Roepstorffc, and C. D. Frith. 2002. Imaging the intentional stance in a competitive game. *NeuuroImage* 16:814–821.

Gallistel, C. R. 1992. *The Organization of Learning*. Cambridge, MA: MIT Press.

Gazdar, G. 1979. *Pragmatics: Implicature, Presupposition, and Logical Form*. New York: Academic Press.

Georgieff, N., and M. Jeannerod. 1998. Beyond consciousness of external reality. A "Who?" system for consciousness of action and self-consciousness. *Consciousness and Cognition* 7(3):465–477.

Gibbon, E. 1776–1788 [1994]. *History of the Decline and Fall of the Roman Empire*. London: Penguin.

Gibbs, R. 1994. *The Poetics of Mind: Figurative Thought, Language, and Understanding*. Cambridge: Cambridge University Press.

Gibbs, R. 1999. *Intentions in the Experience of Meaning*. Cambridge: Cambridge University Press.

Gilbert, M. 2006. *A Theory of Political Obligation: Membership, Commitment, and the Bonds of Society*. Oxford: Clarendon Press.

Goffman, E. 1959. *The Presentation of Self in Everyday Life*. New York: Doubleday.

Goodall, J. 1986. *The Chimpanzees of Gombe: Patterns of Behavior*. Cambridge, MA: Belknap.

Gordon, D., and G. Lakoff. 1971. Conventional postulates. In *Papers from the Seventh Regional Meeting of the Chicago Linguistics Society*. Chicago: Chicago Linguistic Society, 63–84.

Greenfield, P. M., and E. S. Savage-Rumbaugh. 1993. Comparing communicative competence in child and chimp: The pragmatics of repetition. *Journal of Child Language* 20:1–26.

Grice, H. P. 1975. Logic and conversation: The William James Lectures, II. Reprinted in *Studies in the Way of Words*, ed. H. P. Grice, Cambridge, MA: Harvard University Press, 1989, 22–40.

Grice, H. P. 1989. *Studies in the Way of Words*. Cambridge, MA: Harvard University Press.

Grosz, B. J., and C. L. Sidner. 1990. Plans for discourse. In *Intentions in Communication*, ed. P. R. Cohen, J. Morgan, and M. E. Pollack. Cambridge, MA: MIT Press, 417–444.

Gurman, A. S., and D. P. Kniskern. 1991. *Handbook of Family Therapy*. New York: Brunner/Mazel.

Habermas, J. 1976. Some distinctions in universal pragmatics. *Theoretical Sociology* 3:155–167.

Habermas, J. 1979. *Communication and the Evolution of Society*. Boston, MA: Beacon Press.

Haley, J. 1963. *Strategies of Psychotherapy*. New York: Grune and Stratton.

Harman, G. 1977. Review of "Linguistic Behavior" by Jonathan Bennett. *Language* 53:417–424.

Hauser, M. D. 1996. *The Evolution of Communication*. Cambridge, MA: MIT Press.

Hauser, M. D., N. Chomsky, and W. T. Fitch. 2002. The faculty of language: What is it, who has it, and how did it evolve? *Science* 298:1569–1579.

Hinde, R. A. 1972. *Non-verbal Communication*. Cambridge: Cambridge University Press.

Hintikka, J. 1962. *Knowledge and Belief*. Ithaca, NY: Cornell University Press.

Hintikka, J. 1966. Knowing oneself and other problems in epistemic logic. *Theoria* 32:1–13.

Hockett, C. F. 1960. The origin of speech. *Scientific American* 203:89–96.

Holland, A. 1991. Pragmatic aspects of intervention in aphasia. *Journal of Neurolinguistics* 6: 197–211.

Huizinga, J. 1939. *Homo ludens*. Boston: Beacon Press.

Hymes, D. 1971. Sociolinguistics and the ethnography of speaking. In *Social Anthropology and Language*, ed. E. Ardener. London: Tavistock.

Ifrah, G. 1981. *Histoire Universelle des Chiffres*. Paris: Editions Seghers. Translated as *A Universal History of Numbers: From Prehistory to the Invention of the Computer*. London: Harvill Press, 1998.

Inghilleri, P. 1999. *From Subjective Experience to Cultural Change*. Cambridge, MA: Cambridge University Press.

Jackendoff, R., and S. Pinker. 2005. The nature of the language faculty and its implications for evolution of language (reply to Fitch, Hauser, and Chomsky). *Cognition* 97: 211–225.

Jackson, P. L., and J. Decety. 2004. Motor cognition: A new paradigm to study self-other interactions. *Current Opinion in Neurobiology* 14:259–263.

Jacob, P., and M. Jeannerod. 2005. The motor theory of social cognition: A critique. *Trends in Cognitive Neuroscience* 9: 21–25.

Jerison, H. 1973. *Evolution of the Brain and Intelligence*. New York: Academic Press.

Jerison, H., and I. Jerison. 1988. *Intelligence and Evolutionary Biology*. New York: Springer-Verlag.

Johnson-Laird, P. N. 1983. *Mental Models.* Cambridge: Cambridge University Press.

Johnson-Laird, P. N. 2006. *How We Reason.* Oxford: Oxford University Press.

Jones, E. 1953. *The Life and Work of Sigmund Freud,* vol. I. New York: Basic Books.

Kasher, A. 1991. On the pragmatic module: A lecture. *Journal of Pragmatics* 16:381–397.

Kiernan, V. G. 1986. *The Duel in European History: Honour and the Reign of Aristocracy.* Oxford: Oxford University Press.

King, M. C., and A. C. Wilson. 1975. Evolution at two levels in humans and chimpanzees. *Science* 188:107–116.

Kipling, R. 1885. The Betrothed. In *Departmental Ditties and Barrack Room Ballads.* London: Macmillan.

Komarova, N. L., and M. A. Nowak. 2003. Language, learning, and evolution. In *Language Evolution,* ed. M. H. Christiansen and S. Kirby. Oxford: Oxford University Press.

Konolige, K. 1985. Belief and incompleteness. In *Formal Theories of the Commonsense World,* ed. J. R. Hobbs and R. C. Moore. Norwood, NJ: Ablex.

Kuhl, P. K. 1987. Perception of speech and sound in early infancy. In *Handbook of Infant Perception,* vol. 2: *From Perception to Cognition,* ed. P. Salapatek and L. Cohen. Orlando, FL: Academic Press.

Kuhn, T. S. 1962. *The Structure of Scientific Revolutions.* Chicago: University of Chicago Press.

Kummer, H. 1982. Social knowledge in free-ranging primates. In *Animal Mind— Human Mind,* ed. D. R. Griffin. Berlin: Springer-Verlag, 113–130.

La France, M., and C. Mayo. 1976. Racial difference in gaze direction in social interaction. *Journal of Personality and Social Psychology* 33:547–552.

Lakatos, I. 1970. Falsification and the methodology of scientific research programmes. In *Criticism and the Growth of Knowledge,* ed. I. Lakatos and A. Musgrave. Cambridge: Cambridge University Press.

Lakoff, G. 1987. *Women, Fire, and Dangerous Things: What Categories Reveal about the Mind.* Chicago: University of Chicago Press.

Leekman, S. R. 1992. Believing and deceiving: Steps to becoming a good liar. In *Cognitive and Social Factors in Early Deception,* ed. S. J. Ceci, M. DeSimone Leichtman, and M. Putnick. Hillsdale, NJ: Erlbaum.

Levelt, W. J. M. 1989. *Speaking: From Intention to Articulation*. Cambridge, MA: MIT Press.

Levesque, H. J. 1984. A logic of implicit and explicit belief. In *Proceedings of the National Conference of AAAI 1984*. Menlo Park, CA: AAAI Press, 198–202.

Levinson, S. C. 1983. *Pragmatics*. Cambridge: Cambridge University Press.

Lewis, D. K. 1969. *Convention: A Philosophical Study*. Cambridge, MA: Harvard University Press.

Lewis, R. 1960. *The Evolution Man*. Harmondsworth: Penguin.

Lieberman, P. 1991. *Uniquely Human*. Cambridge, MA: Harvard University Press.

Lieberman, P. 2000. *Human Language and Our Reptilian Brain: The Subcortical Bases of Speech, Syntax, and Thought*. Cambridge, MA: Harvard University Press.

London, J. 1907. *Before Adam*. New York: Macmillan.

Louÿs, P. 1898. *La femme et le pantin*. Translated as *Woman and Puppet*. Chicago: Argus Books, 1930.

Manera, V., B. Schouten, C. Becchio, B. G. Bara, and K. Verfaillie. 2010. Inferring intentions from biological motion: A stimulus set of point-light communicative interactions. *Behavior Research Methods*.

Mann, W. C., J. A. Moore, and J. A. Levin. 1977. A comprehension model for human dialogue. In *Proceedings of the V International Joint Conference on Artificial Intelligence*. Cambridge, MA: MIT Press, 77–87.

Marcel, A. J. 1983a. Conscious and unconscious perception: Experiments on visual masking and word recognition. *Cognitive Psychology* 15:197–237.

Marcel, A. J. 1983b. Conscious and unconscious perception: An approach to the relations between phenomenal experience and perceptual processes. *Cognitive Psychology* 15:238–300.

Marshack, A. 1991. The Tai plaque and calendrical notation in the Upper Paleolithic. *Cambridge Archaeological Journal* 1(1):25–61.

Mascagni, P. 1890. *Cavalleria rusticana*. Rome: Teatro Costanzi. Translated as *Cavalleria rusticana*. London: Penguin, 2000.

Maturana, H., and F. J. Varela. 1980. *Autopoiesis and Cognition: The Realization of the Living*. Dordrecht: Reidel.

McNeill, D. 1992. *Hand and Mind: What Gestures Reveal about Thought*. Chicago: University of Chicago Press.

McNeill, D. 1998. Speech and gesture integration. In *The Nature and Functions of Gesture in Children's Communication*, ed. J. M. Iverson and S. Goldin-Meadow. New directions for child development, no. 79. San Francisco: Jossey-Bass, 11–27.

Miller, G. A., E. Galanter, and K. H. Pribram. 1960. *Plans and Structure of Behavior*. New York: Holt, Rinehart, and Winston.

Miller, G. A., and P. N. Johnson-Laird. 1976. *Language and Perception*. Cambridge: Cambridge University Press.

Minsky, M. L. 1975. A framework for representing knowledge. In *The Psychology of Computer Vision*, ed. P. H. Winston. New York: McGraw-Hill.

Minsky, M. L. 1986. *The Society Theory of Mind*. New York: Simon & Schuster.

Mitchell, R. W. 1986. A framework for discussing deception. In *Deception: Perspectives on Human and Non-human Deceit*, ed. R. W. Mitchell and N. S. Thomson. Albany, NY: SUNY Press.

Morgan, J. 1990. Comments on Jones and on Perrault. In *Intentions in Communication*, ed. P. R. Cohen, J. Morgan, and M. E. Pollack. Cambridge, MA: MIT Press, 187–193.

Morris, D. 1977. *Manwatching: A Field Guide to Human Behaviour*. Oxford: Elsevier International Projects.

Murphy, M. 1991. Looking for lesbians. In *Are You Girls Travelling Alone? Adventures in Lesbian Logic*. Los Angeles, CA: Clothespin Fever Press.

Neihardt, J. N., ed. 1932 [2008]. *Black Elk Speaks: Being the Life Story of a Holy Man of the Oglala Sioux*. Albany, NY: SUNY Press.

Nelson, K. 1996. *Language in Cognitive Development: Emergence of the Mediated Mind*. Cambridge: Cambridge University Press.

Norman, D. A. 1988. *The Psychology of Everyday Things*. New York: Basic Books.

Nowak, M. A., and N. L. Komarova. 2001. Towards an evolutionary theory of language. *Trends in Cognitive Sciences* 5:288–295.

Oates, J. 1977. Mesopotamian social organisation: Archaeological and philological evidence. In *The Evolution of Social Systems*, ed. J. Friedman and M. J. Rowlands. London: Duckworth.

Oatley, K. 1992. *Best Laid Schemes: The Psychology of Emotions*. Cambridge: Cambridge University Press.

Pacherie, E. 2006. Towards a dynamic theory of intentions. In *Does Consciousness Cause Behavior? An Investigation of the Nature of Volition*, ed. S. Pockett, W. P. Banks, and S. Gallagher. Cambridge, MA: MIT Press, 145–176.

Passingham, R. E. 1982. *The Human Primate*. New York: Freeman.

Penn, C. 1999. Pragmatic assessment and therapy for persons with brain damage: What have clinicians gleaned in two decades? *Brain and Language* 68: 535–552.

Perner, J. 1991. *Understanding the Representational Mind*. Cambridge, MA: MIT Press.

Perrault, C. R. 1990. An application of default logic to speech act theory. In *Intentions in Communication*, ed. P. R. Cohen, J. Morgan, and M. E. Pollack. Cambridge, MA: MIT Press.

Petitto, L. 1987. On the autonomy of language and gesture: Evidence from the acquisition of personal pronouns in American Sign Language. *Cognition* 27: 1–52.

Piaget, J. 1923. *Le langage et la pensée chez l'enfant*. Paris: Neuchâtel. Translated as *The Language and Thought of the Child*. London: Routledge and Kegan Paul, 1959.

Piattelli-Palmarini, M., ed. 1980. *Language and Learning: The Debate between Jean Piaget and Noam Chomsky*. Cambridge, MA: Harvard University Press.

Piattelli-Palmarini, M. 1989. Evolution, selection, and cognition: From "learning" to parameter setting in biology and the study of language. *Cognition* 31:1–44.

Pickering, M. J., and S. Garrod. 2003. Toward a mechanistic psychology of dialogue. *Behavioral and Brain Sciences* 27(2):169–190.

Pierrehumbert, J. B., and M. Beckman. 1988. *Japanese Tone Structure*. Cambridge, MA: MIT Press.

Pierrehumbert, J. B., and J. Hirschberg. 1990. The meaning of intonational contours in discourse. In *Intentions in Communication*, ed. P. R. Cohen, J. Morgan, and M. E. Pollack. Cambridge, MA: MIT Press.

Piller, I. 2010. *Intercultural Communication: A Critical Introduction*. Edinburgh: Edinburgh University Press.

Pinker, S. 1994. *The Language Instinct*. New York: Morrow.

Pinker, S. 1997. *How the Mind Works*. New York: Norton.

Pinker, S., and R. Jackendoff. 2005. The faculty of language: What's special about it? *Cognition* 95(2):201–236.

Poizner, H., E. S. Klima, and U. Bellugi. 1987. *What the Hand Reveals about the Brain*. Cambridge, MA: MIT Press.

Pollack, M. E. 1992. The uses of plans. *Artificial Intelligence* 57(1):43–68.

Pomerantz, M. A. 1985. Agreeing and disagreeing with assessment: Some features of preferred/dispreferred turn shapes. In *Structures of Social Action*, ed. J. M. Atkinson and J. C. Heritage. Cambridge: Cambridge University Press.

Popper, K. R. 1934. *Logik der Forschung*. Vienna: Julius Springer Verlag. Translated as *The Logic of Scientific Discovery*. New York: Harper & Row, 1965.

Premack, D. 1988. Minds with and without language. In *Thought without Language*, ed. L. Weiskrantz. Oxford: Clarendon.

Psathas, G., ed. 1979. *Everyday Language: Studies in Ethnomethodology*. New York: Irvington.

Puzo, M. 1969. *The Godfather*. New York: Putnam.

Recanati, F. 2004. *Literal Meaning*. Cambridge: Cambridge University Press.

Richman, B. 1976. Some vocal distinctive features used by gelada monkeys. *Journal of the Acoustical Society of America* 60:718–724.

Richman, B. 1987. Rhythm and melody in gelada vocal exchanges. *Primates* 28:199–223.

Rips, L. J. 1994. *The Psychology of Proof: Deductive Reasoning in Human Thinking*. Cambridge, MA: MIT Press.

Rizzolatti, G., and M. A. Arbib. 1998. Language within our grasp. *Trends in Neurosciences* 21(5):188–194.

Rizzolatti, G., L. Fadiga, V. Gallese, and L. Fogassi. 1996. Premotor cortex and the recognition of motor actions. *Brain Research: Cognitive Brain Research* 3: 131–141.

Rizzolatti, G., C. Sinigaglia, and F. Anderson. 2008. *Mirrors in the Brain*. Oxford: Oxford University Press.

Robson, K. S. 1967. The role of eye-to-eye contact in maternal-infant attachment. *Journal of Child Psychology and Psychiatry, and Allied Disciplines* 8:13–25.

Rostand, E. 1897 [1975]. *Cyrano de Bergerac*. Oxford: Oxford University Press.

Sacco, K., R. Angeleri, F. M. Bosco, L. Colle, D. Mate, and B. G. Bara. 2008. Assessment Battery for Communication—ABaCo: A new instrument for the evaluation of pragmatic abilities. *Journal of Cognitive Science* 9: 111–157.

Sacks, H., E. A. Schegloff, and G. Jefferson. 1974. A simplest systematics for the organization of turn taking in conversation. *Language* 50: 696–735.

Sade, D.-A.-F. de. 1791. *Justine, ou les malheurs de la vertu*. Translated as *The Misfortunes of Virtue and Other Early Tales*. Oxford: Oxford University Press, 1992.

Sadock, J. 1974. *Toward a Linguistic Theory of Speech Acts*. New York: Academic Press.

Sartori, L., C. Becchio, B. G. Bara, and U. Castiello. 2009. Does the intention to communicate affect action kinematics? *Consciousness and Cognition* 18: 766–772.

Savage-Rumbaugh, E. S., J. Murphy, R. Sevcik, K. E. Brakke, S. L. Williams, and D. Rumbaugh. 1993. Language comprehension in ape and child. *Monographs of the Society for Research in Child Development* 233(58):3–4.

Saxe, R. 2006. Uniquely human social cognition. *Current Opinion in Neurobiology* 16:235–239.

Scaife, M., and J. S. Bruner. 1975. The capacity for joint visual attention in the infant. *Nature* 253(5489):265–266.

Schank, R. C., and R. P. Abelson. 1977. *Scripts, Plans, Goals, and Understanding: An Inquiry into Human Knowledge Structures*. Hillsdale, NJ: Lawrence Erlbaum.

Schegloff, E. A. 1972. Notes on a conversational practice: Formulating place. In *Studies in Social Interaction*, ed. D. Sudnow. New York: Free Press.

Schegloff, E. A., and H. Sacks. 1973. Opening up closings. *Semiotica* 7:289–327.

Schenkein, J., ed. 1978. *Studies in the Organization of Conversational Interaction*. New York: Academic Press.

Schiffer, S. 1972. *Meaning*. Oxford: Oxford University Press.

Searle, J. R. 1975. Indirect speech acts. In *Syntax and Semantics 3: Speech Acts*, ed. P. Cole and J. L. Morgan. New York: Academic Press.

Searle, J. R. 1983. *Intentionality*. Cambridge: Cambridge University Press.

Searle, J. R. 1990. Collective intentions and actions. In *Intentions in Communication*, ed. P. R. Cohen, J. Morgan, and M. E. Pollack. Cambridge, MA: MIT Press.

Searle, J. R. 1992. *The Rediscovery of the Mind*. Cambridge, MA: MIT Press.

Searle, J. R. 2001. *Rationality in Action*. Cambridge, MA: MIT Press.

Shallice, T. 1988. *From Neuropsychology to Mental Structure*. Cambridge: Cambridge University Press.

Shannon, C. E., and W. Weaver. 1949. *The Mathematical Theory of Communication*. Urbana, IL: University of Illinois Press.

Siegel, D. S. 1999. *The Developing Mind*. New York: Guilford.

Skinner, B. F. 1969. *Contingencies of Reinforcement*. New York: Appleton-Century-Crofts.

Sperber, D., and D. Wilson. 1986. *Relevance: Communication and Cognition*. Oxford: Blackwell, 1995.

Sperber, D., and D. Wilson. 1995. *Relevance: Communication and Cognition*, 2nd ed. Oxford: Blackwell.

Stalnaker, R. 1973. Presuppositions. *Journal of Philosophical Logic* 2:447–457.

Stephan, H., H. Frahm, and G. Baron. 1981. New and revised data on volumes of brain structures in insectivores and primates. *Folia Primatologica* 35:1–29.

Stout, R. 1961. *Kill Now, Pay Later*. New York: Viking Press.

Strawson, P. 1964. Intention and convention in speech acts. *Philosophical Review* 73:439–469.

Suchman, L. A. 1987. *Plans and Situated Actions: The Problem of Hhuman–Machine Communication*. Cambridge: Cambridge University Press.

Thorpe, W. H. 1961. *Bird Song: The Biology of Vocal Communication and Expression in Birds*. Cambridge: Cambridge University Press.

Tirassa, M., F. M. Bosco, and L. Colle. 2006. Rethinking the ontogeny of mindreading. *Consciousness and Cognition* 15:197–217.

Tolchinsky-Landsmann, L., and A. Karmiloff-Smith. 1992. Children's understanding of notations as domains of knowledge versus referential-communicative tools. *Cognitive Development* 7:287–300.

Tomasello, M. 1990. Cultural transmission in the tool use and communicatory signaling of chimpanzees? In *"Language" and Intelligence in Monkeys and Apes*, ed. S. T. Parker and K. R. Gibson. Cambridge: Cambridge University Press.

Tomasello, M. 2008. *Origins of Human Communication*. Cambridge, MA: MIT Press.

Tomasello, M. 2009. *Why We cooperate*. Cambridge, MA: MIT Press.

Tomasello, M., and J. Call. 1997. *Primate Cognition*. Oxford, London: Oxford University Press.

Tomasello, M., M. Carpenter, J. Call, T. Behne, and H. Moll. 2005. Understanding and sharing intentions: The origins of cultural cognition. *Behavioral and Brain Sciences* 28:675–735.

Tomasello, M., A. C. Kruger, and H. H. Ratner. 1993. Cultural learning. *Behavioral and Brain Sciences* 16:495–552.

Trevarthen, C. 1977. Descriptive analyses of infant communicative behaviour. In *Studies in Mother–Infant Interaction*, ed. H. R. Schaffer. London: Academic Press, 227–270.

Tulving, E. 1983. *Elements of Episodic Memory*. Oxford: Oxford University Press.

Tuomela, R. 2002. *The Philosophy of Social Practices: A Collective Acceptance View.* Cambridge: Cambridge University Press.

Turner, R., ed. 1974. *Ethnomethodology: Selected Readings.* Harmondsworth: Penguin.

Varela, F. J., E. Thompson, and E. Rosch. 1991. *The Embodied Mind: Cognitive Science and Human Experience.* Cambridge, MA: MIT Press.

Verga, G. 1884. *Cavalleria rusticana.* Translated as *Cavalleria rusticana.* London: Penguin, 1999.

Voltaire. 1759. *Candide ou l'Optimisme.* Translated as *Candide* London: Penguin, 1947.

von Frisch, K. 1966. *The Dancing Bees: An Account of the Life and Senses of the Honey Bee.* New York: Harcourt, Brace, and World.

Wallman, J. 1992. *Aping Language.* Cambridge: Cambridge University Press.

Walter, H., M. Adenzato, A. Ciaramidaro, I. Enrici, L. Pia, and B. G. Bara. 2004. Understanding intentions in social interaction: The role of the anterior paracingulate cortex. *Journal of Cognitive Neuroscience* 16:1854–1863.

Walter, H., A. Ciaramidaro, M. Adenzato, N. Vasic, R. B. Ardito, S. Erk, and B. G. Bara. 2009. Dysfunction of the social brain in schizophrenia is modulated by intention type: An fMRI study. *Social Cognitive and Affective Neuroscience* 4(2):166–176.

Weigand, E. 1999. Misunderstanding: The standard case. *Journal of Pragmatics* 31:763–785.

Wells, G., and B. P. Robinson. 1982. The role of adult speech in language development. In *Advances in the Social Psychology of Language*, ed. C. Fraser and K. R. Scherer. Cambridge: Cambridge University Press.

Whiten, A., and R. W. Byrne. 1988. Tactical deception in primates. *Behavioral and Brain Sciences* 11:255–256.

Wieder, D. L., and S. Pratt. 1990. On being a recognizable Indian among Indians. In *Cultural Communication and Intercultural Contact*, ed. D. Carbaugh. Hillsdale, NJ: Lawrence Erlbaum, 45–64.

Wiener, N. 1948. *Cybernetics, or Control and Communication in the Animal and the Machine.* Cambridge, MA: MIT Press.

Wilensky, R. 1983. *Planning and Understanding: A Computational Approach to Human Reasoning.* Reading, MA: Addison-Wesley.

Wimmer, H., and J. Perner. 1983. Beliefs about beliefs: Representation and constraining function of wrong beliefs in young children's understanding of deception. *Cognition* 13:103–128.

Winograd, T., and F. Flores. 1986. *Understanding Computers and Cognition.* Norwood, NJ: Ablex.

Wittgenstein, L. 1922. *Tractatus logico-philosophicus.* London: Kegan Paul, Trench, Trubner.

Wittgenstein, L. 1953. *Philosophical Investigations.* Oxford: Blackwell.

Wolpe, J. 1969. *The Practice of Behavior Therapy.* New York: Pergamon Press.

Wootton, A. J. 1981. Two request forms of four year olds. *Journal of Pragmatics* 5:511–523.

Author Index

Subject Index